CONTENTS

ASIA IN EUROPE AND THE MAKING OF THE WEST
*A series in four volumes examining the spread of cultures
from the east into Europe*

Volume 3

SULTANS OF ROME

The Turkish World Expansion

Warwick Ball

For Grethe and Sevgin

SULTANS
OF
ROME

The Turkish World Expansion

Warwick Ball

EAST & WEST
PUBLISHING
LONDON

SULTANS OF ROME
The Turkish World Expansion
First published 2012 by
EAST & WEST PUBLISHING LTD
London
ISBN 978 1 907318 05 4

www.eastandwestpublishing.com

Editor: Leonard Harrow
Produced by Melisende UK Ltd
Printed and bound in Malta at the Gutenberg Press Ltd

SERIES INTRODUCTION

Every culture looks at history in relation to itself, and so it is not surprising that since the nineteenth century our view of world history has been Eurocentric. Perhaps this bias has been overplayed because so many of the world's more powerful nations are rooted in European culture and so the concept of the 'west' and being 'western' has become almost stereotypical and a crude packaging of a whole complex set of cultures.

Whether or not such a view is correct, this questions whether the 'west' is truly 'western'. Or, to put it another way, being 'western' also incorporates a huge amount that is 'eastern'. Hence, regardless of whether the Eurocentric view is correct or not (and in its own terms it can be correct), the traditional view of the European worldwide spread must be balanced by two considerations. First, by the spread of peoples from the east into Europe. And second, that so much of the civilisation we consider to be 'European' is equally Asiatic. In describing the ensuing contact and assessing the affect, much of what it means to be 'European' is challenged. Ultimately, 'eastern' and 'western' civilisations are neither exclusive nor confrontational. In short, it poses the question, what is 'Europe'?

To deny that Arabs and Turks—or Phoenicians, Scythians, Persians, Jews, Huns, and Mongols—are a part of European as well as Asiatic civilisation is not only to fly in the face of evidence, it is to deny some of the greatest achievements of our civilisation: they are integral parts to be acknowledged as much as our Greek, Roman, Norman or Slavic parts. Phoenicians, Persians, Arabs, Turks, Mongols, all form a part of European history, a part that is both European and Asiatic, a part that defines and makes Europe what it is. Arab and Turkish invasions were no more 'attacks on Europe' than Roman or Norman invasions were.

In this series I do not wish to match east against west nor to demonstrate that 'everything came out of the east.' I wish simply to explore the affect of those cultures from beyond the conventional boundaries of Europe that, to a greater or lesser extent, expanded westwards—the counterpart of the 'European expansion'. Since the earliest times, the history of Europe has been inextricably bound up with peoples and cultures from the east. It is an extraordinarily rich and complex relationship. Not only was Europe born and defined out of this relationship, but at every stage in its history it was intimately affected by the lands to the east. This is the story of that relationship: it is the story of Europe itself.

NOTE ON TRANSLITERATION

This book incorporates proper names from a huge range of languages from right across Eurasia, so no single consistent system is possible. I have opted for conventional usage rather than strict forms of transliteration in most cases, but even so, inconsistencies inevitably occur. I have also omitted as much as possible the use of diacritical marks for ease of reading, apart from the modern Turkish alphabet. Since the Chinese names are almost invariably in an historical rather than a modern context, I have used the older Wade-Giles system rather than the modern standard Pinyin (e.g., Hsiung-nu instead of Xongnu), but some inconsistencies will doubtless scream out to the Sinologist. For Persian and Arabic, the modified *Encyclopaedia of Islam* system that has been adopted by the journal *Iran* seems the most sensible, albeit omitting diacriticals, as I have mentioned. This system, however, falls apart when used for the Turk languages of Central Asia, where there is little consensus (e.g., Karakhanid or Qarakhanid? Kagan, Khaqan or Kaghan? All are used—and the latter is an Avar/Juan-juan word in any case, for which no standard exists). For Turkish the modern standard modified Latin alphabet is used throughout, and to aid the reader these modifications are given below. However, where a more familiar form of a Turkish word occurs in English, I have favoured this (e.g., Pasha instead of Paşa). Furthermore, even this system does not necessarily work for the many Turkish and Turkish related languages and dialects, ancient and modern, east of modern Turkey (e.g., the consonant ğ is entirely unsounded in modern Turkish, but becomes gh—approximating to the Arabic *ghain*—in Turkish further east). I can only ask the reader's forbearance on the grounds that none of it makes the slightest difference either to the events or my argument.

THE TURKISH ALPHABET

Up until Ataturk's reforms in 1923, Turkish used the Arabic alphabet. Ataturk's change to the Latin alphabet was not necessarily an anti-Muslim act as many think, it was simply because the Arabic alphabet is completely unsuitable for Turkish: Arabic only has three vowels, and the Turkish language has many, with its grammar entirely dependant upon vowels. Hence, even using Latin, several more vowels had to be invented.

The new Turkish Latin alphabet that was devised might look rather baffling to us, but it is *entirely* phonetic. Hence, using the simple rules below you can easily pronounce any Turkish word correctly.

A a	is pronounced 'a' as in 'gnat'
C c	is pronounced 'geo' as in 'outrageous'
Ç ç	is pronounced 'ti' as in 'contentious'
E e	is pronounced 'ea' as in 'heaven'
F f	is pronounced 'gh' as in 'cough'
G g	is pronounced 'gu' as 'guilty'
Ğ ğ	is pronounced 'p' as in 'ptarmigan' or 'ch' as in 'yacht' or even 'gh' as in 'night'
İ i	(dotted) is pronounced 'o' as in 'women'
I ı	(undotted) is pronounced 'a' as in 'woman'
J j	is pronounced 's' as in 'treasure'
O o	is pronounced 'a' as in 'yacht'
Ö ö	is pronounced 'ugh' as in 'ugh'
Ş ş	is pronounced 'cio' as in 'pernicious'
U u	is pronounced 'oo' as in 'took'
Ü ü	is pronounced 'e' as in 'dew'
Z z	is pronounced 'si' as in 'business'

Now who has the baffling alphabet?

By using the above simple rules you can now translate such strange foreign Turkish words as 'ofis', 'kuaför' or 'şarküteri'.

MAPS

LIST OF PLATES

PREFACE

Europe's identity was above all emotional: Us ... versus Them

(John Hale[1])

Imagine a scene where the two most powerful men in the world of their time—traditional enemies—are sitting down to dine together at table: Sultan Süleyman the Magnificent and his protagonist, Emperor Charles V of Spain. Also present are some of the leading monarchs and statesmen of Europe: Charles' sister Eleanor of Austria and Queen in turn of both Portugal and France, her husband King Francis I of France, Queen Mary I of England, and Rüstem Pasha, Süleyman's Prime Minister. It is an outdoor banquet in the courtyard of a magnificent Neo-Classical palace, the table is sumptuously laid with silver and gold vessels, wine is flowing, music is playing and the 120 or so guests from both Christian and Muslim Europe are opulently attired in finest oriental and European robes—even the many attendants serving at table are colourfully dressed.

But despite the lavishness of the banquet, tensions are visible below the surface. The undercurrents reveal the many strands of interconnections between the participants—and sum up much of the age. Süleyman is frowning as he turns towards his Prime Minister (who was married to his only daughter, Mihrimah) who in turn is— shockingly!—turning his back on Süleyman as he leans over to whisper to a servant. Francis is also scowling as he turns towards his wife, Eleanor of Austria, whom he never loved (and in any case is sister of his enemy Charles V). Like Süleyman, Francis is also turning his back on a monarch, the Catholic Queen Mary of England. Queen Mary ('Bloody Mary') was

1

married to Charles' son Philip II and in turn is trying to catch Francis' attention—and turning her back away from Süleyman (who was later to be courted by Mary's Protestant half-sister, Queen Elizabeth). The one person leaning over to observe these undercurrents is Vittoria Colonna of Naples, who became a patron of Michelangelo. Emperor Charles, on the other hand, is ignoring all as he also turns away to speak to a servant. Many more of the great and the good are present, such as the Italian noblewoman Giulia Gonzaga, looking nervous as the corsair chief Barbarossa stands behind her, talking to one of his Moorish colleagues. Giulia is right to appear nervous, for Barbarossa failed in an attempt to kidnap her and add her to Süleyman's harem (an attempt it is thought may have been put up by Vittoria Colonna's family).

Such an event, of course, never occurred. But it was illustrated in vivid detail: Veronese's massive canvas, *The Wedding at Cana*, completed in 1563 and dominating the refectory of the Monastery of San Giorgio Maggiore opposite the Doge's Palace in Venice (Pl. 1)[2] until it was taken to France by Napoleon, where it now hangs in the Louvre (although a replica has been installed in the monastery). Veronese also portrayed himself and some of his artistic contemporaries, such as Titian and Tintoretto. However, many of the portrait attributions—both of artists and public figures—are doubtful, or at least controversial: there is little if any evidence that Veronese intended them to be portraits, the interpretations are later and Venetian art routinely depicted Turks in any case, even on their churches (e.g., Pl. 71). But the depiction of Muslim Turks in an entirely Christian European context does nonetheless appropriately illustrate much of the aim of this book. First, that the Turkish world-wide spread both anticipated, and was parallel to, that of the Western European: Turks had a worldwide stake along with the Spanish, the English, the Portuguese and others. And second, that an originally Far Eastern people has become an integral part of Europe's own rich inheritance. Although the central figure is, of course, Christ, in a strange way it is the figure of Süleyman who appears to act as a catalyst in one way or another for all the figures around this section of the painting. Veronese's biblical allegory doubtless never intended this and had other purposes, but it is certainly appropriate to our own.

*   *   *

In some ways the inception of this series lies in the 1985 television series and book, *Triumph of the West* by J M Roberts, an attempt by a major British historian to explain how Western civilisation has spread so thoroughly worldwide. It has been discredited, unfairly, by many as Western triumphalism, which it never was, but was a brave attempt by a major historian to confront an uncomfortable fact. It seems timely, therefore, that in completing the present volume, there appeared in 2011 a similar television series and book, *Civilization: The West and the Rest* by Niall Ferguson, a newer generation British historian attempting exactly the same task as Roberts' effort over a quarter of a century earlier. Another book appearing shortly before Ferguson's was *Europe Between the Oceans 9000 BC-AD 1000* by Barry Cunliffe, tackling much the same theme but from an archaeological perspective, seeking the answer to much the same question deeper in the past. Books on the 'why the west has won' theme have become almost a genre in themselves, with many others appearing since Roberts' foray: books by John M Hobson, John M Headley, David Leavering Lewis, Anthony Pagden, Ian Morris and the many by Jack Goody and Felipe Fernández-Armesto are just some of many works now that explore, question or celebrate this relationship.[3] The genre will doubtless continue as the 'West' in turn either trumpets its values or struggles with its conscience. Their purpose has been succinctly summed up by Ferguson in describing his own work: 'This book offers a story … of why one civilization transcended the constraints that had bound all previous ones'.[4]

The title of Ferguson's work also evokes another television series and book, Kenneth Clark's magisterial *Civilisation.*[*] All offer valuable and thoughtful insights on the subject (despite the occasional use by Ferguson and Cunliffe of glib fashionable explanations: Cunliffe, for example, suggesting that Europeans from the earliest times were 'hardwired to be mobile' and Ferguson viewing the explanation of European hegemony in terms of—amazingly!—just six 'killer apps').[5] But however

---

* Ferguson is dismissive of both Roberts and Clark: the former views he disdains as 'self-satisfied'—which they are not—and he erroneously accuses Clark of defining 'civilisation' as applying solely to Western Europe from the Middle Ages to the nineteenth century. Clark famously was unable to define civilisation and was, moreover, confined in his subject matter by the limitations of a television series. Ferguson criticises him furthermore for his 'high and mighty' stance which, from Ferguson's Olympian heights of Harvard, Oxford, Stanford and the LSE is perhaps a bit the pot calling the kettle black! See Ferguson 2011: 1-2, 13.

insightful, such works miss the point. The purpose of our present series is to challenge the very premise of such works: the 'West' is not, nor ever has been, 'one civilization', other civilisations have also transcended such constraints, 'Eastern' civilisations have expanded into the 'West' just as much as vice-versa, there is no such construct as a single 'The West' and—most of all—there is most certainly no such thing as 'the Rest'.

Of course, to deny that 'Western civilisation' (whatever that is)* has spread to every part of the world might appear to be flying in the face of the very evidence in front of our eyes, from blue jeans, Kalashnikovs and Coca Cola to Shakespeare, Beethoven and Leonardo in almost every part of the world, to cite just a fraction of the good, the bad and the irrelevant. But the spread of this or any civilisation is an infinitely more complex process that is a part of a constantly evolving 'one world' in the making, a process that is at once dissolving, dispersing and diverging as well as re-forming and a coming together of all cultures. To take just one example often cited for Western world dominance: Western science and medicine in general, with particular applications such as the development of vaccinations (Niall Ferguson's 'killer apps' Nos. 2 and 4!). Of all the 'Western' scientific breakthroughs that Ferguson lists, few would have been possible without earlier Arab, Persian, Central Asian, Indian, Chinese or Greek developments.† Even as late as the eighteenth century, it was the Ottomans who introduced the practice of inoculation against disease into Europe, one of the most fundamental 'Western' breakthroughs that underpins world medicine today that is frequently cited as one of the pillars of Westernisation.[6] After all, where would Galileo be without Ulugh Beg? Vasco da Gama without Ibn Majid? The Italian Renaissance without Umayyad Cordoba? The Greek Classics without the Baghdad translation school? Western medicine without Avicenna? The list is endless and the above examples are perhaps simplistic without support. The point is, there is neither a 'them' nor an 'us': we are all the products of both.

Perhaps any consideration of the 'Westernisation' of the rest of the world should be balanced against the suggestion that there is only a 'Western civilisation' because it has been 'Easternised', that 'Western civilisation' is a product of the 'East'? (And let us not forget in this

---

* 'It would be a very good idea' as Gandhi famously commented.

† And let us not forget that Greek civilisation cannot be described in terms of exclusive 'Western civilisation'—see *Towards One World* Chapter 2.

context one of the West's greatest definitions, indeed, its main identity, is an Eastern religion.) Of course not. But neither can the rest of the world be viewed in terms of 'Westernisation'.*

Definitions of 'Europe' or 'the West' tend to be highly selective in order to confirm pre-conceived ideas: the good bits with all the nasty bits left out; the 'nice Europe' frequently does not include, for example, Russia[†] or the Ottoman Empire (which, after all, covered up to twenty percent of the mainland of *Europe* at its height); 'Western Europe' does not include Muslim Spain; 'the West' does not include Colombia or Bolivia or Haiti in its exclusive club (but does includes Iceland, Canada and Australia); 'Western values' do not include Nazism, Communism, Fascism, the Massacre of St Bartholomew, the repressive monarchies of Henry VIII or Ivan IV, Robespierre or Vlad the Impaler, or the various tyrannies and dictatorships that have characterised Greece through the ages more than democracy. To airbrush the Turks out of mainstream European history makes almost as little sense as airbrushing out the Slavs. In fact when viewed holistically (which Europe rarely is), there is little to mark 'Europe' much differently to any other randomly selected region in the world: 'Europe' as a definable identity or construct fades away.

*   *   *

This book is the only volume in this series that is narrative history, conforming more or less to a chronological framework rather than thematic. A title *Sultans of Rome* might appear somewhat contrived (although it was a genuine Turkish title as we shall see). But Europe's own greatest legacy—Rome—is deliberately associated here with one of Islam's best known titles to emphasise how closely the two legacies are intertwined.

In attempting to identify what is 'Europe' and 'European', this series, in examining those parts of European culture that are almost invariably

---

* In writing this paragraph it has been interesting to note that my word-processor dictionary recognises 'westernise' and 'westernisation', but there are no such words as 'easternise' or 'easternisation'.

† Up until the forcible union with Spain in 1580, the general Western European attitude to the Portuguese was much the same as that for the Russians: not really a part of Europe. See Hale 2010: 61.

excluded from conventional definitions of Europe, is essentially blurring the boundaries. Ultimately, it is questioning whether there is such a construct as 'Europe', or at least challenging some conventional definitions and indicating some anomalies. The first volume examined peoples from a part of the East that is unquestionably 'non-European'— Arabia—but demonstrated that these peoples—Phoenicians and Arabs—had not only been intimately bound up with European history right from its very beginnings, but came to Europe mainly via the far *west*: the Iberian peninsula.[*] The second examined a people who only entered Europe very briefly—the Persians—but whose contact interacted with and changed European history fundamentally.

Our third volume discusses a people whose origins in the Far East are far beyond both Arabia and Persia, let alone Europe, but who became a part of the history of all three. In charting the Turkish expansion out of their homeland we observe yet another parallel 'world expansion' demonstrating that our present world is the result of something far more complex than just the 'European world expansion', and that a huge amount of national histories from China right through to Europe form a part of this expansion. For centuries, the idea of the 'terrible Turk' dominated the European mind and was viewed as the very antithesis of everything 'European' (although could be transformed into the British fond idea of 'Johnny Turk' at times of political expediency). Whether the Turks really were terrible barbarians or the bearers of great virtue is not the question here (and, like most peoples, Turks are a mixture of both.) Our point is that an 'Eastern' people became for centuries a part of mainstream European history, and remains permanently so.

The historian Margaret Hunt makes a salutary observation when she points out that 'Hardly any broad surveys of European history in English or French cover it [the Ottoman Empire] in any detail; indeed a surprising number of early modern histories of Europe, by tacit agreement, simply stop at the military border of the Ottoman Empire—wherever that happened to be in any given year'.[7] Even the historian John Darwin, in a laudable attempt in his *After Tamerlane* to correct the Eurocentric view of world history that, on the whole, succeeds (and furthermore

---

[*] Since *Out of Arabia* was published, a new academic study and translation of a little known early medieval Latin manuscript, the *Vitae Offarum Duorum*, has identified the late fourth-early fifth-century AD foundations of no less a European state than the English nation by a group of Arab mercenary adventurers. See Swanton 2010.

paints a positive picture of the Ottomans to counter their traditional negative image), is guilty of this when he writes 'The frontier between the European powers and the Ottoman Empire had moved backwards and forwards since the early years of the [eighteenth] century'. The Ottoman Empire *was* a European power and its western border was *never* a 'European frontier'. He makes the mistake again when he writes of 'wars between Europeans and Turks' and the Ottoman Empire as a 'purely Asian state'.[8] Turks were no less European than Bulgarians or Finns—and 'Turks' in any case at that time included Serbs, Greeks, Albanians and many other 'Europeans', while a state that formed up to twenty percent of Europe at its height and was a major player in European politics for several centuries, not to mention conquering most of Anatolia and all of the Middle East from a *European* base, can in no way be called 'purely Asian'. J M Roberts unconsciously emphasised this distinction when he writes 'Hungary ... was safely re-acquired *for Europe* [from the Ottomans] and the Hapsburgs in 1699' (italics added);[9] Hungary never left Europe in the first place, but the Ottomans were still perceived as late as 1996 (when his book was published) as excluded from Europe. One of the very few historians to identify the European character as Muslim as well as Christian is Felipe Fernández-Armesto in his *1492: The Year Our World Began* (2009).[10] Another refreshing exception is Margaret Hunt's *Women in Eighteenth Century Europe* (2010), which gives equal weight to women in the Ottoman Empire as well as eastern Europe and Russia in her full definition of 'Europe'.

In attempting to compress such a huge swathe of history encompassing most of Eurasia—and much else of the world—over the past two millennia or so into a small volume, even the bravest of authors quail, the present one particularly so. The usual warnings involving fools and angels come to mind, and 'as we proceed, the difficulties will inexorably come crowding in again from the very start. After all, if there were no such difficulties, no one would ever take history seriously' as Fernand Braudel famously cautioned.[11] A huge amount is inevitably left out, and a huge amount of important literature remains unread. For this I offer no apology: the author who can read everything remains unborn and is likely to remain so, the advent of the e-book and JSTOR notwithstanding. Some major parts of history are glossed over with a superficiality that would make a specialist cringe, others omitted altogether, as I have tried to keep my theme of an 'Asia into Europe' movement and the resulting implications within workable boundaries. Some important parts of Turk* history—the Khazars, for example, as well as those other Turk tribal movements in the Eurasian steppe—I have reluctantly relegated to Volume 4, steppe history, as being more fitting to discuss in that context, even though they form a part of the general movement of the Turkish peoples (and in the case of the Khazars, an essential part of the origins of the Seljuks, which form an important part of the present volume). On the other hand, I have included here episodes that might have been more appropriate to Volume 1, Arab history: the Barbary Corsairs, for example, or the Revolt of the Moriscos of Spain. I have included them in this volume, however, as belonging within the broader framework of Ottoman history. The point is, no history is encompassed by neat boundaries but remains intimately connected to other histories, Turkish no less than European no less than any other. That, indeed, is the point of this whole series.

In this, I make no claims to originality: it has all been said before. I also offer no apologies for perhaps at times being guilty of viewing Turkish history through rose-tinted spectacles. This is not because I have a head in the sand attitude to the more brutal side of its history (and, like all imperial powers, the Turks have more than their fair share.) It is simply to get away from the negative attitude towards the 'Terrible Turk' that still predominates in so many histories, and hence not a part of the 'good history' of Europe. Of the general theme of my series, one reader wrote to me shortly after the first volume appeared, to say:

> Overall, though, I think you may be flogging a zombie—
> this particular dead idea staggers around, but it is still
> seriously dead. The idea is, of course, that of 'Europe' as
> some well-defined, anciently-rooted internally coherent
> culture. I noted you quoted J M Roberts in evidence
> of this, but reactionary tories (however popular) are
> hardly representative of informed opinion. How about
> Wallerstein, McNeill, Abu-Lughod, and all the other

---

* For the pre-Islamic periods the generic term 'Turk' is used here adjectivally as opposed to the more usual 'Turkish', which is too specific, or the currently fashionable 'Turkic', which is too clumsy (and has no equivalent in Turkish), although I have tended to use 'Turkish' in most Islamic contexts. Similarly 'Turk' is used here for the broad language group rather than 'Turkish', which refers specifically to Osmanli Turkish.

practitioners of grand history? Or, for that matter, the authors of the Penguin atlases of ancient and medieval history, who 40+ years ago set out their maps to cover the whole area north of the Sahara, east of the Atlantic, and west of the Hindu Kush? Recognising that these were the boundaries that made most sense.

Such criticism is, of course, valid and the works cited just some of a long list of worthwhile studies that have refuted conventional assumptions. But sadly, the issues are very much alive and kicking, and not just among a few reactionary popular Tories, but among mainstream histories, not to mention discussions, political issues, current affairs, even 'informed opinion'. Writing any book is essentially self-indulgent, usually written to satisfy the writer (who is usually the last person to be satisfied). But would it were that such books as these did not need to be written. Such as there are, inevitably end up preaching to the converted (who as often as not only wish to read what they already agree with). Would it were that they reached beyond, including even 'informed opinion'. Would it were that the world was not perceived in terms of them and us.

Chapter 1

INTRODUCTION:
TURKS AND TURKISHNESS

THE TRANSIENCE OF DEFINITIONS

This is not a history of a nation or a race. It is a supranational history developed as a symbiotic process of great complexity.

(Doğan Kuban[1])

At first, the term 'Turk' might appear straightforward, an easy definition: we all know what it means, millions today identify with it, and it has conjured up very definite images for many centuries. But 'Turks' are more elusive than other peoples discussed in this series: Iranians, for example, or Arabs—or Chinese, Jews, Egyptians, Russians, Hungarians and many others for that matter. To some extent the term 'Turk' can be compared to 'Roman', which came to mean far more than a citizen of that city and ended up being applied to many different peoples (even to Turks). Or 'German', which encompassed Goths, Franks, Burgundians, Saxons, Austrians as well as a huge range of other peoples, past and present. 'Turks' are even more complex than that. In the quotation above, Doğan Kuban expresses this elusiveness when introducing a book entitled *The Turkic Speaking Peoples*, people who have impacted upon just about every part of the Eurasian continent from the Far East to the Far West—and far beyond.

Such a vast reach has been matched by few imperial powers in history. But the Turks as an imperial power are only a small (albeit important) part of that history. In Europe, this meant almost solely

Ottoman history,* but for much of the rest of Eurasia, Ottoman history had minimal impact and appears relatively late in overall Turkish history. To demonstrate this complexity perhaps we may compare two very different moments in the history of two very different imperial powers at opposite ends of Eurasia.

ASIANS IN EUROPE

1997 marked an event that was viewed as a hallmark in European post-colonial history. This was the year when the last major European possession in Asia famously reverted to Chinese rule: the hand-over of Hong Kong by Britain to China. In its way it was every bit as important to Britain as the independence of India was in 1947, or the withdrawal east of Suez in the 1960s: the sun finally setting on the greatest of the modern colonial empires. It was certainly marked with great emotion in Hong Kong: by the Chinese, by the British and by the polyglot citizens of Hong Kong itself—and all for very different reasons. But amidst all the navel-gazing and historical hallmarking of that end-of-an-era, few would have reflected upon its converse: as the last European possession in Asia reverted to home rule, the last Asiatic possession in Europe looks set to last forever.

Can we speak of such a situation? Indeed, it is so obvious that it is often overlooked: it exists as Istanbul (along with Turkish Thrace, corresponding perhaps to the New Territories if one wished to take the analogy further). Of course, one might well argue that the position is hardly comparable (and 'possession' is an inappropriate term in both cases), as the Turks can be considered European themselves (albeit controversially so by many Europeans), or at least Europe's nearest neighbours. Furthermore, the analogy breaks down upon analysis (and technically, Hong Kong was not the last European possession: Macau is) and can only be taken so far. A closer analogy to Turks in Anatolia and Thrace might be 'British' remaining to this day in North America, Australia and New Zealand. But it does nonetheless illustrate the uneasiness of our conventional 'European' and 'Asian' definitions, as well as demonstrate that the 'Age of European expansion' was never one way.

---

* Although another Turk people, the Khazars, formed a European empire in the Middle Ages—to be discussed in Volume 4 of this series.

Nevertheless, the situation does bear some comparison, for the Turks were originally as far from Istanbul and Turkey as the British were from Hong Kong and China. The Turks are in origin a Far Eastern people, whose original homeland was the borderlands of Mongolia and southern Siberia; their language bears no relation (apart from loan words) to the Indo-European and Semitic languages that currently surround Turkey, but belongs to an eastern group commonly known as Altaic.* Although the Turks are associated nowadays with the country that bears their name—modern Turkey—it is important to remember that the Turkish conquest of Constantinople in 1453 marked the culmination of a long march westwards by the Turks that had already been in progress a thousand years or more by then.

That momentous day in 1453 when Constantinople fell to the Ottomans was one of the great events of history, for it brought to an end the Roman Empire: from its first emperor, Augustus in 33 BC, to its last, Constantine Dragases, the longest lasting empire in history. An end to Rome, but not to Constantinople: a new beginning. For unlike the Crusading hordes of the notorious Fourth Crusade in 1204—the only other army ever to have breached those walls—the Turks under Mehmet the Conqueror and his successors were great builders. In taking Constantinople, the Turks breathed new life into the ancient fabric of the city, enabling it to experience a renaissance such as few other cities have enjoyed.

Or was it an end to Rome? Rome was Europe's greatest empire and greatest legacy—but also its greatest ghost. Ever since it fell, Europe has refused to let it die: there have been several revivals from Charlemagne in the ninth century to Mussolini more dubiously in the twentieth, the title 'Caesar' has been incorporated into the titles of numerous monarchs from Bulgarian and Russian in the east to German and British in the west, and its architecture has been continually revived from Romanesque in the Middle Ages to the flood of Neo-Classical architecture throughout Europe after the eighteenth century that still shows no sign of disappearing. Here, we will see how the Turks also

---

* As well as Turkish, Altaic includes Mongol, Manchu, Tungus and other more obscure languages of the Siberian steppe and forest. It might also be related to Finnish and Hungarian to the west and Korean and Japanese to the east, although this is controversial. Indeed, 'Altaic' may not even be a real group at all, the vast number of loan words between Turk, Mongol and Tungus simply giving the illusion of a group.

became a part of this legacy, a part of this empire that never died, as the title of this book implies.

But Ottoman Constantinople* was no mere 'oriental' civilisation replacing a 'Western' one. Byzantine Constantinople had all of the civilisation of the Classical world and the West behind it, and the Turks brought to it all the civilisation of Islam and the East—and beyond, for the origins of the Turks themselves lay far beyond the eastern limits of the known world in the depths of Siberian myth. Newcomers to the Near East, but hardly newcomers to history—or to civilisation. For the Turks had built great empires and formed great civilisations long before the one they built at Constantinople. The result was a combined civilisation of many different worlds, Eastern and Western, a symbiosis.

WHAT IS A TURK?

In the eighteenth century, Edward Gibbon could define the Turks as 'the mass of voluntary and vanquished subjects who, under the name of Turks, are united by the common ties of religion, language, and manners'.[2] Gibbon here—and his contemporaries—often used 'Turk' interchangeably with 'Muslim', but as his definition implies, it also encompassed Greeks, Armenians, Arabs, Bulgarians and many others. This was still at a time when the Ottoman Empire was near its peak, but with its collapse 'Turk' came to mean little more than a citizen of the Republic of Turkey. Another collapse changed its meaning again, when the collapse of the Soviet Union in 1990 revealed what had hitherto been largely subsumed: the existence of a swathe of Turkish-speaking peoples stretching from the Balkans to China. From one country before that date whose official language was Turkish,† there are now six whose

---

* It is a common popular fallacy—one even reads it in academic studies—that with the conquest, the name of 'Byzantine Constantinople' was changed to 'Turkish Istanbul'. The present writer has even heard a Greek refusing to call the city by 'that Turkish name'. He was without doubt within his rights and it would be an affront to question his sentiments, but it is important to bear in mind that not only is 'Istanbul' just as Greek—and non-Turkish—as 'Constantinople' is ('Istanbul' is a corruption of the Greek *eistanpolis*, 'to the city'), the city was still officially called 'Constantinople' (*Constantinopolis* or *Qustantinniya*) right up until the twentieth century. It was only officially changed to the *Greek* name 'Istanbul' by Ataturk.

† Two, counting the unrecognised Turkish Republic of North Cyprus.

languages are closely related to Turkish: Kyrgyzstan, Kazakhstan, Uzbekistan, Turkmenistan, Azerbaijan and Turkey itself.* In addition, there are some seven or more countries where Turkish-speakers (or at least those whose language is very close to Turkish) form a significant minority: China, Russia, Afghanistan, Iran, Cyprus, Bulgaria and Ukraine (one might almost now include Germany).† This huge spread was brought together in 2005 by a major exhibition at the Royal Academy in London entitled *Turks. A Journey of a Thousand Years*. The exhibition and the accompanying sumptuous catalogue highlighted for the first time to a general British audience the diversity of a people and culture that many—or most—had associated solely with Turkey. A similarly sumptuous publication brought out soon after, *The Turkic Speaking Peoples. 2,000 Years of Art and Culture from Inner Asia to the Balkans*, broadened the sweep even further and doubled the time span encompassed by the Royal Academy exhibition (Map 1). [3]

This modern two-way direction of the Turks—past Ottoman glories in Europe and a future 'new Turkish world' in Central Asia—is appropriately illustrated by the route maps of Turkey's national carrier, Turkish Airlines, over the years. In 1990 it flew to the main western European capitals that one would expect, as well as to New York and to some main capitals in the Far East, with an obvious concentration in Europe on places where there were Turkish guest workers, mainly Germany. There were only a few destinations in the former Ottoman Empire, such as Athens and Budapest in Europe and Tunis, Cairo and Jeddah in the Middle East and North Africa. The only other eastern European destinations were Moscow and Warsaw. To the east, the

---

* A fact quick to be used to advantage by Turkish businessmen, who were among the first following the collapse of the Soviet Union to beat a path to the former republics and bring Western technology and business enterprise and form economic ties based upon mutual language. Today Turkish business remains dominant in all of those countries.

† Uighur in China, Tatar in Russia and Ukraine, Turkmen and Uzbek in Afghanistan, and Azeri, Turkmen and Qashqai in Iran. Indeed, some estimates are as high as one third of the population of Iran being native Turkish speakers. In Russia, Tatar, Chuvash, Bashkir, Nogay, Yakut, Tuvan and other minority languages are described as 'Turkic'. Other countries with 'indigenous' (as opposed to recent immigrant) Turkish speaking minorities include Tajikistan, Georgia, Iraq, Greece, Serbia, Kosovo and Albania; those in Armenia were ethnically cleansed in the 1990s. In addition, most countries in Western Europe as well as the USA, Canada and Australia have large immigrant Turkish communities.

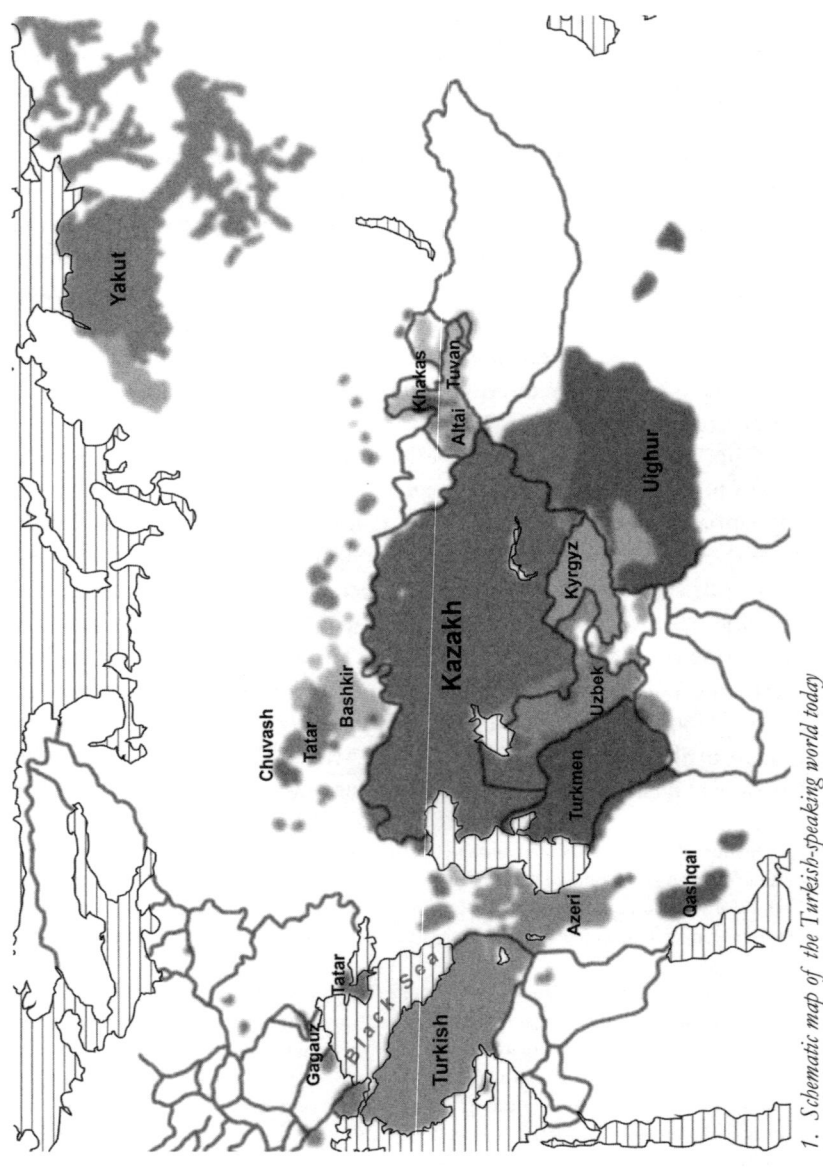

1. *Schematic map of the Turkish-speaking world today*

nearest destination served by Turkish Airlines to Turkish Central Asia was Tehran.

Twenty years later the route map had changed dramatically (Map 2). Now among the largest airlines in the world, by 2011 mainstream destinations served by Turkish Airlines naturally remained (and increased), but in eastern Europe, Turkish Airlines had re-established the spread of the Ottoman Empire, with such destinations as Tirana, Skopje, Podgorica, Pristina, Zagreb, Sarajevo, Bucharest, Budapest, Sofia, Chisinau, Odessa and Simferopol (destinations virtually replicated, significantly, by the old rival in Vienna in the form of Austrian Airlines), as well as Batumi and Tbilisi in Georgia. The former Ottoman Empire to the south and east was similarly embraced with Algiers, Tunis, Tripoli and Benghazi in North Africa, and Aleppo, Damascus, Beirut and Tel Aviv in the Levant, as well as Baghdad, Mosul, Erbil and Sulamaniya in Iraq. The airline hub, one need hardly emphasise, is Ottoman Istanbul rather than Republican Ankara. But more significantly, Turkish Airlines' network had expanded massively eastwards to encompass those places with Turkish-speaking populations. This included all of the capitals of the former Soviet Turcophone republics: Baku, Ashgabat, Tashkent, Bishkek, Almaty and Astana. But it also included Ufa and Kazan in Russia, the capitals of Bashkortostan and Tatarstan respectively, as well as Tabriz, capital of Iranian (Turkish-speaking) Azerbaijan, significantly the only international airline to fly there. Conspicuous by its absence is Kashgar or Urumchi in the Uighur Autonomous Region of Xinjiang: doubtless Chinese fears of the spectre of Uighur separatism (which has support among some elements in Istanbul) make them reluctant to grant Turkish Airlines landing rights there (although they do allow Pakistan International—and allow Turkish Airlines to fly to Beijing, Shanghai, Guangzhou and Hong Kong, well away from Turcophone areas). A highly visible Turkish presence in all of these destinations is reinforced by everything from Turkish brands of beer to Turkish filling stations, automobiles, construction companies and retail outlets—and the Turk-speaking Central Asian republics switching from Cyrillic to the modern Turkish modified Latin script.

Turkish Airlines can hardly be taken to define a 'Turk', but it does nonetheless appropriately illustrate much of both the spread and the history of the Turks, as well as their connections westwards and eastwards. The Turks are first referred to in early Chinese sources, who

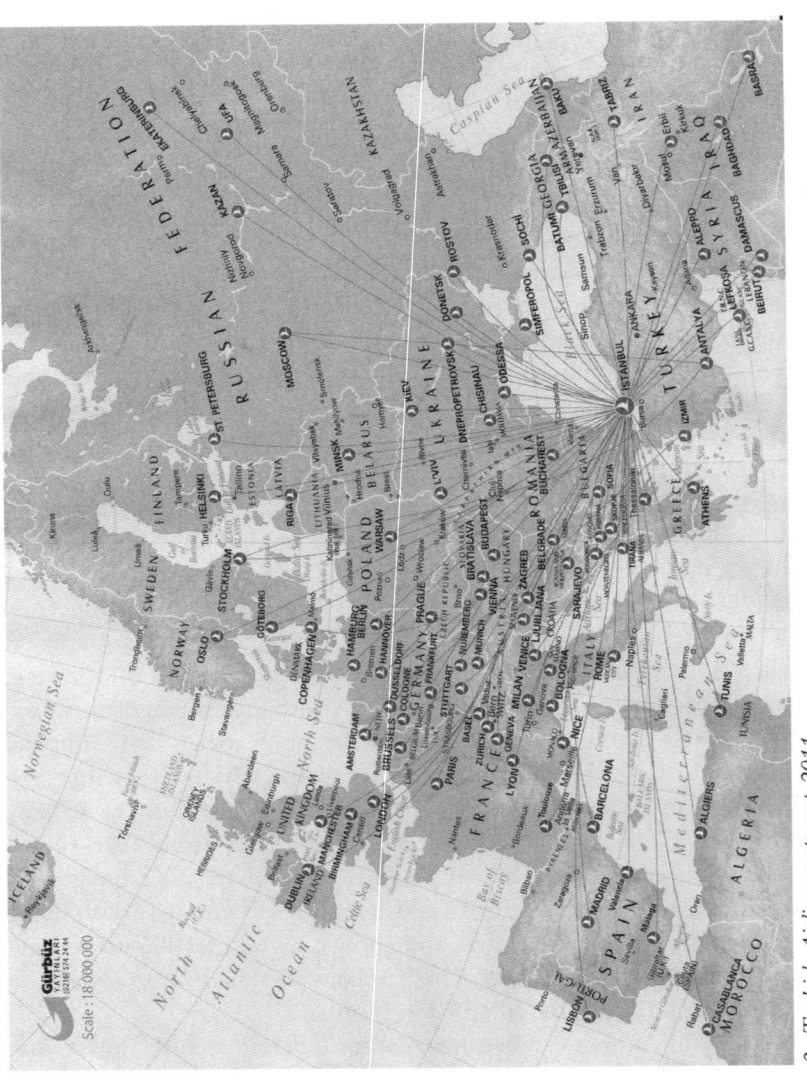

2. Turkish Airlines route map 2011

locate them well to the north of their borders, beyond Mongolia. Turkish origins in general are discussed more in the following chapter. For the moment it is enough to observe that these origins lie in the Far East and that a significant minority of Turks—the Uighurs—are still to be found in China, while the Yakut—probably the closest to the original ethnic 'Turks'—are indigenous to the Russian Far East. Indeed, China is the only country in the world—out of some dozen countries with significant Turkish speaking populations—where the Turk language is still written in the Arabic script (Pl. 3). As one of the five officially recognised languages of China, it appears on all Chinese banknotes.

With Turk origins in the Far East, can one therefore describe the Turks as a Far Eastern people, i.e., a people now conventionally labelled 'Asian'? A modern citizen of Turkey would regard the suggestion as utterly preposterous, and probably rightly so.* After all, compare an ethnic Turk from Keriya in China with a Turk from Istanbul (Pl. 4) and the differences are obvious. In Turkey today, most people appear broadly 'Balkan' or 'East Mediterranean'; many, indeed, appear blond, even Slavic. 'Turk', therefore, is not a racial group. It is also important to emphasise that the 'Turkification' of Anatolia—and elsewhere—was never an ethnic change or displacement but mainly an identity change as the majority indigenous population gradually began to identify with the ruling Turkish minority, just as they had previously identified with Romans or Greeks or Hittites. The social anthropologist Fredrik Barth emphasises how group identity is no more than momentary convenience—usually for gain—and can change: 'an evanescent situational construct, not a solid enduring fact'.[4] The Bulgars, for example, were originally a Turk tribe and so identified themselves as such, but they now have a completely non-Turkish (indeed, positively anti-Turkish for many modern Bulgarians), Slav identity, while those Bulgars who remained on the middle Volga identify themselves as Tatars. Indeed, people might have several identities: a citizen of Turkey might be both a Turk and a Greek, just as a citizen of New Zealand might feel both a New Zealander and a Scot.

On the one hand, the native of Kashgar might regard himself as no less a 'Turk' than the one from Istanbul, and again probably rightly so. On the other hand a Bulgarian would doubtless quite vehemently renounce

---

* And there is an irony that the original 'Asia' of Hittite and Greek sources applied solely to what is now western Turkey—see *Out of Arabia*, the first volume in this series, p. 9.

the label of 'Turk' (and again quite rightly), even though the Bulgars were originally a Turk tribe, so as much a 'Turk' as a Uighur is. The Bulgarians, however, have lost the Turkish language, having being subsumed by the Slavic (although the Tatars of the middle Volga region—almost certainly the original Bulgars—still speak a Turk language).* Turks in Turkey have not, so usually today still regard themselves as 'Turks', even though some generations back they might have been Greek or Slav or Georgian—or, even further back, Phrygian or Lydian or Hittite. That most *Turkish* of institutions during the Ottoman period, the Janissaries, was as a matter of policy made up of boys drawn exclusively from non-Turkish and non-Muslim communities (at least before their decline in the latter period). That most 'Turkish' of royal houses, the Ottomans, by the end had hardly a drop of Turkish (or, indeed, Ottoman) blood in them, as Ottoman princes and sultans bred solely with non-Turkish (and non-Muslim) women, again as a matter of policy—in their last hundred years Ottoman sultans were probably more Slav than Turkish from a purely genetic point of view. What made both the janissaries and the sultans 'Turkish' was their language.

Is a 'Turk', therefore, no more than a speaker of a language? To some extent this is probably the nearest we can get, but it is hardly the full story. During the Ottoman period—surely the peak of Turkish achievement—'Turk' was a term of contempt applied to the peasants of Anatolia: no self-respecting Ottoman Turk would dream of calling himself a 'Turk', 'Ottoman' was the term that was favoured. Hence, Kemal Atarturk's slogan 'Proud be he who calls a Turk' in his attempt to create a Turkish nationalist identity distanced from the Ottoman legacy (and still to be seen emblazoned throughout Turkey today: Pl. 5). The term 'Ottoman' on the other hand applied to all members of the empire, whether Turkish, Greek, Arab, Armenian or Slav. When faced with the wave of militant nationalism that swept the European provinces of the Ottoman Empire in the nineteenth century, Sultan Abdülhamid II remarked in bewilderment, 'But we are all Ottomans'. A 'Turk' therefore was not necessarily a speaker of Turkish (or at least a native speaker).

Probably the nearest one can arrive at defining 'Turk' is simply one of self-identity. Throughout Turkish history there has been a strong sense

---

* The Bulgars—both of the Volga and the Balkans—are discussed more in Volume 4 of this series.

of awareness of being a 'Turk', a common feeling of 'Turkishness' and defining oneself and one's community as 'Turk'. This is true, of course, of many peoples, but with Turks it was perhaps stronger than others. As far back as 443 AD, the Emperor T'o-pa Tao of the Northern Wei Dynasty of China sent an expedition to discover the ancestral cave of the Turk peoples in what is now the far north-eastern part of Inner Mongolia. Although the Northern Wei was Chinese, the dynasty who ruled it was the T'o-pa, a Turk tribe, and despite increasing Sinicisation, Emperor Tao still felt sufficiently aware of his Turk roots.[5] The very first time that the Turkish language was written down was in the eighth century in a series of inscriptions along the Orkhon River in Mongolia, and these texts strongly convey a sense of 'Turkishness' with such phrases as 'the Turks and all the common people' and repeated appeals to 'O Turkish people'.[6] Nizam al-Mulk, the eleventh-century Persian Prime Minister to two Seljuk sultans, describes Alp Tegin, founder of the first major Turkish Islamic dynasty, the Ghaznavid, as 'a Turk, prudent, skilful, popular', and Alp Arslan, the founder of the Seljuk Empire, is quoted as saying 'Today God has favoured the Turks'. In writing of these dynasties Nizam al-Mulk's text is littered with the Seljuk rulers' strong sense of Turkishness, referring to the *ummat al-turk* or 'Turkish nation', the political expediency of an Iranian prime minister pandering to a Turkish dynasty notwithstanding.[7] The early Seljuk rulers in Central Asia would often be described as 'leader of all the Turks' in strong contrast to traditional Islamic titulature, where a ruler would usually 'leader of the faithful' or 'lord of the four quarters' or 'sultan of east and west' and not ethnically defined (unlike Christian European rulers: 'King of the Franks', 'Tsar of all the Russias', etc.). The great seventeenth century Ottoman traveller, Evliya Çelebi, describes his 'saintly' ancestor, the twelfth century Central Asian mystic Ahmad Yassavi, as a 'Turk of the Turks'.[8]

Perhaps the best definition of what it is to be a Turk was given by Gurbugha, a Turkish commander in Anatolia addressing Frankish envoys from the First Crusade when he asked: 'Are your lords ready to become Turks? … If so, they may stay here. We will give you cities and horses, you will become horsemen like us, and we will extend our friendship to you'.[9] In other words, merely a self definition: anybody could 'become Turk'. In some ways perhaps the wisest answer to modern Turkish identity was made by a Turkish friend who stated 'we are all Anatolians'.

So, a Turk, an Ottoman, an Anatolian; a term to proud of, a term of contempt; a speaker of a language irrelevant of political borders, a member of an empire regardless of language; an ethnicity, an identity, an idea. In other words, the term 'Turk' has many meanings or none, and has changed as perceptions of changed: transitory, as so many definitions are.

TURKEY AND 'EUROPE'

To some extent, the above subheading is a geographical tautology: a large part of Turkey—including its largest city—is a part of Europe. More important, a large part of its history was European: the Ottoman Empire was a European power, and the Ottomans conquered south-eastern Europe *before* they conquered 'Turkey'.

The concept of 'Europe', fortress Europe, is a modern one, perhaps even twentieth century, born out of the problems of trying to define and reinvent.* The European conflicts of the twentieth century are both a cause and a symptom, and the process is still ongoing, making it difficult to either recognise its proper processes or its underlying causes. As recently as the nineteenth century Turkey was quite easily accepted as 'European' and regarded as a part of Europe: the 'sick man of Europe' 'to take her [Turkey's] proper place in the general councils of Europe' in the words of Sir Stratford Canning, Britain's ambassador to the Porte in 1832.

Contrary to Canning and other nineteenth-century diplomats, a senior European Union official and former President of France, Valéry Giscard d'Estaing, in alluding to Turkey's Muslim population in a newspaper interview in 2002, famously stated that Turkey is 'not a European country' and that not recognising this 'would be the end of Europe'.[10] Although EU officials quickly distanced themselves from his remarks, there is little doubt that in alluding that Islam has no place in Europe, Giscard d'Estaing was reflecting widely held views. More significant was Giscard d'Estaing's position at the time of his remarks: not so much as one of France's more prominent citizens, but his position responsible at that time for drafting an official EU constitution.

---

* Although Pope Pius II defined Europe in terms of a Christian fortress in opposition to Islam in general and the Turks in particular. (By 'Christian' and 'Europe' he doubtless excluded Orthodox Europe). See Cardini 2001: 133.

Whether or not Turkey ought to be allowed to enter the European Union is hardly the issue here. (Although the Dutch historian Peter Rietbergen cautions that 'Precisely the interpretation and use of Europe's past will determine the course of its future.'[11]) The real issue, even apart from the timing of Giscard d'Estaing's contentious remarks—which came at a time of acute Muslim-Western tensions—is the possibility (even when it is the merest implication) that the definition of 'Europe' be constitutionally enshrined as non-Muslim, or at least non-Turkish—and by extension a Christian union. This not only ignores that two of the great periods in European civilisation—Constantinople in the age of Sultan Süleyman the Magnificent and Andalusia in the age of Caliph Abd ar-Rahman III—were Muslim. It also effectively ignores the ten million or so Muslims already living within western Europe—more than the population of a number of EU countries.* It also contradicts one of the EU's most 'sacred' goals: that of secularism.

In fact such attitudes are merely voicing old and carefully nurtured prejudices. Historian Andrew Wheatcroft emphasises this when writing of the old Habsburg-Ottoman conflicts:

> The contrast between what actually happened and these carefully fabricated myths is startling. Once more the Siege of Vienna in 1683 is becoming an inspirational metaphor of perpetual struggle, of West versus East, of Muslim versus Christian, just as it was hundreds of years ago. Once more the event is serving a polemical purpose. Now it buttresses the idea that a new Battle for Europe is being fought. The Turks of the twenty-first century must not be allowed to enter the European Union because this will destroy Christendom. They would succeed where their Ottoman predecessors had failed in 1683.[12]

The still hugely common fallacy of explaining all of history in terms of some entirely mythical 'East-West conflict' has been explored more

---

* With the largest number—four million—in Giscard d'Estaing's own country. See Nielson 1998: 20.

in Volume 2, a fallacy that Ian Almond rightly dismisses as 'nothing more than a Disney version of history'.[13]

At the risk of a digression, I might end with a personal anecdote (and I beg the reader's forbearance). Some years ago, in conducting a group down the west coast of Turkey, the issue of 'Europe' recurred in several guises. To begin with, we were visiting the outstanding Classical remains for which that coast is famous. Indeed, Turkey has more remains from the Greek and Roman past than any other country, immediately begging the question of where 'our' Classical past comes from: Europe or Asia. Travelling along the eastern shore of the Sea of Marmara (towards Troy) we passed the Turkish island of Marmara (famous for its ancient marble quarries, the much prized 'Proconnessian' marble) just off the coast, and I posed the question: is the island a part of Europe or Asia? The answer was unanimous: Asia. Some days later on passing the Greek island of Samos, even closer to the Turkish mainland than Marmara (one can almost lean out and touch it), I posed the same question. Again, the answer was unanimous: Europe. Nobody was wrong, but the point is: the definition of 'Europe' is not so much geographical as perceptual.

Chapter 2

DESCENDANTS OF THE SHE-WOLF

He came naked, by night, alone and very hungry; yet he was not afraid! Look, he has pushed one of my babes to one side already. And that lame butcher would have killed him and would have run off to the Waingunga while the villagers here hunted through all our lairs in revenge! Keep him? Assuredly I will keep him. Lie still, little frog. O thou Mowgli—for Mowgli the Frog I will call thee—the time will come when thou wilt hunt Shere Khan as he has hunted thee.

(The She-wolf on the adoption of the child Mowgli in Rudyard Kipling, The Jungle Book*)*

Some Classical sources of the first century AD refer to a group of people known as the *Turcae* dwelling on the southern Russian steppe north of the Sea of Azov. These have been viewed by some authorities as the first references to Turks. However, there has been no consensus on this, with no firm evidence of Turks appearing in the region until the sixth century. Early Turk history has been reconstructed from a combination of literary, linguistic and archaeological sources, with virtually all of the available evidence pointing further east in Mongolia or Siberia as the original Turk homeland. To see how a nation of Siberian forest dwellers would eventually become masters of twenty percent of mainland Europe (even occupying, at one point, a part of the British Isles), one must begin with the Chinese.

HUNS AND WOLVES, CAVES AND PRINCESSES

The earliest mentions of the Turks in history are in Chinese sources at the end of the third century BC, where they are referred to as the *T'u-chüeh* in relation to the *Hsiung-nu*, a great steppe empire to the north who obsessed the Chinese and whom many have identified with the Huns of later history.* The T'u-chüeh were a tribe located somewhere to the north of the Hsiung-nu, whom the Chinese regarded as ancestors of the Turks. But analysis of the very few Hsiung-nu words that have survived in Chinese transcriptions shows this to be not so—indeed, the Hsiung-nu language is unlikely even to have been Altaic. Evidence is extremely slim either way and the Chinese sources are vague and contradictory.†

Many in both Turkey and Hungary today believe they are descended from the Huns, fallaciously for both peoples (perhaps slightly less so in the case of Turks): hence 'Attila' is a not uncommon boys' name in both countries.‡ Turks in modern times have also claimed descent—again fallaciously—from Scythians, Hittites and Sumerians, the latter from an early twentieth-century misunderstanding of the nature of the Sumerian language. Hence, when Ataturk made the adoption of surnames compulsory, many Turks adopted Sumerian surnames such as 'Akurgal' and 'Sümer'.

When trying to work out the complex Hsiung-nu-Turk connections from the Chinese sources, it is important to remember, first of all, that the Chinese probably lumped all 'them barbarians out there' under the one label anyway, regardless of ethnic origin, much as we used to lump all non-Europeans as 'Indians'. It must also be remembered that our tendency to group different peoples together almost solely on linguistic grounds is very a recent one, and such criteria may not have even occurred to the Chinese, nor seemed very relevant (and may still be largely irrelevant, as the term 'Anglo-Saxon' applying to peoples as diverse as English, Scots, Australians and Americans indicate). Most of

---

* Albeit controversially. The Huns and their origins are discussed more in Volume 4 of this series, *The Gates of Europe*.

† The Hsiung-nu language might have been related to Kettish, a very obscure Siberian forest language that became extinct in the nineteenth century.

‡ As far back as the fifteenth century, King Matthias Corvinus of Hungary was calling himself a 'second Attila' and proposing an alliance with Mehmet the Conqueror on the grounds of shared ethnicity. See Almond 2009: 142. The Huns are discussed in more detail in Volume 4.

all, our very tendency to look for ethnic inter-connections and origins might in itself be fallacious, as not only are there many entirely unrelated groups in the Mongol-North Chinese-Siberian region, but there would have been even far more in early antiquity.

The sources preserve many of the traditions relating to Turk origins. According to these, the original homeland of the Turks was the sacred Ötükän Forest (or in some versions the Ötükän was a sacred mountain, usually, but not always, associated with a forest) where there were several related Turk tribes, such as the 'White-clothed Turks', the 'Yellow-head Turks', the 'Skiing Turks' and the 'Ox-hoofed Turks'. The latter are further described as a northern people in a land of extreme cold, all indications suggesting a northern origin in the forest belt (a location also corroborated by an independent Tibetan source; 'Skiing Turks' hardly indicates the tropics). The Chinese sources also refer to 'black' and 'yellow' Turk tribes, and early Turk inscriptions refer further to 'Blue Turks'.[1]

These traditions related in the Chinese sources also preserve several legendary versions of Turk origins. According to one, the Turks were originally a separate clan of the Hsiung-nu confederation who fought and fell out with the Hsiung-nu king. The T'u-chüeh were defeated, their chief killed and the young prince captured, mutilated and then abandoned to die. The prince was adopted by a blue-grey she-wolf and brought up in a cavern. Out of the resulting union were ten boys who became ancestors of the Turk race. The Turks eventually emerged from the cavern to become blacksmiths for the *Juan-juan*, a later steppe confederacy (probably related to the Avars, who invaded south-eastern Europe) who succeeded the Hsiung-nu. Another version also has reference to a cavern as the original home, but the liaison was with the daughter of a lake spirit, with the resulting offspring the ancestors.

A different tradition relates how a Hsiung-nu king had two daughters too beautiful to be married to mere mortals. He accordingly built a tower for them in an uninhabited forest far to the north and asked heaven to provide husbands. One day a wolf came and howled at the foot of the tower day and night, excavating a cave as a dwelling. The younger (and more beautiful) princess realised that this was her intended, so climbed down and lived in the cave with the wolf. The offspring became the ancestors of the Turks.*

---

* Perhaps the origin of the wolf-whistle? If mythic descent from a bestial union with

Several suggestive factors emerge from these legends regarding Turk origins. The ancestral cavern occurs in several versions and seems to be peculiar to the Turks—the traditional story surrounding the founder of the Turki Shahi dynasty of the eastern Hindu Kush in the ninth century, for example, relates how he hid in a cavern and then appeared as a miraculous being. The ancestral caverns are presumed to be indirect references to iron-ore mines—and one recalls the tradition where the Turks were originally iron-workers for the Juan-juan. In later history the Turks were certainly proficient in weaponry—one of the reasons for their success in warfare—and references to 'iron' (Turkish *demir*) are popular in Turkish names, such as Demirji and Demirel, or more distantly Teimur (Tamerlane) and Mongol Temujin (the name of Chingiz Khan).

The supposed ancestral cave was actually discovered in antiquity by an expedition sent by the Northern Wei Dynasty of China, which was itself Turk in origin (see below). This was the cave of Ka-Hsian (or Gaxian), deep in a forest in a ravine in the remote Xingangling Mountains in the far north-east of present day Inner Mongolia. It is a large natural cave with a Chinese inscription at the entrance. This inscription records how reports of the ancestral cavern had reached the Turk Emperor T'o-pa Tao of the Northern Wei Dynasty in 443 so he sent an expedition to investigate. The inscription describes the cave, the ancestral origins of the Northern Wei kings in a sacred cave, and their migration southwards to become the T'o-pa (or Tuoba) tribe of Turks and thence into China. It further records how local people at the cave were still worshipping the T'o-pa ancestors and their mythic descent from an ancestral bear within the cave at the time of the expedition. It was rediscovered by the Chinese in recent times.[2]

The ancestral totemic wolf occurs in several ancient mythic origins, often amongst people quite varied and unrelated in origin, although most can be traced back to steppe traditions (and werewolf myths are probably also related to the same totemic wolf traditions). That relating to the Romans is well known, as is the Indian version famously related by Rudyard Kipling (which has been adopted as a totem for the Boy Scout movement). It also occurs widely amongst Eurasian steppe peoples,

---

a wolf seems perverse to our modern mind, one must remember that according to Greek myth all Europeans are descended from the union of a Phoenician princess (Europa) with a bull (Zeus in disguise)—a favourite subject in often almost erotic detail of many a Renaissance and later painting.

such as the Hsiung-nu and the Wu-Sun on the western borderlands of China—even Chingiz Khan, according to the Mongol *Secret History*, was descended from a blue-grey wolf, and an alternative derivation of his name *Temuchin* means 'wolf'. The Luwians, a Bronze Age pre-Hittite Indo-European people of Anatolia, have similar wolfish origins, and wolfish myths were also associated with Hun origins according to some ancient authorities.* Modern Turkish far-right political movements use the wolf as a symbol—the Turkish right-wing movement of the seventies, for example, called themselves the 'Grey Wolves'. None of these different people sharing wolfish origins are necessarily connected: the fact the Luwians, the Romans and the Turks all in the end were associated with Anatolia is pure coincidence.†

The apparent 'colour-coding' of Turk tribes ('White', 'yellow', 'blue', 'black' Turks etc.) is a long and venerable tradition, and recurs in later historical Turkish tribes such as the *Karakhanids* ('Black Khans'), the *Ak Koyunlu* and *Kara Koyunlu* ('White-sheep' and 'Black-sheep' Turkmen), the *Kizil Bash* ('Red Head'), etc. Historical sources also refer to many other tribal groupings and confederations such as the Türgesh, Karluks, Kirghiz, Uighurs, etc., which are all 'Turk' broadly, in much the same way that Goths, Prussians, Bavarians, Saxons, etc. are all loosely 'German'.

The references to forest homelands, as well as to 'White-clothed', 'Skiing' and 'Ox-hoofed' Turks, all suggest a northern, sub-arctic origin of forest dwellers, presumably in northern Mongolia or the Siberian forest belt (Pl. 6). Some authorities have located the ancestral homeland in the Minusinsk area of Siberia where large numbers of metal objects, many in the characteristic 'animal style' of the Eurasian steppe art, have been recovered from burials dating from about 500 BC to the sixth century AD. This fits in with the migration of the Turk nation southwards on the eve of the foundation of the First Turk Empire (see next chapter). The Yakut of today along the Lena River of north-

---

* The Luwian is from the Indo-European root word *lupu* = 'wolf'—cf. 'lupus', 'lupine' etc., and Lycia/Lukoi in western Anatolia is from the same root, as are such 'wolf places' as Lycopolis in Egypt and the Lyceum in Athens.

† Ustinova (2002) has a very thorough summary of Indo-European wolfish and werewolf associations and foundation myths from Hittite references and Scythian burial customs right across to ancient Rome and ancient Irish and Icelandic mythologies, all of which are traced back to Zoroastrian Avestan sources. She makes no mention, however, of the Turks.

eastern Siberia are a Turk related group, the only 'Turks' still left in the ancestral homeland.

In the first millennium BC, therefore, the Turks were probably just a nomadic nation in the area to the north of the Great Wall who, along with other loosely related tribes, would occasionally raid into the more settled areas of China. Then, from about the second century BC, we see various movements of people from this area as a result of the Han Chinese efforts at pacifying the region and evicting the nomadic tribes from their borders. Such efforts by the Chinese alternated between diplomatic and military, negotiation and invasion, occasionally combining both, as well as—most visibly—architectural: the series of long land walls aimed at hemming in the nomads and later lumped together under the Great Wall. Nothing is more confrontational than a wall as modern history demonstrates (with its Iron Curtain, Berlin Wall and Palestinian Wall) as much as the past. The Chinese construction of the Great Wall—together with their related military campaigns—resulted in a massive disruption of steppe peoples whose ramifications were felt ultimately right across Eurasia (Pl. 7). The Turks were probably one of the groups of people that were displaced by these activities, and many Turkish tribes moved away from their original homelands in the wake of the Hsiung-Nu migrations.

But such disruption can also rebound, and 'Great Walls' throughout history rarely succeed in their purpose: the Roman *Limes*, the Maginot Line, Berlin Wall and even the Great Wall are ultimately monuments to their failure. For by their very nature they usually cut across rather than mark boundaries, creating ever greater confrontation and hostility. The Great Wall, it has been argued, created the very conditions it aimed to solve: in alienating the steppe nomad it simply made them more hostile: it created the 'barbarian'. Faced with no alternative, the steppe nomad had little choice but to penetrate the Great Wall and enter China. Hence, after the Great Wall, China was frequently overrun by nomads from beyond the Wall, from the Hsian-bei (a Hun-related group) of antiquity to the Mongols of the Middle Ages, to the Manchus of modern times. Groups of Turks were amongst the first to move from their traditional lands down into China.

TURKS AND BUDDHISTS: THE NORTHERN WEI OF CHINA

Before the emergence of the Turks as a major steppe power, an eastern Turk tribe, the Tabgach (or Tabgaj; Chinese T'o-pa), had spread across northern China and Inner Mongolia in the late third century AD. This occurred after their diaspora from the mythical cavern following the disruption caused by the Great Wall and its associated politics and the collapse of the Hsiung-nu confederation. They entered China in the fourth century AD as a part of the Hsian-bei confederacy, a very loose alliance of steppe tribes who emerged after the collapse of the Hsiung-nu (and probably incorporated some Hsiung-nu remnants). The T'o-pa or Tabgach Turks* emerged as the leaders of this confederacy and founded the Northern Wei Dynasty of China in 386 centred on Pingcheng, modern Tatung, which they made their capital in 398. Approximately twenty percent of the Northern Wei elite were Turks.

The Northern Wei rulers were enthusiastic supporters of Buddhism—the first Chinese dynasty to be so—and Emperor T'o-pa Tao was the first to elevate Buddhism to an official state level since the time of the Kushans of Afghanistan in the second century AD. In particular, the T'o-pa kings embraced the peculiarly Mahayana element in Buddhism where the secular ruler is invested with the authority of the Buddha. This element took spectacular form in the Buddhist caves constructed throughout the fifth century by the Northern Wei dynasty at Yungang outside their capital at Tatung (Pls 8 and 9), as well as at the Longmen Caves near their later capital of Loyang, where each T'o-pa king erected a giant statue of Buddha representing the Buddhist authority invested in himself: each giant Buddha statue, in other words, represented both Buddha and the emperor. This was the first time that giganticism—colossal Buddha statues—had been introduced into Buddhist art, and was to have enormous consequences for subsequent Buddhist art and Turkish history.

Pingcheng remained the Northern Wei capital throughout the fifth century, but the court became progressively more Sinicised as they distanced themselves from their tribal origins. As part of this process the Emperor Hsiao Wen-ti moved the capital in 494 to the old Chinese

---

* There is some dispute as to whether the T'o-pa were really Turk. However, see Sanping Chen 2005, who confirms their Turk language. Tabgach also remained a Turkish name, such as in the Karakhanid ruler Tabghach Bughra Khan in 1069.

capital of Luoyang; the Hsian-bei and To-pa languages and dress were outlawed and the Tabgach/T'o-pa were forced to adopt Chinese names. The Hsian-bei military revolted in 524 and the Northern Wei Dynasty collapsed in 534. There was some revival with the East and West Wei Dynasties later on, but without its Turk element.

The great French historian of Eurasia, René Grousset, compares the various steppe invasions of China after the 'Classical' period of the Han Dynasty (206 BC—220 AD) to the 'barbarian' invasions of the Roman Empire at the end of antiquity. These invasions were the Hsiung-nu, Hsian-bei, Juan-Juan and eventually the T'o-pa (the names need hardly concern us here, merely the pattern), steppe tribes who eventually established states within the boundaries of the former Chinese Han Empire, just as the Germanic tribes did in the former Roman Empire. A rump China was left in Loyang as the ancient capital of Chang'an was occupied by the barbarians, just as a rump 'Rome' was left in Constantinople after Rome fell to the Goths. The T'o-pa Turks, the last 'wave' of the steppe peoples to invade China, brought about a revival of Chinese civilisation under the Northern Wei, and Grousset compares this to the European revival under the Franks and the eventual 'Carolingian renaissance', with the adoption of Buddhism by Emperor T'o-pa Tao compared to the adoption of Christianity by Clovis.[3]

The comparison, while appropriate, is an uneasy one: like all historical parallels, there are no neat fits and it breaks down upon analysis. Nonetheless, we can draw important lessons from the history of the Northern Wei. Already we have seen the transformation of a Turk group from steppe nomad to sedentary power, from the conqueror of an empire to its reviver. The decision by T'o-pa Tao to combine secular and religious authority in the person of the ruler and translate this into massive, visible architectural statements was to have huge ramifications for later Turkish architecture. Never mind the comparison between the Northern Wei and the Merovingians, it is their comparison with the Seljuk conquest of Iran and the Ottoman of Constantinople that form the more relevant analogy here: the T'o-pa/Northern Wei symbiosis was a 'dress rehearsal' for much that was to characterise later Turk history. We thus leave the earliest history of the Turks as a Far Eastern people on the threshold of world history.

Chapter 3

THE TURKS MOVE WESTWARDS

THE PRE-ISLAMIC TURK EMPIRES

The two centuries during which the Turks were the dominant power in Inner Asia seem to mark a turning point since, for the first time in recorded history, an essentially nomad empire bordered simultaneously on three major sedentary civilizations: those of China, Iran, and the Western world as represented by Byzantium. A more or less permanent link was established between these three civilizations, allowing the free flow of trade and with it, one must presume, a range of ideas and information.

(Denis Sinor[1])

We have seen in the previous chapter how the Turks, barely removed from their forest origins, had already impacted upon one of history's major ancient civilisations, that of China. Their subsequent spread westwards to affect the history of the remainder of the Eurasian land mass—and in the context of the present study, Europe in particular—is inextricably bound up with the nature of the Inner Eurasian steppe lands that lie between China and Europe (Pl. 19). This, however, is an entire subject in itself, and the relationship of the steppe nomads (of whom the Turks were a major element) to Europe will be examined in the fourth volume in this series, when the steppe nomads and their empires will be explored more deeply.*

---

* *The Gates of Europe.*

For the moment we may observe that to some extent the steppe can be compared more to a sea than to land: like the seas, the steppe has been subject to the constant movement of peoples who are eventually 'beached up' in the lands on its rim. Historian Michael Khodarkovsky takes the metaphor further when he compares the caravan cities to sea ports, the caravans themselves to ships, and the nomadic raiders to pirates.[2] But one must caution against the terms 'hordes' and 'waves' frequently used to describe such movements. Such terms give a very false impression of movements that were as often as not very gradual, usually taking place over several generations, frequently peaceful, and with assimilation and accommodation on the way, even though the end result might result in long-term change. In fact it is rare that a single definable culture or people emerge on the steppe, despite the preponderance of tribal and national names; such names were usually just that of a prominent group that incorporated many other tribes. Archaeologist Philip Kohl, when discussing the prehistory of the steppe, emphasises that 'The cultures that ethnographers study are not pure, pristine entities developing in a vacuum. Rather, they are almost always hybrids, fissioning or coalescing, assimilating or modifying the customs of the neighbouring peoples with whom they constantly interact.'[3]

In other words, the very nature of the steppe has never been static, but has seen sweeping movements of peoples throughout its history. Hence, the Turk migrations from their homelands were never any conscious tribal decision to 'go west young man' but were just one— albeit one of the more important—of the many groups of people swept up in this perpetual *Volkswanderung*. Subsequent Turkish dynasties such as the Ottoman or the Timurid states are therefore frequently characterised as somehow 'nomadic', as 'yet another pillaging mounted horde [from the steppe]'.[4] But it is a cardinal mistake to overstate the nomadic nature of Turkish dynasties and states, just as it would be a mistake to characterise the Arab caliphate as nomadic because of its Bedouin background, or the early English and Russian states as nomadic because of their Viking background. Turkish movements throughout were as much symbiosis and assimilation as conquests, so were equally characterised by sedentary civilisations as by nomadism, as we have seen in their early history in the Northern Wei. This symbiosis was to continue as they moved westwards.

A Eurasian empire: the First Turk Empire (Map 3)

Early Turk history has been reconstructed mainly from Chinese sources, supplemented by the Turk runic inscriptions on the Orkhon River in Mongolia and the occasional Byzantine source. These are often contradictory and their interpretation—particularly of the Chinese sources—is frequently disputed, so the modern accounts vary in detail and dates. But the following account represents a broad consensus.

The collapse of the Hsiung-nu Empire at the end of the first century AD in the steppe to the north of China resulted in various tribal movements and dissolving and re-forming alliances, with no particular group filling the vacuum. Eventually a new confederation emerged in the fourth century dominated by the Juan-juan tribes. The Turks were described in Chinese accounts of the Juan-juan as a group of iron-workers in the Altai Mountains subject to the Juan-juan Confederacy. The confederation was seriously weakened first of all by a major defeat inflicted upon them by the Northern Wei in the mid-fifth century, with the *coup de grâce* delivered by a Turk revolt in 552 led by Bumin, who destroyed their power and inherited their title of Kagan. By 555 the remaining Juan-juan were forced to flee westwards.[*] As a consequence, the Turks quickly filled the vacuum in the steppes, emerging as the First Turk Empire, or Kaganate (after the title of the ruler, the *kagan*, first used as the title of the Juan-juan ruler) covering a vast area stretching from the borders of Manchuria in the east to the Talas River (mainly in present-day southern Kazakhstan) in the west. One of the reasons for their rapid success was the metal armour worn by their elite cavalry known as 'wolves', thus recalling both their traditional skills and their mythic origins—and anticipating later history. The Turks had arrived on the threshold of world history—and had created the very first Eurasian empire.

The first kagan was Bumin (or T'u-men, a non-Turk name), the only one to rule over a united empire, for on his death he was succeeded by his two sons Muhan (553-72), who ruled the eastern half of the empire, and Ishtemi (553-?) who ruled the western half. The eastern empire comprised mainly Mongolia, but Muhan soon extended it to incorporate most of Manchuria. Ishtemi, the Kagan of the Western Turks, is known

---

[*] The Juan-juan eventually came into Europe, where they are known as the Avars. This is discussed more in *The Gates of Europe*, vol. 4 in this series.

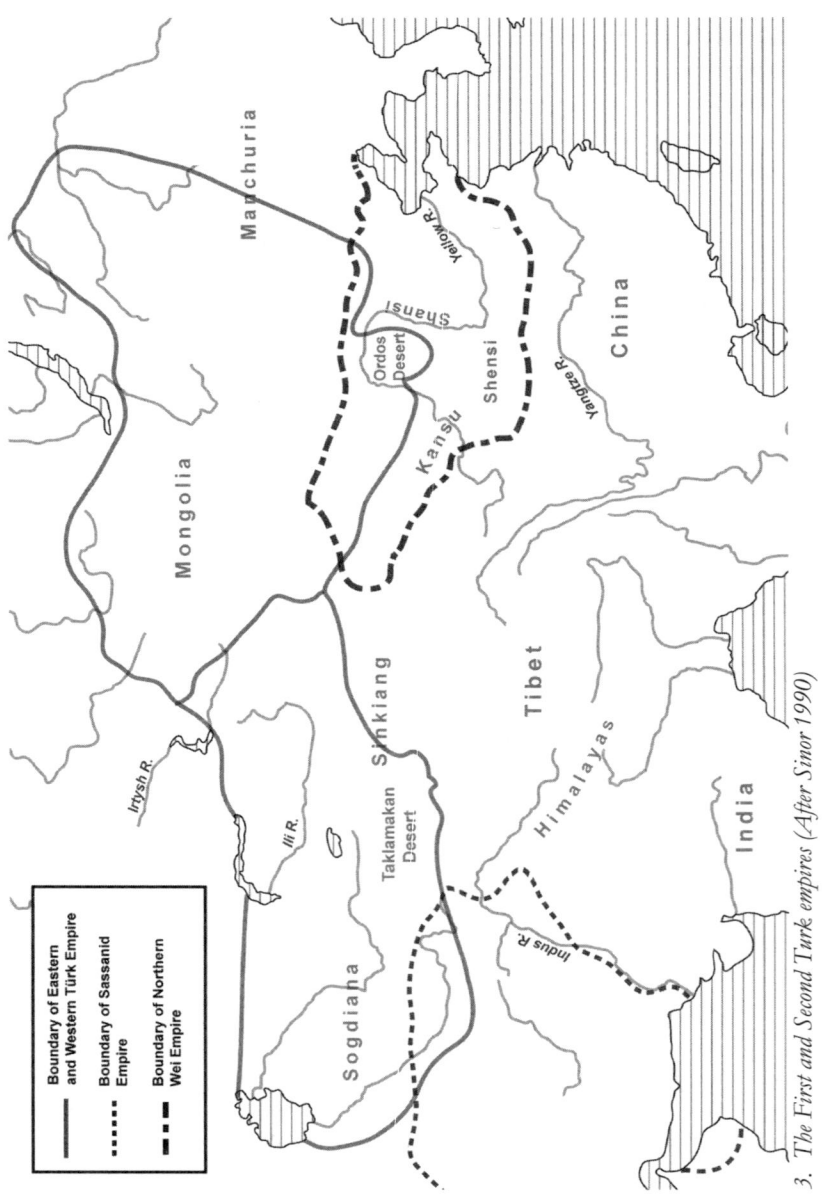

3. *The First and Second Turk empires (After Sinor 1990)*

from Byzantine sources and was one of the rulers who overthrew the Hephthalite Empire (a steppe people related to the Huns) of Central Asia and the Indian borderlands of the fifth-sixth century, in alliance with Khusrau I Anushirvan of Iran. By about 555 his empire probably extended as far as the Aral Sea and possibly even as far as the Volga.

Ishtemi also sent several diplomatic missions to Constantinople, the very first contact of the Turks with the city with which they were eventually to be identified above all others. The very first Turk we know about to enter Constantinople was the envoy Aksel in 563, but the main mission was led by a Soghdian (one of the Central Asian peoples subject to the Turks), Maniakh, in about 568 to the Emperor Justin II. Maniakh was to propose a grand alliance between the Byzantine and Turk Empires to outflank their mutual enemy, the Sasanian Empire of Iran, as well as to pursue another mutual enemy, the Avars (descendants of the Juan-juan), at that time raiding Byzantine territory in the Balkans. Maniakh had an audience with Justin II, during which he played (what he thought) his ace card: a proposal to bring Chinese silks direct to Constantinople by-passing the Iranians' extortionate taxes. Justin was unimpressed, and to emphasise his point conducted Maniakh personally around his own imperial silk factories. Nevertheless, Justin responded with a diplomatic mission led by Zemarkhos to the Turks in 569 and several more exchanges were made (described by the Byzantine historian Menander) until 576 when the good relations collapsed with a Turk raid on Byzantine possessions in the Crimea.

In the Byzantine accounts of these momentous first contacts between Turk and Roman, the Turk ruler is called 'Silziboulos', which is otherwise unknown in Turk and Chinese sources. He may be a relatively minor Turk provincial ruler, which seems unlikely, or it may be just another name for Ishtemi. Be that as it may, Ishtemi was succeeded as Emperor of the Western Turks by his son Tardu, who ruled until 603.

The Kagan of the Eastern Turks, Taspar (572-81), was converted to Buddhism by a Chinese monk. Buddhism then spread among the Turks, although it faced some resistance from the native Turk shaman cults, and there was increasing Chinese cultural influence, to some extent similar to the Sinicization of the Turks under the Northern Wei. On the whole, however, both Kaganates were marked by religious tolerance. During the time of Taspar, the Gandharan monk Jinagupta translated many of the sacred Buddhist texts into both Turkish and

Chinese at the great monastery at Kucha in the Tarim Basin in China, and Zoroastrianism, Christianity and Manichaeism also flourished under the tolerant Turk rulers, as well as the indigenous heaven worship of the steppe. The kagans (even those who were Buddhist) were regarded as semi-divine whose blood must not be shed, even if they were to be executed, a practice that the Ottomans still continued centuries later (strangulation by silk cord being the convenient way of side-stepping this inconvenient rule).

The Eastern Turks were instrumental in bringing about the end of the Sui Dynasty of China and helping the establishment of the T'ang Dynasty in the early seventh century.* Indeed, the T'ang themselves were of mixed Chinese and steppe (Hsiung-nu) descent that included Turks in their administration (and it is notable that the T'ang were almost unique in Chinese dynasties in not building any part of the Great Wall system). However, there was increasing conflict between the Western and Eastern arms of the Turk Empire in the early seventh century, and the Eastern Turk Empire collapsed with the death of its Kagan Hsieh-li (619-30). The very nature of the empire, remaining essentially a steppe confederation rather than a centrally ruled state more characteristic of sedentary empires, meant that it was always prone to dissipation in any case, and this inherent weakness was to characterise most Turk polities until the Ottomans. Much of the Eastern Turk Empire was absorbed into the T'ang Empire and many Turks settled in the Chinese borderlands after this collapse, the ancestors of the Turk populations of China today. The Western Turk Empire absorbed much of the Central Asian territories and was strengthened greatly by the Eastern collapse.

Indeed, the Western Turk Empire was expanding rapidly, particularly with the defeat of the former Hephthalite Empire centred in northern Bactria. By 616/7 a Turk army had even penetrated deep into Sasanian Iran as far as Rayy, just south of Tehran. In 619 the most powerful of the Western Turk Kagans succeeded to the throne, T'ung yabgu Kagan. Under T'ung yabgu the empire reached its greatest extent, incorporating the Tarim Basin, Ferghana, Bactria, and parts of Afghanistan and northern Pakistan, with T'ung yabgu himself advancing as far as the

---

* This was indirectly a part of a greater war being fought far to the west between Sasanian Persia and Byzantium, that drew the Turks in and had an effect as far east as China, which I bravely describe in the second volume of this series, *Towards One World*, as 'the greatest war in the history of the world.'

Indus in 625. This resulted in a shift of gravity for the empire, with Tukharistan—ancient Bactria—and its capital at Qunduz on the Oxus becoming the centre of the empire. There was an increase in Turk immigration into these areas, particularly in and around the Hindu Kush.

THE LAST FLOWERING OF GANDHARAN ART

T'ung yabgu was furthermore known to be favourably inclined towards Buddhism, and the vigorous Buddhist art of Central Asia continued to be patronised by the Turks. Many of the isolated mountain valleys of the Hindu Kush as well as the plains surrounding them came to be ruled by petty Turk princes; princes, however, who not only absorbed the cultures they encountered but patronised them on a massive scale, and there was a consequent explosion of Buddhist art in the Hindu Kush area, a renaissance of the great days of Gandharan art.

The art style known as 'Gandharan' (after the ancient Achaemenid province of that name straddling the present Pakistan-Afghanistan border region) was a hybrid style that took form in the last few centuries BC and fused Indian and Greek art under the Indo-Greek kingdom. Although the kingdom itself collapsed in the first century BC, the art proved particularly vigorous, continuing to develop and flourish reaching its height under the Kushan Empire in the first few centuries AD. The predominant elements were the Buddhist religion and Greek sculpture, although Roman styles also penetrated under the Kushans, when the art is often labelled 'Romano-Buddhist' (indeed, the sculpture is startlingly similar to Roman sculpture of the same period).

The best known of the Buddhist centres patronised by the Western Turk Empire was Bamiyan with its colossal Buddhas (Pls 11-12). Deservedly famous though the great standing Buddhas are, they have nonetheless detracted from the numerous other remains of Buddhist art at Bamiyan: a third standing Buddha (at Kakrak), three seated Buddhas, rumours of a colossal sleeping Buddha (first reported by the Chinese pilgrim Hsiuen Tsiang in the seventh century), one excavated stupa with the unexcavated remains of several more, and numerous frescos and reliefs.

In the architecture and art generally of Bamiyan there exists a surprising paradox. For Bamiyan was only a minor principality in the

Western Turk federation, the capital of which was at Qunduz in north-eastern Afghanistan, where no monuments on such a scale have been discovered. It has been suggested that Bamiyan may have been a dynastic centre for the Western Turks,[5] in much the same way that Surkh Kotal (a massive terraced dynastic shrine in northern Afghanistan) functioned for the Kushan Dynasty centuries previously (a tradition perhaps ultimately originating with the ancient Achaemenid dynastic centre of Persepolis: architecture embodying the authority of the ruler). In this respect the concept behind the colossal Buddhas at Bamiyan resembles that of the earlier Northern Wei colossal Buddhas at Yungang in China, where each Buddha represents the ruler, invested with the authority of Buddha in Mahayana Buddhism. The tradition of combining the authority of secular ruler with that of the religion in a colossal dynastic monument was to become a feature of the Turks as we shall see. Whether or not this is true, Buddhist architecture reached a peak at Bamiyan. The caves cut out of the mountainside housed thousands of devotees; the colossal statues were the ultimate embodiment of the Buddha image, while the painting and sculpture combined Hellenistic, Iranian and Indian elements that influenced subsequent Chinese at one end of the world and Islamic at the other in one of the most extraordinary statements of both political and religious self-confidence in the world.

Above all, Bamiyan was not the only 'principality' to benefit from this last great flowering of Gandharan art under the benevolent—and religiously tolerant—rule of the Turk Kagans. There were many more, usually small petty states, often no more than an isolated mountain valley or a princely court, but all enjoying astonishing artistic patronage with a huge outpouring of works of art. At Tepe Sardar near Ghazni, for example, the largest stupa complex in Afghanistan was built almost literally encrusted with sculptures—Hindu as well as Buddhist. Other such centres of late Buddhist art were the giant sleeping Buddha at Ajina Tepe in Tajikistan and stupa complexes at Funduqistan and Kandahar (Pl. 13) in Afghanistan. Many subject peoples, such as the Soghdians north of the Oxus, underwent a renaissance under their Turk rulers—indeed, the achievements of the First Turk Empire was to a large extent the result of a Soghdian-Turk symbiosis, just as Ottoman civilisation was largely a Greek-Turkish symbiosis.

REVIVAL AND RESURGENCE: THE SECOND TURK EMPIRE (MAP 3)

A new alliance was entered into between the Turks and the Byzantine Empire under Emperor Heraclius against the Sasanian Emperor Khusrau II Parviz, but T'ung yabgu was killed in a revolt of the Karluk (another Turk confederation) in 630, so effective use was never made of the alliance. Following his death the empire slowly disintegrated, with eastern parts of the empire passing nominally under T'ang rule and western parts becoming increasingly encroached upon by the subsequent Arab invasions. It is likely, however, that disintegration would have been inevitable even without T'ang or Arab encroachments, as the 'empire' was, at best, never more than a large-scale tribal confederation, and not a centrally ruled and organised state. This is not to say that it was merely a barbaric horde: many of the Turkish princes, particularly in and around the Hindu Kush mountains of Afghanistan, were great and cultured patrons of the arts as we have observed, and many subject peoples, such as the Soghdians around Bukhara, Samarkand, the Ferghana Valley and Tashkent, underwent a renaissance under the benevolent overlordship of their Turk rulers (Pl. 14). Many petty Turk principalities also managed to hang on for another century or so, particularly in the Hindu Kush, but the last Kagan of the Western Turks, Chen-chu, was killed in battle against the Chinese in 659.

With the collapse of both arms of the First Turk Kaganate there followed a period of fragmentation and demoralisation. The Turk tribes were re-united by Elterish Kutlugh (682-92), an adventurer who set out initially with just seventeen men to establish the Second Turk Kaganate. Between 697 and 691 it expanded westwards into Mongolia and the empire soon came to be centred on the Orkhon River. For the first time contemporary Turk sources survive recording these events in the form of a series of rock inscriptions in Turk runes on the Orkhon River. Elterish was succeeded by his brother, Kapghan Kagan (691-716), who consolidated the Second Kaganate and entered into a rapprochement with the Chinese. His rule is regarded as the height of the Second Turk Empire. Two more brothers succeeded Kapghan: Költegin and Bilgä Kagan (716-34), who ruled together. Under them the Second Kaganate reached its greatest extent, but it collapsed quickly on the death of Bilgä, with the last kagan killed in 745. The Second Turk Empire had lasted barely sixty years.

The period of the collapse corresponds to the dramatic expansion of the first Arab caliphate under the Umayyads into Central Asia, and this doubtless was a contributory cause. But it would be a mistake to over-emphasise this. Nomadic empires were rarely more than loose tribal confederations on a large scale, which by their nature are always subject to fragmentation: there was rarely the highly centralised rule that characterise the great sedentary empires of antiquity. Hence, they were inherently unstable, and it is likely that the Turk Empire would have collapsed even without the Umayyad Caliphate. It would also be a mistake to over-emphasise the 'Turk' nature of the empire (although this was without doubt its predominant characteristic). Nomadic states and confederations usually took the name of the dominant tribe or ethnicity—in this case the Turks—but this does not mean that the confederation comprised solely those people: it would comprise many often very disparate tribes and peoples, both nomadic and sedentary, Huns and Mongols as well as Soghdians and Chinese.

Nevertheless, even after the collapse the western parts of Inner Eurasia were increasingly dominated by disparate Turk tribal groups, with new minor confederations emerging such as the Karluks. There was a general dispersion of Turk tribes westwards, such as the Pechenegs to the Black Sea steppe and the Oghuz Turks (or Ghuzz in the Arab sources) to the Aral Sea region. The Oghuz, originally from Mongolia, were probably a tribal confederation rather than a single tribe, and were to figure largely in the rise of the Seljuks as we shall see. Many of the cities such as Panjikent (Pl. 14) were probably still ruled by Turk elites over indigenous Soghdian populations, although there is no evidence of tensions, and further south in the remoter valleys of the Hindu Kush petty Turk princes continued to rule their small fiefdoms as we have seen. But on the broader steppes outside such enclaves, the Turk tribes increasingly formed the majority population, albeit mostly pastoral nomads. The period of the Turk Empires was thus one of ethnic change, marking the final disappearance of the Scythian and other related Indo-European speaking groups of antiquity and the advent of the Turkish groups, which still characterises most of Central Asia to this day.

INDIAN SUMMER

There was a brief Indian summer of Turk kings in the Hindu Kush that witnessed a final flourishing before Islam. One of the petty rulers who survived the Kaganate collapse was able to rally Turk forces around Kabul to create a new dynasty known as the Turk Shahis of Kabul. Not only did the Turk Shahis and their successors create an island of stability in the ashes of Kaganate collapse, they resisted the first Muslim incursions and encouraged the last creative upsurge of the Gandharan style. The dynasty was founded by Barhatigin who seized Kabul in about 666 after an Arab raid from Seistan. It was certainly the Muslim Arab invasions that forced Barhatagin to found his dynasty and defend both the region and its rich cultural identity from the new religion—with some success, as he routed an Arab army in 683 and again in 698-9. By a series of skilful negotiations backed up by military force the Turk Shahis of Kabul were able to safeguard their mountain stronghold and stave off the invading Arabs, as often as not by drawing them into their territory only to cut off their rear by blocking the passes.

The last Turk Shah of Kabul was Lagartuman, who was forced in the end to buy off the Arabs of Seistan with tribute. It might have been this climbdown that prompted his chief minister, the Brahman Kallas, to overthrow Lagartuman in about 843 bringing about the end of the Turk dynasty and starting his own, the Hindu dynasty. This vigorous dynasty of Hindu kings in Kabul was able to stave off the Arab advance a while longer and even initiate some monumental building programmes. But the Muslim advance was ultimately unstoppable (albeit not reaching parts of Afghanistan until the 1880s) with Kabul falling under the rule of the Muslim Saffarid dynasty of Seistan in the mid-tenth century.

The Turk Shahs of Kabul are little more than a footnote in the expansion of the Turks westwards. Normally they would hardly rate even that in the present pages—many other early Turk states we have omitted altogether—if not for one important factor: the existing Turk element in eastern Afghanistan was to be a vital background in the rise centuries later of one of the most important Turkish dynasties in early Islam: the Ghaznavids. We will be discussing the Ghaznavids further in the next chapter, but for the moment it is worth remembering that the Ghaznavid dynasty did not rise in a 'Turkish vacuum' in eastern Afghanistan.

FOLLOWERS OF THE PROPHET MANI:
KINGDOM OF THE UIGHURS

During the middle of the seventh century AD we see a resurgence of Chinese power in Sinkiang in the western borderlands of China under the T'ang Dynasty. This brought the region more firmly under Chinese control after a period of being ruled by many different isolated local dynasties, both Hsiung-nu and Chinese. But at the same time or a little later, we see the emergence of a new people to the region, the Uighur Turks.

The first mention of the Uighurs is in Chinese sources of the third century BC. These refer to them as a group known then as the Ting-ling to the north of and subject to the Hsiung-nu, along with the nearby Chien-k'un (identified with the Kirghiz). Both the Ting-ling and the Chien-k'un are identified by the Chinese as two of the five Turk tribes. By the seventh century AD the Uighurs were a subject people of the Eastern Turk Kaganate living in the region of the Selenga River to the north of the Kaganate. They were regarded by the Chinese as distinct from the Turks themselves, in fact as descendants of the Hsiung-nu (who were in any case regarded—mistakenly—by the Chinese as connected to the Turks).

The Uighur Empire lasted from 744 to 840, ruled from its capital at Karabalghasun on the Orkhon River. The Uighur Turks were originally centred in western Mongolia as subjects of the Eastern Turk Empire. In 742 a coalition of Uighur, Karluk and Bismil tribes (all Turk) defeated the last of the Eastern Turks and a new kaganate was formed. It was led by Alp Bilgä Kagan, a Bismil, who was in turn overthrown by a Karluk-Uighur coalition. The Uighurs in turn ousted the Karluk and established the Uighur Kaganate in 744 ruled by Kutlugh Bilgä Köl Kagan. The Uighurs regarded themselves as continuing the Turk Kaganate rather than replacing it, with Kutlugh himself tracing descent from Bumin Kagan. Effectively, therefore, it was a Third Turk Empire. Kutlugh died in 747 and was succeeded by his son Bilgä Köl or El-Etmish Bilgä Kagan (747-59). Under him the Kaganate underwent considerable expansion and consolidation. In particular, the Uighurs intervened successfully in a Chinese civil war, aiding the ruling T'ang to suppress the rebellion led by the Soghdian Lu-shan and successfully helped to recapture their capital of Loyang. As a result T'ang China was for a short time a dependency of the Uighurs.

The Kaganate reached its height under Bilgä's son Tängri (or Mou-yü) Kagan (659-79), although the power behind the throne was Tängri's brother Bögü Khan, son of Bilgä and a Chinese princess. Tängri and Bögü also converted to Manichaeism as a result of Soghdian proselytisation, and Bögü was accordingly awarded the title *Zahan-i Mani* ('Emanation of Mani'). There was a resultant increase in Soghdian influence at both the Uighur and T'ang courts, causing resentment in both camps. Manichaeism had originally arrived in eastern Central Asia with refugees escaping from both Zoroastrian Persian and Christian Roman persecutions in the West after the fourth century, and flourished under the Uighurs.* Under the reign of Kutlugh Bilgä Kagan (790-5) the office of *ögäsi* or 'grand vizier' was instigated, an institution that was to become a feature of Turkish rule in later centuries. The capital was the old Turk capital of Karabalghasun on the Orkhon River, and Uighur inscriptions there record the achievements. Karabalghasun is described by the Arab traveller Tamim ibn Bakr in 821, when the majority religion of the city was Manichaeism. Another important Uighur city was Bay Baliq on the Selenga River.

The Uighur weakening of China, exacerbated by the Tibetan invasions of the same time, enabled Sinkiang to be penetrated more and more by the Uighur Turks, to eventually displace the 'native' Tokharian population (a people speaking an isolated Indo-European language). One of the greatest of the Uighur kagans, Tängridä Kagan, defeated the Tibetans and pushed them back beyond the Kunlun Mountains. There was a slow decline after his death, aggravated by a severe winter in their homelands and grazing grounds on the Orkhon in 839, leading to the eventual Uighur defeat by the Kirghiz in 840 and subsequent dispersion.

This dispersion resulted in Uighur tribes migrating westwards to Beshbaliq (Beiteng) and Turfan, establishing a second Uighur kingdom in about 860 with its capital at Khocho, modern Karakhoja in the Turfan oasis (Pls 15-17). The kingdom was never big enough, nor did it accommodate enough non-Uighur Turk tribes, for it to be styled a 'Fourth Turk Empire', and the title 'Kagan' was soon dropped in favour of *Idiqut*. This can be translated as 'Holy Majesty' (an alternative name for their capital today is still *Idiqut Shahri* or 'Idiqut City')—perhaps a reference

---

* The world spread of Manichaeism and impact of its ideas is explored more in Chapter 9 of Volume 2 of this series.

to their patronage of Manichaeism. The kingdom soon expanded to include all of the northern Tarim basin. There is no evidence, however, that this took the form of violent invasions and destruction of the native Tocharians. On the contrary, the new arrivals appear to have co-existed quite peacefully with the older Tocharian population for several centuries. The native population eventually lost its distinct identity and became absorbed by the Uighurs, although in turn the newcomers were sedentarised by the Tocharians. The process, therefore, seems to have been one of gradual assimilation, eventually resulting in the extinction of the Tocharian language, much as Turkish in Anatolia eventually displaced the older Greek and Anatolian languages there. They certainly absorbed many of the Tocharian cultural traits in the process, adopting the Tocharian form of Buddhism so wholeheartedly that there appears little change in the artistic record to mark the ethnic transition. The entire contact was a classic case of Turkish cross-fertilisation; the result was a brilliant civilisation.

Manichaeism continued to flourish under the Uighurs, becoming virtually the state religion of Sinkiang after the ninth century, surviving down to the thirteenth (Pl. 18). The Manichaeans were not the only minorities fleeing religious persecution in the west who found protection under the tolerant Uighurs. Second to them were the Nestorian Christians. Although Christian, Nestorianism was condemned as heretical by the orthodox court in Constantinople and its followers persecuted by their fellow Christians, causing them to flee eastwards along the trade routes. They flourished in Sinkiang after the ninth century, giving rise to later European legends of the lost Christian kingdom of Prester John, and even spread to Mongolia where many of the leading Mongols after Genghis Khan practised Nestorian Christianity. In addition to Manichaeism and Nestorianism, Buddhism continued to flourish in the Uighur kingdom, although it began to die out after the tenth century. Zoroastrianism, Confucianism and various pagan religions were also openly practised in this extraordinarily attractive and tolerant civilisation of the Uighurs. As well as its vibrant and varied religious life, the arts were extensively patronised; painting and music especially featured highly, with the paintings leaving their mark in the astonishingly rich cave and temple paintings which are a feature of Sinkiang's heritage today (Pl. 18). The Uighurs also adopted the Soghdian form of the Aramaic script and passed it onto the Mongols, who still use it today (Pl. 19).

To the end, the Uighurs preserved their distinct culture and religion even when almost all other Turks were converting to Islam. Between the tenth and thirteenth centuries they maintained stiff and successful resistance to the Islam of the Karakhanid Turks of Kashgar just to their west. The Uighur kingdom came under the Western Liao Dynasty in the mid-twelfth century, and in 1209 Barchuk Art Tegin voluntarily submitted to Genghis Khan. Rebels took Beshbaliq in 1270 and Khocho in 1284, which brought an end to the Uighur kingdom.

THE END OF THE BEGINNING

In this brief summary of the origins and early history of the Turks, several characteristic features become apparent. First concerns the definition of 'Turk': peoples as diverse as Türgesh, Karluks, Kirghiz and Uighurs all, as we have observed, seem to be lumped under the name 'Turk', and soon Karakhanids, Oghuz, Seljuks, Kazakhs, Uzbeks, Ottomans and a host of other names would be added to the list. True, all of these groups are ethnically and linguistically related, but the name 'Turk' seems to emerge effectively as 'pan-Turk', a term that both transcended and united all Turk groups. Equally, early Turk history incorporated many non-Turk cultural elements: Soghdian, Mongol, Hsiung-nu, Hun, Chinese and many others, and later Turk history would see many more included, from Indians in the east to Bulgarians in the west. Careful analysis of many early Turk names, even those of major rulers such as Bumin, Ishtemi and Silziboulos, furthermore reveal them to be of non-Turk origin. Ishtemi's full title was Sri Yabghu Kagan, a composite one: Sri (Hindu), Yabghu (Iranian) and Kagan (Avar). Clearly, right from the very beginning Turk culture was multi-ethnic and multi-cultural, characterised by a readiness to absorb non-Turk elements, traits that were to characterise their civilisation in subsequent millennia.

At the same time, there was a very clear common Turk identity, a consciousness of being *Turk*, that in some ways anticipates later Turkish nationalist ideas. The idea of the common Turk identity comes across very strongly in the Orkhon inscriptions and constantly recurs—in the eleventh century *Siyasatnama*, for example, a strong self-awareness of 'Turks' is a recurrent theme.* In some ways these two characteristics—the

---

* The *Siyasat-nama*, or *The Book of Government or Rules for Kings*, was a 'Mirror for Princes'

readiness to incorporate other cultures on the one hand and the emphasis on a Turk identity on the other—seem contradictory, but both were to be a feature of subsequent Turkish history.

The collapse of the Second Turk Empire brings about the end of the beginning of the Turks in world history, but already their achievement was impressive. The wealth of the 'neo-Gandharan' artistic revival in the Hindu Kush, the Soghdian renaissance north of the Oxus and the upsurge in Buddhism and Manichaeism east of the Pamirs are more than ample testament to their already significant legacy. But their effect on the subsequent history of Inner Asia was, if anything, even more significant. In the words of a major historian of the Turks, Denis Sinor:

> The Türks achieved and maintained for a period, long by Inner Asian standards, the political unification of a stretch of land that reached from the confines of China to the borders of Byzantium. They intervened with lasting effect in the destinies of China, Iran and Byzantium; they conveyed knowledge between the Greek, Iranian, Indian and Chinese worlds. In the Western world, for centuries, their name was used as a common denomination of barbarians, irrespective of their language, whereas for the peoples of Inner Asia the name Türk became, and has remained, the hallmark of the unity of peoples sharing a common language.[6]

Even this achievement was simply a curtain raiser of greater things to come.

---

written for the Seljuk kings by the great Persian prime minister Nizam al-Mulk (translated by Hubert Darke, London 1960).

1   *Detail of* The Wedding at Cana *by Veronese supposedly depicting Sultan Süleyman the Magnificent sitting down to dine with Emperor Charles V of Spain. (© Réunion des musées nationaux Agence Photographique)*

2   *A modern mosque built entirely in the Ottoman imperial style at Verkhnyaya Pishma, a Tatar area outside Ekaterinburg in the Urals. This is closely modelled on the vizirial mosques of the sixteenth century built by the great Ottoman architect Sinan, such as the Hadım Ibrahim Paşa Mosque in Istanbul, of which this is a virtually exact copy. Even the marble is imported from Turkey..*

3   Uighur Turks in a street scene in Kashgar. Note the bilingual sign in Chinese and Uighur Turkish, the only country in the world where Turkish is still written in the Arabic script.

4   What is a Turk? Not a race: compare the Uighur Turks from Keriya in China on the left to a Turk from Istanbul on the right.

5 *Statue of Ataturk in Artvin with his slogan 'Proud be he who calls himself a Turk'.*

6 *The Siberian forest, the probable original homeland of the Turk people, still with Turk related ethnic groups today, such as Tatars and Yakut.*

7 The Great Wall of China at Qingshihe across the Ordos steppe.

8   The Yungang caves outside Tatung (Datong), the first 'Turk' capital, where the T'o-pa emperors of the Northern Wei Dynasty first introduced giganticism into Buddhist art.

9   The giant Buddha statue at Yungang built by the Northern Wei Emperor T'o-pa Tao, representing the authority of the Buddha invested in himself: the statues is, in effect, both Buddha and T'o-pa Tao.

10   The Inner Eurasian steppe belt, here in south-western Siberia, where the first Turk empires flourished.

11   *The valley of Bamiyan in Afghanistan, dominated by the two giant Buddha statues built by the Western Turks.*

12   *The large Buddha statue at Bamiyan.*

13   *The Buddhist stupa at Kandahar.*

14   *The Sogdian city of Panjikent in the Zarafshan Mountains (Tajikistan), which flourished under the Western Turk Empire.*

15   *The vast remains of Khocho, modern Karakhoja (Chinese Gaochang) in Sinkiang, capital of the later Uighur kingdom. Also known as Idiqut Shahri after the title of the Uighur king, and Shahr-i Daqianus or 'Decius City' after the legend of the Seven Sleepers of Ephesus preserved in the Qur'an.*

16   *Another view of Karakhoja, with a Buddhist stupa in the foreground.*

17   The central Manichaean temple at Karakhoja.

18   The Manichaean-Buddhist cave monasteries of Bezeklik outside Karakhoja.

19   The Uighur script used in modern Mongolian at the site of Xanadu.

20   The old town of Kashgar, the first Karakhanid capital, where the first mass conversion of Turks to Islam took place.

21   *Victory minaret in Uzkend in Ferghana, the second Karakhanid capital.*

22   *The Kalan Minaret in Bukhara, built by the Karakhanid prince Nasr.*

23   The victory minarets at Ghazni in Afghanistan.

24   The vast forecourt to one of the palaces at the Ghaznavid winter capital of Lashkari Bazar.

25   *The entrance to one of the palaces at Lashkari Bazar.*

26   *The Seljuk dome chamber built by Malik Shah's vizier, Taj ul-Mulk, at the Friday Mosque in Isfahan.*

27   Seljuk brick decorated minaret at Damghan in Iran.

28   A detail of one of the Seljuk brick decorated tombs at Kharraqan in Iran.

29 The port of Antalya, with the lovely fluted Seljuk minaret of Sultan Alaeddin Keykubad in the foreground.

30 The Seljuk harbour at Alanya, one of the best preserved medieval harbours in the Mediterranean.

31   The great Genoese and Seljuk fortress of Sudak in Crimea.

32   The Ince Minare Madrasa at Konya.

Chapter 4

THE LURE OF ISLAM

SLAVES, MERCHANTS AND CONQUERORS

True nobility belongs to the man of wisdom and intellect
... The wise ruler puts his realm in good order so that
the common folk become rich, and he in turn makes their
wealth a fortress for himself ... a thousand virtues are
required for the world-conqueror ... with these virtues
the world-ruler clears away the fog and grasps the realm;
he wields the sword and lops off the neck of his foe; he
governs his territory and his people with law and justice.

(Yusuf Khass Hajib of Balasaghun on Turk rulership[1])

The so-called 'Abbasid Revolution' of 750, which saw the establishment
of the Abbasid dynasty and the move of the Caliphate from Damascus
to the new city of Baghdad, seemed to turn Islam's back upon the
West. Up until that time the capital of Islam was in the Hellenised city
of Damascus with its Mediterranean orientation; its main outward
expansion was focussed towards the west, with Constantinople a major
goal and the Roman Empire a model. But with the move to Baghdad
Islam turned more eastward: expansion westward largely stopped, there
were no more major campaigns against Constantinople, and the main
focus for expansion was eastwards. To some extent the event was similar
to Constantine's move of the capital of the Roman Empire from Rome
to Constantinople: Rome, like Damascus, was weighed down by its pagan
past; Baghdad, like Constantinople, was a completely new city founded
for the new religion; both largely turned their backs upon the West.

This move also internationalised Islam. Hitherto, Islam was associated almost entirely with—or at least dominated by—the Arabs. But the Abbasid Revolution originated in the eastern Iranian world and incorporated many eastern and non-Arab disaffected elements within it, which meant that Islam was no longer dominated by the Arabs and the western Islamic lands: Islam became more universal. More importantly, it expanded more among the native non-Arab populations. This would have immense ramifications for the Middle East and for Islam generally. It was to be a reinvigorated Islam in the hands of a people from Central Asia who had no common cultural experience with the Arabs who were to transform the Arabs, the Middle East, Islam and eventually much of Europe and the Mediterranean, when the Turks came out of Central Asia some centuries later.

TURKISH SLAVES AND MASTERS

It was the ruler of one of the minor principalities on the eastern fringes of the Abbasid Caliphate who first brought Islam to the Turks and the Turks into the Middle East. Abdullah ibn Talha (830-45) was the head of the Tahirid dynasty of Khurasan, the state that straddled northeastern Iran and the western parts of Central Asia. He raided deep into the Oghuz steppe country (now corresponding roughly to Kazakhstan) bringing back some two thousand Turkish slaves from the Oghuz tribe. Two hundred of them were presented to the Caliph al-Mutawakkil in 847, the first Turks to enter Iraq. The Samanid dynasty who ruled Bukhara (a native Central Asian Iranian dynasty who had converted to Islam) was quick to realise the potential of the Turkish slave trade too, and the trade became a major commercial enterprise between the Central Asian Muslim kingdoms and the Caliphate during the course of the ninth and tenth centuries.

Turkish slaves then began entering the Middle East in greater numbers. They made a huge impact upon the Muslims who first encountered them—in more ways than one. To begin with, they appeared to stand for everything barbaric, exotic and foreign—indeed, amongst the Arab and Persian writers of the time these Turkish slaves soon became an image of both exotic beauty and barbaric cruelty, imagery that anticipated the European romantic metaphor for the noble savage a thousand years later. In this context it is essential to understand that under Islam, slaves enjoyed considerable legal rights and privileges, and were rarely 'slaves' as the term was later understood—and abused—in European contexts, such as those of the Middle Passage transported to the Americas (who enjoyed no rights whatsoever). But beautiful or barbaric, it soon became apparent that these Turkish slaves from the remotest wilds of Central Asia made poor agricultural labourers and even worse domestic servants, the fate of most slaves in early Islamic society. They were, however, natural warriors.* Consequently, more and more of these Turkish slaves were—upon conversion to Islam—incorporated into Muslim armies as mercenary slave units. The demand for more became insatiable and the trickle of Turkish slaves became a flood. But their fighting skills were too good and soon the inevitable was to happen: the Turks became the masters, eventually to dominate the Middle East until the fall of the Ottoman Empire at the end of the First World War.

This first happened at the very centre of the Abbasid Caliphate in Baghdad. From the early ninth century the Caliphs, mistrustful of their mainly Arab army increasingly dominated by powerful family factions, began to surround themselves with private bodyguards of Turkish slaves (known as *ghulams* and later as *mamluks*). These Turkish slaves, by not belonging to any of the various families or tribes vying for influence at the court, could be relied upon to owe allegiance solely to the Caliph himself, and hence grew into a powerful praetorian guard. By the middle of the ninth century, clashes in Baghdad between the Arab population and the increasingly powerful Turkish soldiers prompted the Caliph al-Mu'tasim to move the capital itself further upstream on the Tigris to the entirely new city of Samarra. The power of the Turkish *ghulams*, however, continued to increase unabated until they became the main power in the Caliphate: Caliph al-Mutawakkil was assassinated by his Turkish guard in 861, and thereafter was a rapid succession of Caliphs made and unmade by the Turkish soldiers more or less at whim. The Caliphate effectively became a puppet of the Turkish slaves, one of the main contributory causes to the decline of the Abbasids. The Islamic world was beginning to become a Turkish one.

---

* In contrast, Turkish prisoners of war who were taken by the T'ang Chinese and enslaved were solely as domestic or agricultural slaves, never as soldiers. See Schafer 1963: 40-3.

PROSPERITY, POWER AND CIVILISATION: THE LURE OF ISLAM

The Muslim Arabs defeated a Chinese army in 751 in a battle on the Talas River west of the Tien Shan Mountains. While Arab arms would never penetrate further east than this, despite the victory, it did mark the beginnings of the Islamisation of the Inner Asian steppe and the gradual retreat of the other religions. Zoroastrianism, Manichaeism and Nestorian Christianity were eventually to disappear altogether in Central Asia. Buddhism remained only among the Mongols and related groups of Inner Asia (albeit mainly due to separate Buddhist proselytisation from Tibet after the fourteenth century: modern Mongolian Tantric Buddhism is substantially different from the initial Mahayana Buddhism of the early Turks). The indigenous steppe religions of heaven worship and various forms of shamanism retreated largely to the Siberian forest belt (although elements remain in some aspects of Central Asian Islam, particularly the Sufi movements).

It must be emphasised first, however, that this process of Islamisation was spread over a very long time, with the ancient religions of Inner Asia still probably the majority religions until the tenth century or even later: Buddhism and Manichaeism simply died out slowly. And second, the nature of this conversion was largely peaceful and persuasive. Christian propaganda has for centuries misrepresented Islam as 'spread by the sword'. It is not in dispute that this occurred (and occurred in most religions, including Christianity), but by far the greatest extensions of Islam were peaceful.*

There was a brief resurgence of a pagan dynasty in Central Asia with the arrival in the twelfth century of the Qara Khitai or Western Liao, a dynasty from Manchuria who conquered a vast empire stretching from Peking to the Aral Sea. The Qara Khitai overthrew the Karakhanids and even inflicted a crushing defeat against the Seljuks, until they in turn melted away with the Mongol invasions. They hardly merit a mention in the present context, except that they remain notable as one of the very

---

* There is evidence that many of the Buddhist communities in Sinkiang came to a sudden and violent end: in Karakhoja, the later Uighur capital, the bodies of slaughtered priests were found and most of the religious archives and furniture of the monasteries were simply abandoned as if the clergy left suddenly, to be rediscovered by archaeologists almost intact at the end of the nineteenth century. This destruction, however, was almost certainly not at the hands of the first Muslims, but more likely the result of the Mongol invasions in the thirteenth century.

rare examples of a steppe confederation that actually *resisted* conversion to one of the three major monotheistic religions.[*]

But the Qara Khitai and the Seljuks are to get ahead of ourselves. To take up the historical narrative once more, in the tenth century Turk Pecheneg tribes were driven westwards into the Volga-Ural area by the neighbouring Oghuz Turks, who soon occupied the steppe-land from the Aral Sea eastwards to Chimkent near the foot of the Tien Shan Mountains. Oghuz pressure on the Pechenegs forced them to cross the Volga and put pressure on both Byzantine and Khazar lands. East of the Oghuz were the Karluk Turks, who extended eastwards to the Ferghana and Ili valleys. The Karluks in turn had migrated westwards when they fell out with the Uighurs in 747 at the time of the overthrow of the Second Turk Kaganate and the establishment of the first Uighur kingdom.

Their conflict with the Uighurs led the Karluk into an alliance with the Tibetans, but the adoption of Manichaeism by their Uighur enemies, which the Karluk associated with the subject Soghdians (hence inferiors), led many to look to Islam. In 893 the Samanid ruler of Bukhara, Isma'il, campaigned against the Karluk of the Talas River, bringing back many prisoners and converting them to Islam, a major policy of the Samanids as we have seen. Large numbers of both Karluk and Oghuz had in any case by then converted voluntarily: conversions seem to have been mainly pacific through contact with Muslim merchants and settlers in the Turk lands. An important part was also played by the various Sufi brotherhoods in Central Asia. The Sufis (from Arabic *suf*, 'wool', referring to the garment they wore; the common Persian term was *darwish* from which we obtain our word 'dervish') represented a more mystic, spiritual side of Islam. The Turks were probably more attracted to the dervishes because of their resemblance to their own native shamans—indeed, many of the Central Asian Sufi movements probably incorporated elements of shamanism. The more mystical nature of Sufism was also closer to Buddhism, previously the main established religion in the Turkish lands of Central Asia—again, many of the early Sufi movements incorporated elements of Buddhism. For these various reasons, therefore, many Karluk Turks had accepted Islam

---

[*] Such as the Turks (Islam), the Khazars (Judaism) or the Kievan Rus (Christianity). See Biran 2005. The Qara Khitai are discussed more in the fourth volume of this series, *The Gates of Europe*.

by the ninth century, according to Arabic reports. The situation was probably very similar to that of the Germanic tribes on the borders of the Roman Empire in late antiquity: as for the Germans, a major religion practised by a great power represented for the Turkish tribes the lure of prosperity, civilisation and power.

The centre of the Karluk confederacy in the ninth and tenth centuries was Balasaghun on the Talas River. With the defeat of the Uighur Kaganate further east in 840 at the hands of the Kirghiz, the Karluk chief seized the supreme Turk title and proclaimed himself Kagan. The population was mixed Turk and Soghdian, and religion would have been mixed as well: in addition to Islam and Manichaeism, there was a considerable Christian minority (we read of a large church at Balasaghun that was later converted to a mosque). Within the Karluk confederacy, a new clan was soon to emerge uppermost: the Karakhanids.

RISE OF THE BLACK LORDS (MAP 4)

The Karakhanids—their name means 'Black Lords'—were probably already one of the ruling clans of the Karluk. The defeat of the Karluk Kagan by Isma'il of Bukhara in 893 led the Karakhanids and their allied tribes to withdraw their support and migrate to the Kashgar region. There, in the middle of the tenth century, one of the Karakhanid chiefs, Prince Satuk, took one of those momentous steps that were to have enormous repercussions not only for the Turks but for the world at large. At the minor town of Artush, just north of Kashgar, Satuk converted to Islam, the first Turkish prince to do so, along with his followers. This was followed up by his conquest of Kashgar and a mass conversion to Islam of the Turks tribes under his command—'200,000 Turkish tents' accepted Islam virtually overnight according to the traditional *History of Kashghar* (Pl. 20). Satuk died soon after in 955 and the claim was almost certainly exaggerated, but his establishment of the first Turkish Islamic state makes this little known prince on the fringes of China one of the most significant Turkish princes in history.

In the last quarter of the tenth century the Karakhanids began to encroach upon the territory of Bukhara, ruled by the Iranian Samanid dynasty that had been established by Isma'il and at that time was the foremost power of Central Asia. By this time the Karakhanids had split into two, with the eastern branch centred on Balasaghun in Semirechye and the western branch at Uzkend in the Ferghana Valley, where a minaret and several monumental tombs still stand (Pl. 21). The Samanid state in Bukhara was crumbling fast under the ineffective rule of Nuh II (976-97). The Karakhanid prince Harun Bughra Khan marched on Bukhara in 992, and on 23 October 999, his successor Nasr Ilig took Bukhara and ended the rule of the Samanid dynasty, thus bringing about an end to several thousand years of rule by Iranian peoples in Central Asia. There would not be another independent Iranian state in Central Asia until the establishment of Tajikistan in 1990. The Karakhanids consolidated their victory by moving their capital once more, to Bukhara. The spectacular great victory tower, the Kalan Minaret, built by Nasr (whose name itself means 'victory' in Arabic) still soars over Bukhara today (Pl. 22).

The Karakhanid era in Central Asia also marks another major development. Under the Karakhanids in the eleventh century the Turkish language was for the first time written down using the Arabic script, which it continued to use until its replacement in Turkey itself with the Latin script by Ataturk and Cyrillic in the Turkophone countries of the Soviet Union (although most of these countries have adopted the Latin script since independence; Turkish is still written using the Arabic script in the original Karakhanid heartland in Sinkiang: see Pl. 3). Up until then, Turkish was essentially an oral language (apart from its occasional usage of runic symbols on inscriptions) and the Arabic script used solely for Arabic and Persian. The period thus marks the beginning of modern Turkish literature. It was also under the Karakhanids that Mahmud al-Kashghari produced, in about 1077, his magisterial *Compendium of Turk Dialects*. Although written in Arabic it aimed to disseminate all aspects of Turkish culture to a broader public in the Islamic world.

THE GHAZNAVIDS AND FIRST INCURSIONS IN INDIA

The Samanids had been relying increasingly upon Turkish mercenaries in their army, so that by the mid-tenth century the predominately Turkish guard in their army held real power while the reigning Samanid prince was little more than a figurehead. Upon the death of the ruler in

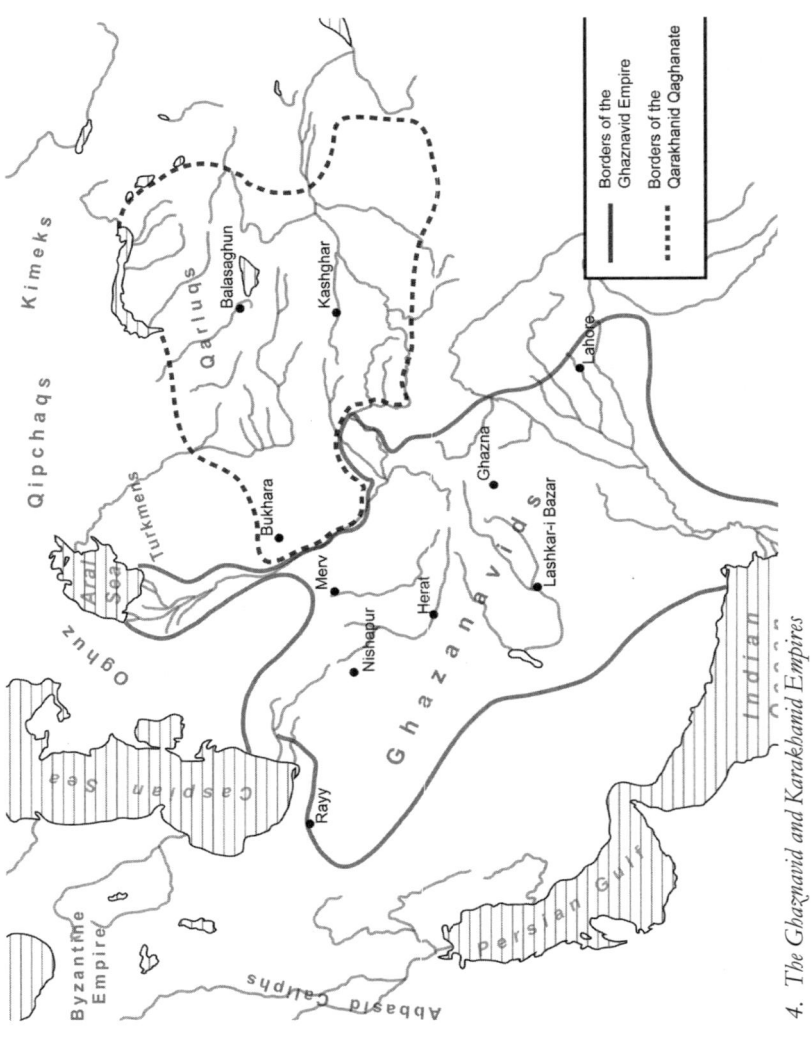

4. *The Ghaznavid and Karakhanid Empires*

Bukhara, Abd al-Malik in 961, the Turkish head of the Samanid army, Alp Tegin, attempted a coup. It failed, but the following year Alp Tegin fled southwards to Ghazna (in present-day eastern Afghanistan) near the borderlands with India to establish his own power base (Pl. 23). A Turkish slave of Alp Tegin, Sebuktegin,* established Ghazna as a separate kingdom after 977; his son, Sultan Mahmud of Ghazna, established it as a great empire after 997. The first Turkish Muslim empire had come into being, and the Muslim world would never be the same.

This fact alone ranks the Ghaznavid Empire as one of the more important empires of the Middle Ages. There are further reasons as well. The Ghaznavids, particularly under their greatest ruler, Mahmud of Ghazna, were the first to bring Islam down onto the plains of India on a substantial scale.† Thus, an additional overlay to the already multi-layered nature of Indian civilisation was added, probably the single most important event for India since the Indo-Aryan invasions nearly three thousand years previously in the way that it permanently affected the nature of Indian civilisation. The Ghaznavids were more than mere invaders, however. True to the legacy of the pre-Islamic Turk princes who ruled the petty states of the Hindu Kush under the Second Turk Empire, the Ghaznavid kings became great patrons as well. Just as their forbears had ushered in a renaissance of Gandharan civilisation, their Ghaznavid successors patronised a renaissance of Persian civilisation. Mahmud of Ghazna attracted to his court the great Persian epic poet Firdawsi, the Khwarazmian universal scientist al-Biruni, and a large number of other poets, artists, scientists, mathematicians and men of learning. The term 'renaissance' is chosen carefully here: not until popes of Rome and the merchant houses of Florence would the world see patronage again on such a grand scale. The place Firdawsi holds in world literature cannot be over-estimated, a position he holds in Persian literature similar to that of Homer in Greek or Shakespeare in English. He is also regarded by Iranians for single-handedly saving not only their pre-Islamic history, but the very Persian language itself. Al-Biruni accompanied his patron Mahmud on his campaigns in India, learnt Sanskrit and compiled the largest general compendium on India before

* The Turk suffx *–tegin*—as in Bartegin, Alptegin, Sebuktegin, etc.—means 'prince'.
† Although it was not the first time that Islam had penetrated the Subcontinent: an Arab invasion in the mid-eighth century by Muhammad Ibn Qasim had established Islam in Sind.

the modern period. He also compiled a world chronology, calculated the circumference of the globe, and wrote a history of his native Khwarazm (now lost). These are just some of the almost entirely Persian scholarship patronised at the court at Ghazna—poetry, history, literature, painting, mathematics, science—and the historian G E Tetley rightly emphasises the essentially Persian character of the Turkish Ghaznavids, as opposed to the Seljuks who were at pains to stress their Turkish identity.[2] Mahmud of Ghazna became the greatest potentate of the Islamic world whose achievements out-shone even the Caliphs of Baghdad of the time. For this, a new title had to be coined that henceforward would be associated mainly with Turkish sovereigns: he was probably the first Muslim ruler to be awarded the title 'Sultan'.

While emphasising the importance of the Ghaznavids in tracing the world expansion of the Turks and Turkish history generally, at the same time it would be a great mistake to overstate the 'Turkish' nature of the Ghaznavid state. Ethnic Turks never formed more than a ruling elite and even in the army probably formed little more than the officer core and elite cavalry units, with the bulk of the army made up of local levies. The court language of Ghazna was Persian, not Turkish, it was Persian culture that was patronised and the bulk of both the court and the ruled were the indigenous Iranians of Central Asia. There was no mass movement of Turks and ethnic displacement of the populations at the heart of their empire (and even today the Ghaznavid heartlands remain ethnically Iranian—i.e., Tajik—and Pashtun); there was no Turkification such as later occurred in Anatolia. However, it is precisely this polyglot nature of the state and the symbiosis between incoming ruler and indigenous ruled that is also most characteristic of Turkish dynasties: their ability to embrace and reinvigorate the older cultures of the peoples they encountered, whether Chinese, Gandharan, Persian or Byzantine. It remained a characteristic of subsequent Turkish polities and remains so today with Turkey's embracing of European ways.

The Ghaznavid Empire was brought to an end by a native dynasty from the remote mountain fastness of Ghur in western Afghanistan. The Shansabanid dynasty—usually known as the Ghurids, after their homeland—were never absorbed successfully into the empire by Mahmud, due mainly to the inaccessibility of the terrain. During the course of the twelfth century, the Shansabani princes of the remote mountain principality of Firuzkuh on the upper Herat River unified the rival mountain valleys of Ghur and began to threaten the position of the Ghaznavids by raids out of their mountain strongholds. Then in 1173-4 the greatest of the Ghurid sultans, 'Ala ud-Din, sacked Ghazna in an orgy of destruction. For this 'Ala ud-Din was awarded the title of *Jahan-suz* or 'world-burner'.

There is little to see of Ghazna today, due as much to 'Ala ud-Din's destruction as to Genghis Khan's a short time later. The most conspicuous remains are two minarets or victory towers (Pl. 23), interpreted as victory towers, covered in elaborate brick and terracotta decoration, built by Mas'ud III (1099-1114) and Bahram Shah (1118-1152). Rather more of an impression of Ghaznavid magnificence can be seen at their winter capital of Lashkari Bazar to the south-west of Kandahar. Here, the remains of vast palace complexes line the banks of the Helmand River for an astonishing distance of nearly fourteen kilometres, far exceeding in both size and opulence any European palace, either contemporary or later. The northern part of the site consists of the remains of three vast palatial complexes built at the height of the Ghaznavid period, each surrounded by immense walled enclosures which were ornamental gardens and hunting parks. The largest and most elaborate palace is the southernmost one, which incorporated a magnificent audience hall originally decorated in frescos and carved stucco, with a small private mosque adjacent completely covered in carved stucco. Together, the city covers some twenty square kilometres, much of it palatial buildings, although many more remains lie scattered in the surrounding region, making this figure a conservative estimate of the total area of occupation (Pls 24-5). The only comparable contemporary remains in the Islamic world are at the Abbasid capital of Samarra in Iraq, which it resembles in many ways.

The Oxus then formed the boundary between two rival Turkish states: the Ghaznavids to the south and the Karakhanids to the north. But a third and greater Turkish power was forming further to the north that was soon to challenge both—and take the Turkish nation westwards to the Mediterranean and ultimately into Europe: the Seljuks. We thus end our overview of the Turks entering Islam once again with a new beginning. The Turks, in being enslaved by the Arabs, had become their masters; in being converted to Islam, they had become its champions.

Chapter 5

THE SULTANS OF ROME

THE SELJUKS AND THE WEST

There had everywhere definitely been collusion as much as resistance to the Turkish conquest. ... In brief, the Greeks had created a Turkish sultan *within* the Byzantine Empire.

(Claude Cahen[1])

Hitherto we have followed the Turks from their original forest homeland in Siberia to the threshold of European and world history. It has been necessary to follow their long march fairly closely. This is mainly because Turkish origins are so little known—and the importance of these origins even less appreciated—in relation to wider European history. It is essential to emphasise various aspects of this complex journey that relate to our present theme: that a Far Eastern people can become a European people, and that Europeans were not the only ones who travelled, conquered and settled world-wide. With the advent of the Seljuks, the Turks begin to enter the mainstream of European history, so it is not intended—nor necessary—to relate events in such detail. Instead, we will just highlight particular events and themes—both in Seljuk and subsequent Ottoman history—that affects how we redefine 'European'.

ORIGIN OF THE SELJUKS

The old Oghuz tribal areas to the north and west of the Karakhanid state had undergone gradual Islamisation over the tenth century, probably following much the same pattern as amongst the Karluk: Muslim merchants and missionaries bringing Islam hand in hand with the lure of civilisation and wealth—and awakening the Oghuz to the even greater lure of the central Islamic lands further west. The Oghuz, or Ghuzz, were a tribal confederation made up of twenty-two sub-tribes originally from Mongolia, part of the general diaspora of Turkish tribes following the collapse of the Turk Empire in the eighth century. Between the eighth and tenth centuries they ended up in the steppe region between the Aral Sea and Volga and were absorbed into the Khazar state, where they formed an important element. In 965 the Oghuz contributed to the destruction of the Khazar state on the Volga, elevating them to pre-eminence amongst the steppe Turks.

Indeed, there had probably been considerable interaction amongst the Oghuz and Khazars. Duqaq, the father of Seljuk (eponymous founder of the dynasty), was a high ranking official at the Khazar court and his son a commander in the Khazar army. The Khazar elite had adopted Judaism[*] although Islam and Christianity were widely tolerated and practised in the kingdom. The Khazar state collapsed in 965 with the sack at the hands of the Rus of their capital of Itil on the Volga Delta; a revolt by Seljuk and his Oghuz followers at the same time might have also contributed to the collapse. Seljuk was certainly accused of plotting to overthrow the Khazar Kagan, and so escaped with a small group of a hundred followers eastwards to Jand on the lower Syr Darya river just east of the Aral Sea. There he consolidated his power and converted to Islam, and a series of victories against pagan Turk tribes attracted more to his banner.

Seljuk's flight is traditionally viewed as the emblematic origin of the Seljuk dynasty; it might, however, be a retrospective gloss to demonstrate a parallel with Muhammad's flight from Mecca and the beginning of the Islamic era in order to emphasise Seljuk's Islamic credentials.[†] There is after all some suggestion that Seljuk's family were—at least at first— Jewish: his sons were named Mika'il, Isra'il and Musa—Michael, Israel and Moses—which, while not unknown as Muslim names, is at least

---

[*] This and its implications are discussed more in volume 4, *The Gates of Europe*.

[†] The flight of a charismatic leader with a small band of followers that soon created a great empire is a common 'mythic-heroic origin theme' of a number of empires, not least Turk, such as Elterish Kutlugh and the establishment of the Second Turk Empire (Chapter 3) or Babur and the origin of the Mughal Empire (Chapter 6).

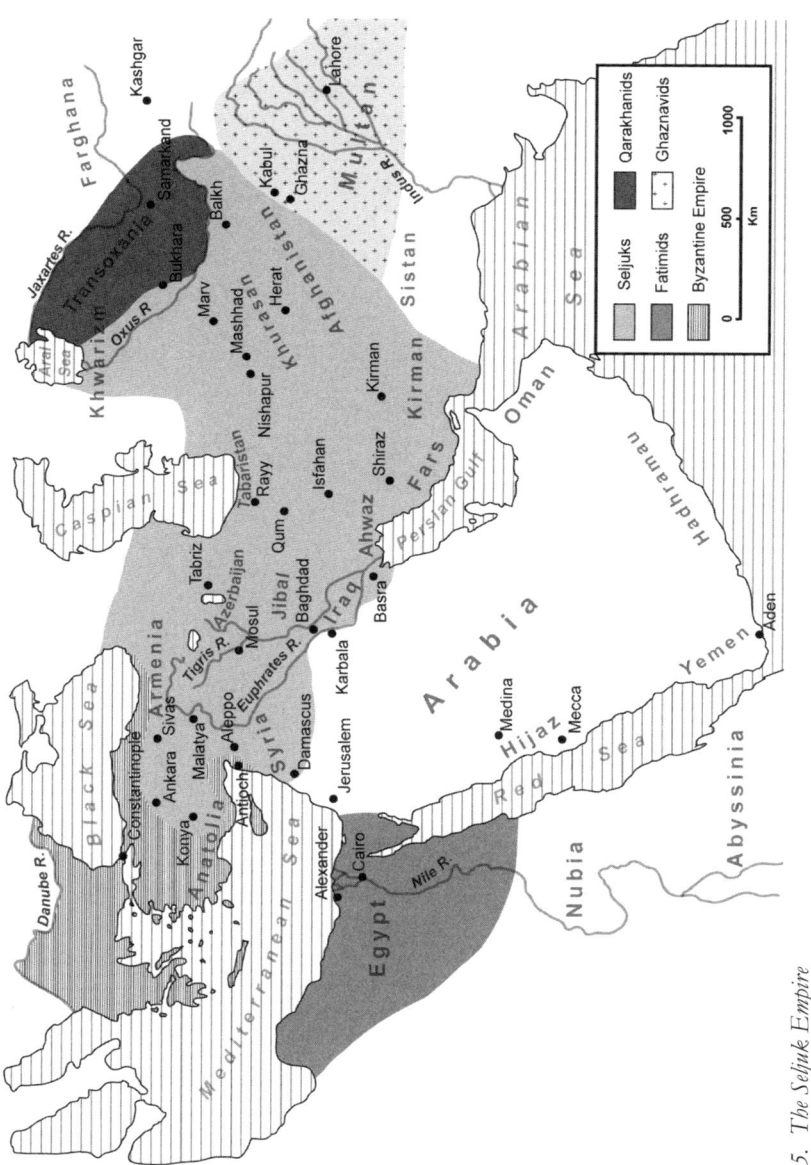

5. *The Seljuk Empire*

Kashgar

Farghana

Jaxartes R.

Samarkand

Bukhara

Transoxania

Khwarizm

Oxus R.

Balkh

Kabul

Ghazna

Multan

Lahore

Sistan

Afghanistan

Khurasan

Herat

Marv

Mashhad

Nishapur

Rayy

Tabaristan

Isfahan

Kirman

Shiraz

Fars

Kirman

Arabian Sea

Oman Sea

Aral Sea

Caspian Sea

Tabriz

Qum

Azerbaijan

Ahwaz

Persian Gulf

Baghdad

Jibal

Iraq

Basra

Mosul

Tigris R.

Euphrates R.

Karbala

Armenia

Sivas

Aleppo

Syria

Damascus

Jerusalem

Arabia

Medina

Mecca

Hijaz

Hadhramaun

Yemen

Aden

Red Sea

Black Sea

Constantinople

Ankara

Malatya

Konya

Anatolia

Antioch

Alexander

Cairo

Nile R.

Egypt

Nubia

Abyssinia

Mediterranean Sea

Danube R.

Qarakhanids

Seljuks

Ghaznavids

Fatimids

Byzantine Empire

1000

500

0

Km

suggestive. The Khazar connection is questioned by some authorities, but otherwise there seems no reason to invent it in the traditional histories of Seljuk origins, so it is probably true, even if Seljuk himself was not Jewish.* Be that as it may, by the time he emerged in about 985 as the leader of the Oghuz he was a Muslim, consolidating both his religion and his powerbase by raids against the pagan Turks. This move is almost an exact repetition of Satuk's conversion and the beginning of the Karakhanid state recounted in the previous chapter; indeed, it might well reflect mutual foundation myth borrowing.

In the year 1017-18 there occurred one of those great disruptions in Inner Asia resulting in a classic steppe knock-on effect. The chain was set in motion by the expansion of the Qara Khitai Empire from its eastern Mongolian homeland. This displaced the Mongol Qun tribes, in place disrupting the Turk Qay, Sari and Kimek tribes further to their west. As a result the Kimek and Kipchek Turkish tribes exerted pressure on the northern areas of Oghuz control, displacing many Oghuz tribes in the process. The collapse of the Samanid state, mainly at the hands of the Karakhanids to their east (reviewed in the last chapter) but also partly by the Ghaznavids to the south, led to a power vacuum in Central Asia. This rather confusing list of names and events need not concern us so much as its result: the chain of migrations forced the Seljuks to turn southwards.† A major victory by Tughril Beg, Seljuk's grandson, against the Ghaznavids at the Battle of Dandanaqan north of the Oxus in 1040 opened up the rich lands of Khurasan to Seljuk raids. The same year sees Tughril Beg capture the great Khurasani metropolis of Nishapur (now in north-eastern Iran), which led to him being awarded the title of 'Sultan'. In 1063 his successor, Sultan Alp Arslan, was able to unite the remainder of the Oghuz tribes under his family in a full scale invasion of the lands to the west. The Turks were coming, and coming to stay.

It is at about this time and in this area that we learn of yet another Turkish tribal—or national—name that still figures largely today: the Turkmen, who have given their name to the modern country of Turkmenistan in the same area that saw the rise of the Seljuks. The origin

---

* It is in any case notable that the Ottomans were particularly accommodating towards the Jews—see Chapter 8 below.

† The nature of the steppe that created such 'knock-on' effects is explored more in the fourth volume of this series, *The Gates of Europe*. There is also some evidence of a period of aridity in the Aral Sea region after 900 that might have prompted Seljuk migrations southwards to the area around Bukhara and Samarkand.

and exact meaning of 'Turkmen' is very vague; it is often taken to be synonymous with the Oghuz Turks, and is first used in connection with the Seljuks as a general designation for the Turkish tribes of Central Asia who supported the Seljuk conquests, but the exact difference between 'Turkmen' and 'Turk' remains unclear.* The only vague differentiation that seems to emerge is that 'Turkmen' were specifically Muslim convert Turks, while 'Turk' was more generic; the Oghuz could be either Muslim or pagan.

TOWARDS THE MEDITERRANEAN

The Seljuk conquest of Iran was neither long drawn out nor necessarily even very destructive: there was no wholesale sacking of cities or slaughter of armies that characterised other invasions. This is not to say that it was bloodless, but overall it appeared more constructive than destructive. For under the Seljuks the land of Iran became the intellectual and political centre of a great empire stretching from the Mediterranean to Central Asia—largely replicating the spread of the Achaemenid Empire in antiquity (Map 5). The first Seljuk capital was at Merv, in what is now Turkmenistan, but it was soon moved to Nishapur in north-eastern Iran. The capital was moved again to Isfahan in the centre of Iran (Pl. 26), but the Turkish lands of Central Asia remained the heartland of the Seljuk empire, with the great cities of Nishapur, Tus, Merv, Herat, Balkh and Bukhara becoming amongst the greatest cities and intellectual centres of Asia. The Seljuk Sultans went on to defeat both the Arab Caliphs of Baghdad and the Byzantine Emperors of Rome, eventually to rule most of Western Asia. The sultans themselves, particularly Alp

---

* As well as in Turkmenistan, Turkmen are to be found in the adjacent province of Gurgan in north-western Iran and in north-western Afghanistan centred upon Andkhui. They are also to be found throughout Turkey, although usually in a nomadic context, but in Iraq the Turkmen are sedentary, mainly in and around the city of Tell 'Afar. Turkmen themselves seem unclear as to their identity: on questioning Turkmen in Tell 'Afar in the 1980s what was their difference to Turks they could not say, apart from emphatically being *Turkmen* rather than Turks (and, interestingly, I observed some of them once being able to converse—just—with some Uighur Turk labourers from China at the time working in a nearby Chinese construction camp). I put the same question to a citizen of Turkmenistan shortly after its independence, and again the answer was uncertain, although she did pose the question: 'Perhaps we are Parthians?'

Arslan and Malik Shah, were great patrons of the arts as well, leaving behind in the exquisitely decorated brick monuments throughout Iran some of the greatest masterpieces of Islamic architecture (Pls 26-8).

It is also important to realise that the Seljuk move westwards—into Iran, Iraq and ultimately Syria and Anatolia—was not so much a direction as a deflection, determined as much by the still strong Ghaznavid empire (despite the Battle of Dandanqan) and its successor, the Ghurid empire, blocking invasion routes to the east, as by any greater attractions in the west. In other words, the Seljuk advance westwards must be viewed as largely opportunistic, made possible by the weakened Abbasid Caliphate in the Near East and various petty states in Iran; it was not the result of any long-term strategic policy nor inevitability. Otherwise, the Seljuks might just as easily turned south-eastwards towards far richer pickings in India, just as the Ghaznavids before them had, and the Mughals afterwards would.

Their conquests were also extraordinarily rapid. The historian G E Tetley illustrates this when she writes how one of the Sultans, Malikshah:

> ... in the space of one year (481/1090) he made his second visit to Syria, travelled to Antioch and Latakia and watered his horses in the Mediterranean, appointed governors for Aleppo, Antioch and Mosul, and returned to Iran; he then went to Samarqand, captured it and took the Khān prisoner, continued to Uzkend and left governors in every city as far as the borders of Khitā and Khutan (approximately the farthest extent of the Qarakhānid dominions), made a visit to his governor in Khwārazm, and finally returned to Isfahān. Even in modern terms this is a formidable amount of travelling.[2]

Clearly, a nomadic element still remained in the early Seljuks.

THE BATTLE OF MANZIKERT

We must, however, pass reluctantly over the Seljuk legacy in Iran with their magnificent architecture to focus more on their legacy in the land that is nowadays most closely associated with the Turks: Anatolia in particular and the lands to the west in general. We may start with a date. The year 1066, the date of the Battle of Hastings, is a date ingrained into all British minds as formative to their own history. Five years later and half a continent away was another date and battle that was probably even more formative: 1071, the Battle of Manzikert, fought between the Romans led by Emperor Romanes IV Diogenes and the Seljuks led by Sultan Alp Arslan. Of the symbolic importance of this battle, historian Carole Hillenbrand emphasises how it 'has worked and is still working the yeast in the Muslim and especially in the Turkish mind. It simply will not stay in the past'.[3] The two battles, Hastings and Manzikert, whilst unconnected, nonetheless bear comparison. Both dates are crucial (or at least iconic) to the arrival of two peoples—respectively the Normans and the Turks—who in some ways share similar characteristics. Both were originally perceived as barbarian, and both originated well beyond the areas they came to dominate: the one from the fringes of Europe, the other from the fringes of Asia. Both founded kingdoms far from their original homelands: the Norsemen in Russia, France, England, southern Italy and Sicily,[*] the Turks in all the lands we have reviewed above and several more we are still to review. Both were to be major protagonists in the greatest event of the European Middle Ages that brought the two peoples face to face: the Crusades.

And both Normans and Turks faced each other at the Battle of Manzikert in 1071. Although often in confrontation with the Byzantines, the Normans fought on their side at the Battle of Manzikert, albeit ambivalently, thereby sowing seeds of mutual suspicion between Greek and Frank that was to plague the subsequent history of Crusader relations with Constantinople. Romanes Diogenes' army also included Turks: Pecheneg and Cuman Turks from southern Russia (although many of the Turks in the Byzantine army deserted to the Seljuks).[4]

Manzikert is routinely regarded by many in the West as a classic example of Turkish-Islamic aggression against Christendom: of Islam spread by the sword, the first of an unstoppable and aggressive wave that

---

* Interestingly, there was even an abortive attempt in 1082 to establish a Norman kingdom in Anatolia at Byzantine expense under Bohemond, the son of Robert Guiscard, founder of the Norman kingdom of Sicily (unwittingly retracing the route of their adoptive 'ancestors', the Gauls, who founded the kingdom of Galatia—which, like the two Galicias in Spain and Poland, means simply 'Gallic'—in central Anatolia in the third century BC: curiously, Ankara was a Gallic capital some twenty-two centuries before it became a Turkish one).

would not be turned back until the wave finally broke against the walls of Vienna. But Manzikert is more a symbolic than significant turning point. Seljuk raids into Anatolia had begun forty years earlier, Byzantine power had already declined there, much of Anatolia was already depopulated, holy war was never an object—indeed, the battle had never been sought in the first place by the Seljuks, who had no desire at that time to extend their conquests into Anatolia, nor to confront the still legendary name of the Roman Empire.* The frontier was stable and the Seljuks posed no threat to Byzantine lands in Anatolia—Alp Arslan even extended a peace offer to Romanes Diogenes on the eve of the battle. The Seljuks were far more concerned with expanding their empire at the expense of the Muslim Near East rather than that of Christian Byzantium. The Battle of Manzikert came about mainly because of the short-sighted and confrontational policies of Emperor Romanes IV who made the common mistake of many an unwise ruler in seeking war in order to divert attention from failed policies at home. Manzikert resulted in a complete rout of the Romans and the capture of their emperor by Sultan Alp Arslan, but even after their undisputed victory when the way into Anatolia lay unprotected, there was no opening of the flood-gates. The Turks continued to turn their backs upon Anatolia, anxious to placate Constantinople, and released the emperor after a ransom was paid (it was the Byzantines themselves who shortly afterwards despatched the unfortunate Romanes Diogenes). Indeed, Alp Arslan informed the captive Romanes Diogenes,

> Did I not give permission to the envoys of the caliph that they should seek you out, draw up peace terms with you and respond therein to your request? Did I not now send a message to you and make an offer to you that I would withdraw from you, and you refused and so on. What thing caused you to infringe [the treaty]?[5]

Byzantine defeat was more symbolic than actual: more destruction to Byzantine property and lives resulted from the civil war after the

---

* Although now conventionally referred to as the 'Byzantine Empire', it is important to emphasise that neither the 'Byzantines' themselves nor the Seljuks ever used this misnomer, referring to it correctly as the 'Roman Empire' throughout: the Byzantines at least were fully aware of the immense historical weight of that name—and so in the end were the Seljuks, as we shall see.

battle than from Manzikert itself, and the Seljuks never followed up their victory. Alp Arslan himself left immediately afterwards to campaign in Central Asia where he eventually died, and his successor, Malik Shah, showed little or no interest in Byzantine possessions in Anatolia. Manzikert, in other words, did not open the floodgates to Turkish colonisation; it actually changed very little at all.

In fact the iconic nature of Manzikert is largely retrospective spin. There are no accounts from the Seljuk perspective, and most Muslim accounts of the battle are later, recasting it retrospectively as a triumph of Islam. Many of the surviving Muslim accounts date from the time of the Crusades, a time of Muslim-Christian confrontation, so Manzikert was recast in that mould. Perhaps the main legacy of Manzikert was the perspective it cast upon the Turks themselves by their fellow Muslims. Once Arab and Persian writers realised that their Turkish conquerors— previously despised as uncivilised barbarian steppe nomads—were here to stay, they went out of their way to extol Turkish virtues: physical, heroic and—above all—religious. [6]

THE ROMANS CREATE A SULTAN (MAP 6)

So despite Manzikert, there was no immediate Turkish threat to Anatolia, leaving the Byzantines free to concentrate on what they did best: dispute each other for the succession to their throne. The various quarrelling factions led by the great Byzantine aristocratic houses saw the Turks not so much as enemies but, on the contrary, as potential allies and a convenient source of additional troops in the fight for the imperial purple. Individual Turkish warlords and their private armies joined forces with some of the Byzantine warlords. A distant relative of the Seljuk Sultan, Kutlumuş, was settled with his sons and followers around Nicaea by one of the Byzantine contenders. A rival faction led by Alexius Comnenus (who would ultimately be successful) even called upon Kutlumuş and his Turks as allies to fight against the Normans in Europe. Although nominally a Byzantine subject, Kutlumuş in practice remained virtually independent, to the annoyance not only of the Byzantines but also of his distant relative, the Seljuk Sultan Malik Shah, who did not wish his cousins to become his rivals. Despite this, one of Kutlumuş' sons, Süleyman, unofficially styled himself 'sultan'. The title was not only recognised by Alexius Comnenus when he became emperor, but actually legitimised by him. 'In brief, the Greeks had created a Turkish sultan *within* the Byzantine Empire.' [italics added][7]

In proclaiming himself a rival Seljuk sultan in Anatolia, Süleyman was not only defying the true Seljuk sultan, Malik Shah, but also the caliph himself, the only one with the authority to award the title. Rival sultans and rival Seljuks—but what is even more astonishing is the title that the Anatolian Seljuks were to add to sultan: they proclaimed themselves Sultans of *Rome*.[8] The significance of the name 'Rome' might not have been appreciated by the Seljuks. Rome—or *Rūm* in Arabic and Turkish—was by that time little more than a geographical designation corresponding broadly to Anatolia: the land of the Romans, i.e., the Roman Empire (as the Byzantine Empire was officially and correctly known). But equally, the significance might well have been appreciated: the Byzantines, of course, were only too aware of the significance of the Roman title and all that it implied (hence their earlier reluctance to recognise the revived Roman imperial title in the West with Charlemagne) and earlier Caliphs had also been fully aware of its import. Later Seljuk sultans themselves married into the leading Roman aristocratic families of Constantinople, and Sultan Süleyman's ultimate successor (in spirit, if not dynastic), the Ottoman Sultan Mehmet the Conqueror, was also very acutely aware of the immense Roman name and legacy that he was stepping into (as we shall see).

In 1081, with Süleyman proclaimed sultan in Nicaea, his ally Alexius Comnenus proclaimed himself Emperor of the Romans. Alexius encouraged Süleyman to attack his fellow Christian rivals in both Armenia and Antioch. But in creating and encouraging the Sultanate of Süleyman, the Emperor Alexius had asked for more than he had bargained, as Sultan Süleyman and his Turks encroached more and more upon Byzantine territory. The true Seljuk sultan, Malik Shah, also resented Süleyman simply as a Turk who was beyond his control, hence a potential threat to his own line. Negotiations were opened between Sultan Malik Shah and Emperor Alexius to form an alliance *against* Süleyman, with Malik Shah offering to restore all of Anatolia to Byzantine rule and aid in the eviction of the Turks: a Turkish-Greek alliance to rid 'Turkey' of Turks! The negotiations broke down with the death of Malik Shah and the subsequent quarrels of his successors, so the Seljuk Turks in Anatolia, now succeeded by Süleyman's son and successor

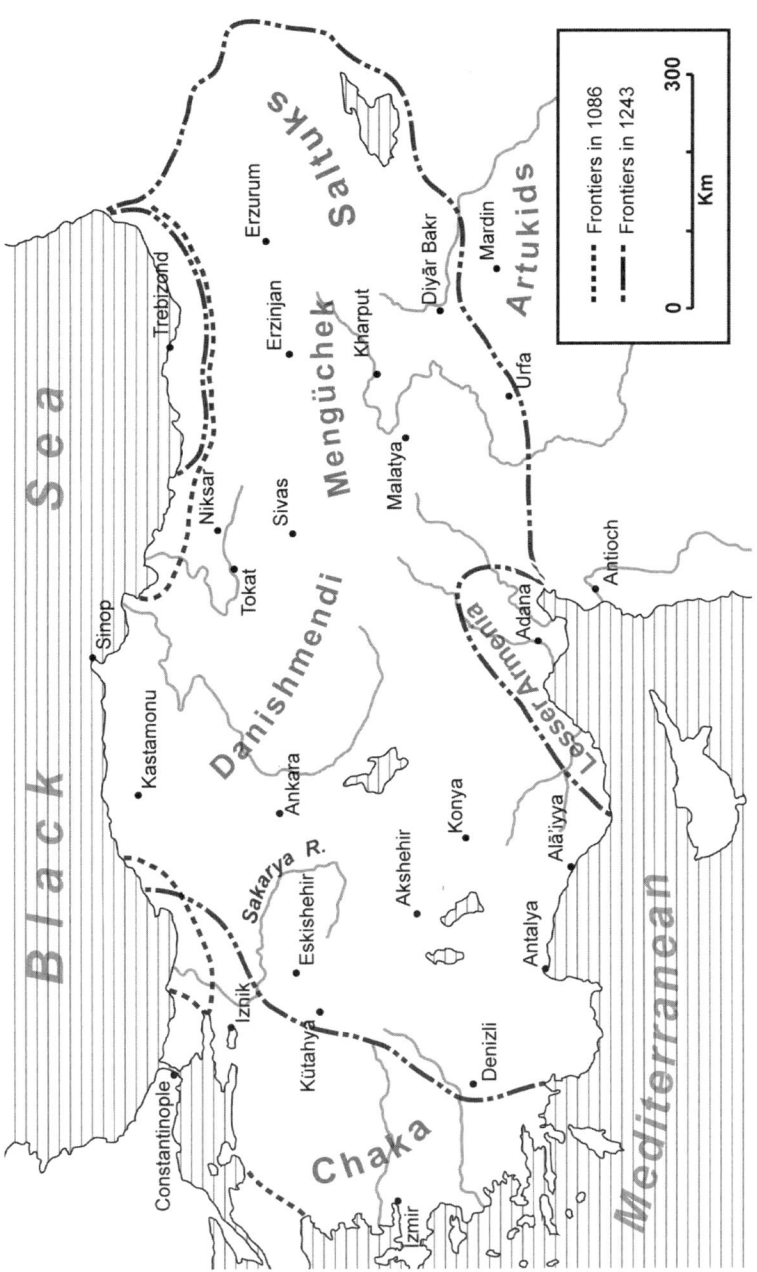

Frontiers in 1086
Frontiers in 1243

Km
0   300

Black Sea

Mediterranean

Saltuks

Artukids

Mengüchek

Danishmendi

Lesser Armenia

Chaka

Erzurum
Trebizond
Diyār Bakr
Mardin
Erzinjan
Kharput
Urfa
Malatya
Niksar
Sivas
Antioch
Tokat
Sinop
Adana
Kastamonu
Ankara
Konya
Akshehir
Alā'iyya
Sakarya R.
Eskishehir
Antalya
Iznik
Kütahya
Denizli
Constantinople
Izmir

6. *Seljuk Anatolia (after Turan 1970)*

Sultan Kılıç Arslan I, were allowed free rein in the west, capturing all the great ports of Classical antiquity on the Aegean: Clazomenae, Phocaea, Smyrna, Chios, Samos and Mitylene.

Alexius managed to retake these ports, and in the ensuing complex and constantly shifting power struggles of different groups in Anatolia, Byzantine as well as Turkish, Alexius even for a short while formed an alliance with Kılıç Arslan. But the Anatolian Turks were ultimately both too unruly and too strong for Alexius and his increasingly embattled Roman Empire, so he pulled out his last card: Alexius appealed to the Christian powers of western Europe. Alas, in doing so much to restore the ailing Roman Empire, Alexius I is ultimately a tragic figure. For Pope Urban II responded in a way that Alexius could never have conceived: in 1095 Urban preached the First Crusade at the Council of Clermont. Having created one menace with the Seljuk Sultanate, the Emperor Alexius created an even greater one in the Crusades. Between them, Crusaders and Turks were ultimately to bring about the final collapse of Constantinople and the Roman Empire.

SHIFTING ALLIANCES: TURKS, BYZANTINES, ARMENIANS AND CRUSADERS

The Crusades hardly form a part of the present story. They are characterised as the ultimate Christian holy war against Islam, and are still today evoked as part of the perceived struggle between East and West. But even during the height of the Crusades, the true picture of Christian-Muslim relations was far more complex and far less confrontational. As early as 1107, for example, Alexius and Kılıç Arslan I formed an alliance and Kılıç Arslan sent a contingent of his Turks to aid Alexius's war against the invasion of Epirus by the Norman adventurer, Bohemond (that perennial thorn in the side of Byzantine emperors). Even Alp Arslan himself, in the very same year as Manzikert, was far more concerned with attacking fellow Muslims in Syria. The picture was further complicated by the establishment of another Turkish principality in Anatolia in about 1095, the Danishmends of Sivas, who fell in and out of both war and alliances with both Byzantium and the Seljuk state. Hence, the shifting relationships throughout the twelfth century between rival Turkish Anatolian principalities, Byzantium, the

Armenian kingdom of Cilicia and Crusader possessions in the Holy Land would see Christians forming alliances with Muslims against fellow Christians and vice-versa; the neat pattern of Christian-Muslim conflict of popular Crusader perception is myth.

In 1130 the brother of the Emperor John II Comnenus, Isaac Comnenus, fled Constantinople and took refuge with the Turks. His son became Muslim and married the daughter of Sultan Masud I, uniting the two houses of Seljuk and Comnenus by marriage.* We thus have two 'Roman Emperors' in the twelfth century: both in Anatolia, both related by marriage, one an emperor, the other a sultan, one a Christian, the other a Muslim, both occasionally at war and occasionally in alliance, both claiming the name (or at least the legacy) of Rome.

The relationship between the Seljuk and Byzantine 'Romans' continued to be a complex one of falling in and out of alliances throughout the twelfth and well into the thirteenth century. In 1167 Kılıç Arslan II was allied to Byzantium in its war against Bulgaria, but by 1176 they were at war again and the ensuing battle at Myriocephalon saw a major victory by the Seljuks against Byzantium, ensuring the permanence of the Turkish state in Anatolia. Under Sultan Kay Khusraw I the Seljuk state was consolidated and expanded. The capture of Antalya in 1207 (Pl. 29) established an outlet to the Mediterranean in one direction (especially after the construction of the magnificent harbour further along the coast at Alanya (pl. 30)—and the Venetians were quick to beat a path to the Seljuk door and conclude a trade agreement, Christian solidarity against the infidel notwithstanding and their capture of Sudak in Crimea ensured outlets in the Black Sea and southern Russia in the other direction (Pl. 31).

In 1230 the supremacy of the Seljuks of Rome was challenged by a new threat from the East. This was an invading army of over a hundred thousand Khwarazmians from the lower Oxus in Central Asia under their brilliant leader Jalal ad-Din Mankobirti (one of the few who had defeated a Mongol army in open battle). The Khwarazmians were both Muslims and Turks—indeed, from the original homeland of the Seljuks themselves—but the Suljuk Sultan Kay Kubad I gathered

---

* There is even an (unverified) suggestion that Osman, the eponymous founder of the Ottomans, was a descendant of the Comnenids. Given the long and established tradition of Greek-Turkish aristocratic marriages, such a suggestion is at least credible. See Almond 2009: 126.

73

together a coalition force that brought together traditional enemies such as Armenians, Franks and Ayyubids from Syria under the Seljuk banner—a 'Crusade' in all but name and object—that inflicted a decisive defeat on the Khwarazmians in eastern Turkey. Both Christians as well as Muslims hailed Kay Kubad's triumph.

Ultimately, however, it was a hollow triumph. For the Khwarazmians themselves were fleeing an even greater menace from the deeper East: the Mongol invasions. The Seljuk victory simply served to weaken the Khwarazmian buffer and hasten the Mongol onslaught. By 1243 they were at the gates of Anatolia and even Seljuk power could not withstand the Mongols. The Seljuks were annihilated at the Battle of Köşedağ, and the Sultans of Rome became clients of the Mongols. Ironically it was this invasion in the thirteenth century rather than the initial Seljuk invasions of the eleventh that accelerated Turkish migrations into Anatolia and ultimately brought about its Turkicisation. For the Turkish tribes from Central Asia were forced to flee the Mongol juggernaut, as well as the Turkish tribes from Iran swept before them.

MUSLIMS AND CHRISTIANS, TURKS AND GREEKS

During the height of the Seljuk Sultanate in the thirteenth century the Christian Greek population of Anatolia still outnumbered the Turkish Muslim by as much as ten to one according to William of Rubruck, a contemporary observer of the Seljuk state. And by and large the two populations lived alongside each other: there is little if any evidence of forced conversions, and marriages between Greeks and Turks were common. The mothers of both Sultans Kay Khusraw I and Kay Khusraw II were Greeks (or rather 'Romans' as the Greeks of Anatolia have always called themselves) and were allowed to freely practise their Christianity after their marriages. Many leading Seljuks married into Byzantine aristocratic families, and the sultan himself usually had an entourage of Byzantine aristocrats. Whenever there was conflict within the Seljuk royal house it is significant that princes would invariably flee for protection to the Christian Greeks rather than their co-religionists in the Muslim powers of Iran, Syria or Egypt.

Seljuk civilisation was thus a syncretic one, with both Greeks and Turks at once contributing to it and sharing in its benefits. The legacy is an impressive one. The Seljuk court at Konya (ancient Iconium) at the heart of the Anatolian plateau attracted artists and men of learning from throughout the Islamic world (Pls 32-4). Probably the best known was the great Persian mystic poet and musician Jalal ad-Din Rumi ('the Roman'—although he was an Iranian originally from Balkh in Central Asia) who founded the Mevlana order of Sufis (Pl. 34). Jalal ad-Din's poetry was, of course, in Persian, his own native language as well as the court language of the Seljuks. But significantly, Jalal ad-Din also wrote verse in both Turkish and Greek, and on his death Greeks as well as Turks came to his funeral; Christians and Jews as well as Muslims.

Architecture is the Seljuks' most visible legacy (as anyone who has travelled in Turkey will attest; Pls 32-7). It is not possible here to give an account of Seljuk architecture, but several aspects are relevant to our present theme. An original Seljuk contribution to Islamic architecture was the development of the *madrasa* or college for teching law and other disciplines based mainly on the Qur'an (Pls 32-3, 35).[9] Although the institution of the madrasa existed before, the characteristic building was introduced by the Seljuks from Central Asia. It was then promoted as a means to counter Shi'ism in the Near East, specifically the Fatimids who ruled parts of the Near East and the Buyids who ruled much of Iran (although the madrasa was eventually to become as much a feature of Shi'a architecture as Sunni). The madrasa form might have been copied from the Buddhist monastery complexes of Central Asia, which some of the earlier madrasas outwardly resemble. They were usually built from wealthy individual patronage and endowments, and in Seljuk Anatolia became major institutions in virtually every city (and often in the countryside as well).

Closely allied to the madrasas were other endowments, such as hospitals, asylums and charitable kitchens, often associated with a madrasa in an elaborate architectural complex which would also include a monumental tomb of the founder. These foreshadowed the great religious complexes of the Ottomans which we will examine later (Chapter 8). As centres of both learning and research they also foreshadowed the university colleges of medieval Europe (although whether they actually inspired the first European universities, which they pre-date, is debated).

A peculiar feature of so many of these Seljuk architectural religious complexes is that many were endowed by or dedicated to leading Seljuk *women* (Pl. 37). This might appear surprising in traditional Islam, so may have been caused by many leading Seljuks having Christian wives as already observed. However, it is precisely traditional Islam rather than Christian marital influence that brought this about, combined with a separate Turkish tradition reaching further back into their Central Asian nomadic roots. This aspect of female endowments and the position of women generally among the Turks is explored separately in Chapter 8.

In fact it would be a mistake to read too much of a religious message into the Seljuk conquests or their architectural legacy. The Seljuks were not as hostile to Shi'ism as was previously thought, and were not necessarily the religious zealots they are often portrayed as being. They were after all comparatively recent converts and large numbers of them at least still retained some pagan (and Buddhist) elements—indeed, many of the Turks accompanying the Seljuk armies may still have been open pagans.[10] Both before and after Manzikert the Turkish raids into Anatolia and the Caucasus were aimed at Muslim settlements as much as Christian: there was no jihadist agenda. They were directed at Anatolia and the Caucasus primarily because of the rich pasture that these lands offered to the still nomadic Turkmen that their vast herds of horses, sheep and goats demanded.* A secondary consideration was that the Seljuk rulers themselves encouraged their often troublesome and unpredictable Turkmen allies to raid in this direction so as to divert their depredations from the settled—and hence more stable and wealthy— urban areas of Iran, Iraq and Syria. The result ultimately would be the Turkification of the eastern—and richest pastures—of the Caucasus, modern Azerbaijan,† and Anatolia.

---

* Exactly the same consideration meant that all Mongol capitals of Iran in the fourteenth century would be the grassy lands of north-western Iran, up until that time a political periphery.

† Azerbaijan is an interesting example of how history—and even the hard evidence of archaeological remains—can so easily and quickly be falsified (or at least distorted) to become accepted wisdom. A false descent of the Azerbaijani Turks arose shortly after the independence of the Republic of Azerbaijan from the Soviet Union through the misinterpretation of some ancient petroglyphs at Gobustan overlooking the Caspian Sea south of Baku. These petroglyphs were the subject of an expedition by the well-known Norwegian explorer and navigator, Thor Heyerdahl in the 1980s, who interpreted one particular (undated and unsubstantiated) petroglyph as a Viking vessel, supposedly left there by the historically well documented Viking river trade down the Volga River and into the Caspian in the Middle Ages. From this has risen a recent popular Azerbaijani myth that they are descended from the Vikings. Although

The reaction of the older established Muslims of the Near East to the newly arrived Turks was in a way even more ambivalent than that of the Christians. The Arab and Persian attitudes ranged from sycophantic court panegyrics extolling their physical beauty and military prowess to resentful contempt for barbaric, uncivilised ex-slaves who could not speak any intelligible language. But the Turks had out-Arabed and out-Persianed what they considered to be their own prerogative: Islamic success. 'If the Persians, quick-witted and subtle like the Greeks of the classical world, were scornful of what they saw as the barbarism and backwardness of the Turks, the Turks, while generally accepting the superiority of Persian culture, were, like the Romans, confident of their military strength and ability to rule'[11]in the words of Gillies Tetley. Such ambivalence towards the Turks still exists in Arab and Iranian lands today.

As well as confounding traditional perceptions of Islam as being anti-Christian, confrontational and unrelated to 'our own' Roman legacy, Seljuk Anatolia confounds the traditional idea of the Turkish march westwards as being a simple case of conquest, rapine and aggression. On the contrary, Anatolia and the Byzantine Empire was never their first object, Holy War was never their prime consideration, the Sultans of Rome were a product of the 'West' as well as the 'East', and one of the main scholars of the Turks, the French historian Claude Cahen, emphasises that 'there had everywhere definitely been collusion as much as resistance to the Turkish conquest'.[12] The subsequent history of the Ottomans was to underline all of these points and more.

---

historically a nonsense, it is easy to see how such a myth can prove to be popular in post-independence Azerbaijan searching for an identity: an identity that is separate from their recent overlords, the Russians (indeed, particularly attractive in view of the fact that the Vikings were the founders of the Russian state: the 'Viking-Azerbaijanis' could look upon themselves as somehow the founders of Russia rather than the other way round), as well as distinct from their nearest neighbours, Turkey, Iran and Armenia. Although hardly elevated to official history, it is nonetheless notable that one of the most prestigious buildings in the old city of Baku has been given to the Norwegian Embassy.

Chapter 6

A TURKISH WORLD

TURKISH-SPEAKING DYNASTIES FROM EGYPT THROUGH TO INDIA

In the history of Eurasia, a Turk can be a Pecheneg, a
Cuman, an Oghuz or Guz, a Yakut, a Turcoman, a Kalmuk
(or Kalmyk), a Seljuk, a Karakhanid, a Ghaznevid, a
Kazakh, a Karakoyunlu, an Akkoyunlu, an Özbek, a
Kirghiz, a Uighur, an Ottoman, a Kashgai, a Mamluk—or
even something else in the vast nomenclature of tribal
or dynastic appellations. He can also be Baburshah,
the founder of the so-called Mughal Dynasty, with his
autobiography written in Turkic, or, more distantly a Wei
emperor, or a Hsiung-nu chieftain within the confines of
the Great Wall, a Hunnic warrior (perhaps with the name
Attila), a pagan Bulgarian king besieging Constantinople
… even a member of the first royal family of Arpads
of Hungary.

(Doğan Kuban[1])

Before we discuss the Ottomans it is worth pausing and assessing
the Turkish reach so far. We have already observed how they formed
dynasties in China and throughout Inner Eurasia before Islam. We have
seen how in spreading into Central Asia they formed some of the more
important states of medieval Islam: Karakhanid, Ghaznavid, Seljuk,
Khwarazmian. We have seen how in spreading west they influenced
events in the Middle East; we will soon see them influencing events
throughout Europe and beyond. Eastwards they had brought about

dynastic changes in China, and in extending their conquests into India under the Ghaznavids they brought about the most profound changes in the subcontinent since the Indo-Aryan invasions some three thousand years previously. The list quoted by the art historian Doğan Kuban at the beginning of this chapter might be a little over-stated in some instance—Huns and Hsiung-nu, for example, were probably not Turk—but equally there are many more names that could be cited, both those that we have already encountered as well as many we have yet to mention: Kuban might also include the Western Turk kagans who built Bamiyan, for example, or the Tulunids of Cairo or Tughluqids of Delhi. By the early seventeenth century a contemporary commentator, Mustafa Ali of Gallipoli, names the four main Islamic states in the world of his time: Ottoman Turkey, Safavid Persia, Mughal India and Uzbek Central Asia.[2] Notably, all were dominated by dynasties whose mother tongue was Turkish. Turk populations are overwhelmingly Muslim throughout, but not exclusively so: the Yakut of Siberia are Shamanist, for example, the Karaim of Crimea and Lithuania are Jewish, and the Gagauz of Moldova are Orthodox Christian.

The account in this chapter is nothing more than a brief overview of the main Turkish dynasties from about the twelfth century until the height of the Ottomans. Anything more detailed would be beyond the scope of this book, and numerous smaller Turkish dynasties and states are passed over, such as the Artuqids of northern Iraq or the picturesquely named Qara Qoyunlu and Aq Qoyunlu Turkmen—the 'Black Sheep' and 'White Sheep' Turkmen—of the Iranian-Anatolian borderlands or the numerous petty sultanates of India. Also not given here are the numerous Turkish-speaking (and Turkish-related) populations that are found not only in the ancient homelands of the Turks in innermost Asia but the vast diaspora extending throughout Eurasia from the Tatars of Ukraine and Russia to the Yakuts of Siberia.* This is not because they are necessarily less important or had less of an impact. Our purpose here is mainly to highlight just how much of the European 'Age of Expansion' was anticipated and paralleled by a 'Turkish world expansion'—in turn anticipating an Ottoman Age of Expansion in Chapter 9.

---

* Also omitted are the various earlier Turk and Turk-related states of the Eurasian steppe, such as the Bulgars, the Khazars or the Golden Horde. These are explored further in the fourth volume in the series (*The Gates of Europe*).

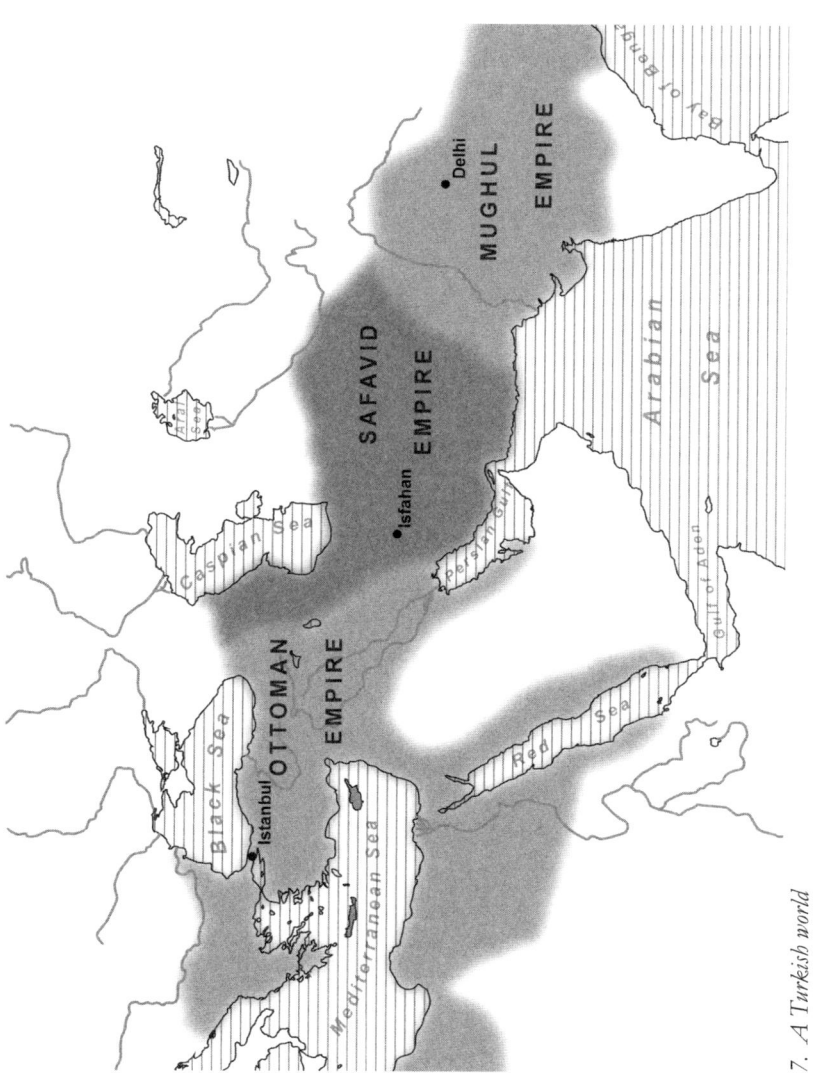

7. A Turkish world

SLAVES WHO RULED EMPIRES: FROM DELHI TO CAIRO

The Ghaznavids would not be the last Turks to rule in India. The dynasty that eventually overthrew them, the Ghurids centred on western Afghanistan in the late twelfth and thirteenth centuries, continued the tradition of incorporating Turkish slaves into their armies. One of these slaves, Qutb ud-Din Aybak, became governor of India under the Ghurid sultans in the early thirteenth century. Qutb ud-Din broke away from the Ghurids and established his own rule in India, but continued the tradition of bringing in Turkish slaves from Central Asia to rule and eventually succeed. Hence, the dynasty was known as the *Mamluk* or Slave dynasty (after the Arabic *mamluk*, 'slave') which ruled throughout the thirteenth century as sultans of Delhi. They were succeeded by two further Turkish dynasties of Delhi sultans, the Khaljis from 1290 to 1320 and the Tughluqids throughout the remainder of the fourteenth century. The southern outskirts of Delhi today are littered with the vast monuments and colossal remains of the former capitals of these Turkish sultans, such as the Qutb Minar, the largest minaret in the Islamic world (and even that dwarfed by an unfinished minaret adjacent), or the gigantic walls of the city of Tughluqabad, as well as numerous tombs and minor monuments (Pls 39-40). After the Central Asian homelands of the Turks were devastated in the thirteenth century by the Mongol invasions, India was one of the few places in Eurasia to escape the Mongol holocaust, so under the patronage of its Turkish slave sultans was one of the few parts of the Islamic world to provide a refuge and to flourish during this dreadful period.

The Mamluks of Delhi anticipated a far better known institution, also known as the Mamluks. These were the Mamluks of Egypt from 1250 to 1517. In fact a Turkish ex-slave, Ahmad Ibn Tulun, ruled Egypt virtually independently of Baghdad very early on in Islam in the late ninth century (the mosque he built in old Cairo is one of the greatest of early Islam: Pl. 41), and slavery of the most extraordinary sort the world has ever seen was to characterise Mamluk rule of the thirteenth century. For the Mamluks were at once slaves, slavers and rulers at the same time. The Ayyubid dynasty (founded by Saladin's father), predecessors of the Mamluks, maintained a by now established tradition of Middle Eastern rulers whereby they supported their rule by ranks of professional slave guards drawn from the Turks and Circassians of Central Asia and southern Russia. The Ayyubids became increasingly dependant upon this 'Praetorian Guard' to stay in power until inevitably the slaves seized power themselves, forming their own government.

Even after seizing power the Mamluks maintained their slave status: the court, most of the administration and the top ranks of the army were drawn from slaves. Indeed, slave status was essential for high office, especially under the latter line of Mamluks, when each successive sultan would be a slave specially chosen for the purpose; succession was rarely dynastic. Under this extraordinary system, the free born—even the sons of former Mamluk sultans—would be second-class citizens. And by and large, the system worked extremely well, rather like the system of adopted emperors of Rome's golden age. Without the commitment to inherited lines of rulers, each Mamluk sultan would be chosen largely on talent—or at least strength. That the system succeeded is demonstrated by its length of rule, from 1250 to 1517—nearly three hundred years, the longest any government had remained in power in Egypt since the Romans.

The Mamluk achievements were correspondingly impressive (Pl. 42). They extended their rule outside Egypt to eventually incorporate all of Palestine, Lebanon, Syria and Yemen. They were one of the few peoples ever to defeat the hitherto invincible Mongols—twice, in the Battle of 'Ain Jalut ('Goliath's Spring') near Nazareth in 1260 and again at the Battle of Marj as-Saffar, south of Damascus, in 1303. In 1400, the invasion of Tamerlane was finally and decisively beaten, and the borders of Mamluk Egypt were extended southwards to the Sudan and Yemen and westwards to Cyrenaica, but perhaps their most symbolic victory was against invaders from the West, not East. This was during the Fifth Crusade, when the Mamluks finally evicted the last Crusaders from the Holy Land. Just as the Second Crusade produced a great leader of the Saracens in the person of Saladin, so did the Fifth Crusade in Baibars, originally a Turkish slave who became sultan in Egypt in 1261. But Baibars was a very different stamp to Saladin, and whilst 'a statesman of the highest calibre' in the words of Sir Steven Runciman, 'was unimpeded by any scruple of honour, gratitude or mercy.'[3] He accordingly pursued the Franks with the ruthlessness and relentlessness of a vendetta and, with his successor Sultan Qalawun, finally brought an end to the extraordinary history of the Crusader possessions in the Holy Land. It was Qalawun's son Khalil al-Ashraf who finally took Acre in 1291, with the last of the Franks finally being expelled from Tortosa later that same year. The Crusades had come to an end. Just as it was the Turks who sparked off the Crusades in the first place, it seemed fitting that it was the Turks who would see their end. Henceforward, the Near East became a Turkish world: the Arabs, it seemed, had forfeited Islam to these newcomers from far-off Central Asia.

Inevitably, however, the Mamluks were seen as rivals by an emerging new Turkish power on the Middle Eastern scene who were to dominate the region down to modern times: the Ottoman Turks. When the Mamluk and Ottoman armies finally met in pitched battle near Aleppo in 1516, the effect was devastating and the Mamluks were slaughtered. Syria and Egypt were incorporated into the Ottoman Empire by Sultan Selim I ('the Grim'). Henceforth, the Arab lands were to be ruled once again from Constantinople, but as an Ottoman backwater rather than a Byzantine hinterland.

UNDER THE SHADOW OF GENGHIS KHAN: THE EXTRAORDINARY HOUSE OF TAMERLANE

With the decline of the Mongol Empire the Central Asian heartland became a political vacuum of conflicting rival groups and families, all fighting to succeed the Mongols. It was Tamerlane at the end of the fourteenth century who filled this vacuum. Although he traced his descent (albeit tenuously) back to Genghis Khan on his mother's side, Tamerlane was not a Mongol as is often thought. He was a Turk of the Chaghatai Khanate born in about 1336 in the well-watered region of Chaghanian south of Samarkand with its capital at Kish (present Shahr-i Sabz). During the course of the 1370s Tamerlane was able to unite the various warring factions in the region and raid Iran and Afghanistan. It was during one of these raids in Seistan that a leg wound gave his nick-name: Timur-i Lang or 'Timur the Lame'. With success the raids soon became more confident and more far-reaching, becoming full-scale campaigns of conquest to establish a new great Central Asian empire.

Tamerlane's invasions seemed like the Mongol devastations all over again. Central and western Asia, barely reviving, saw its carefully rebuilt cities and resettled populations ruthlessly destroyed once more, and even cities that had escaped the earlier holocaust were destroyed. Baghdad at one end of Asia was captured in 1393 and Delhi at the other end five years later. 1402 sees one of Tamerlane's greatest victories at the Battle of Ankara against the Ottoman Turks when Sultan Bayazit was killed (and incidentally giving Constantinople an eleventh hour reprieve from the Ottomans for a further fifty years). At first, Tamerlane stood in awe of the memory of the mighty Mongol Empire that had gone before him and he hesitated to challenge even the shadow of Mongol power that survived in northern Central Asia. He never claimed the supreme title of 'Khan', for example, or even 'Sultan', but remained content with the more modest 'Amir' throughout, even though he built almost as great an empire as his mighty predecessor. But after a victory against a Mongol force, Tamerlane stood unchallenged, no longer under Genghis Khan's great shadow. It can only be guessed at how great an empire Tamerlane might have created. His death at Otrar in 1405 interrupted his most ambitious campaign to date: the conquest of China (birthplace of his wife, Bibi Khanum, whom his great mosque in Samarkand commemorates: Pl. 43).

Tamerlane's destruction was never quite as wholesale as that of the Mongols. Horrific though it was, Mongol destruction nearly always had a purpose (usually sheer terror and extortion admittedly). With Tamerlane, on the other hand, one senses barbarity that was far more gratuitous: the pyramids of decapitated heads were as much to satiate sheer cruelty as to punish. But Tamerlane, unlike Genghis Khan, was as great a builder as he was a destroyer. Tamerlane instigated another great period for the arts and architecture, and his dynasty remained as rulers until the nineteenth century. His capital city of Samarkand remains one of the great monumental cities of Asia, and a visible legacy of the dynasty's founder (Pls 43-7).

Although the personality of Tamerlane himself is marked—indeed, marred—as much by acts of barbarity as by building, in the dynasty he created he left behind one of the most talented families in Asia's history. His son, Shah Rukh, moved the capital in the early fifteenth century to Herat, establishing one of the most brilliant schools of Persian painting—as well as other arts and sciences—in Iranian and Central Asian history. Today, gems of Timurid architecture can still be found not only in the great cities of the Timurid Empire—Samarkand, Bukhara, Herat and Mashhad—but in the remote countryside of Iran and Afghanistan as well, such as at Kuhsan or Balkh or the vast shrine of Ahmad Yassavi in the remote steppe at Turkestan in Kazakhstan, perhaps the most spectacular building of Tamerlane's era of giganticism (Pl. 46). These monuments, often to be found in mere villages, are masterpieces that sometimes excel those of Samarkand and Isfahan. This perhaps more than anything is a true mark of Timurid greatness: a great rural as well as a great urban civilisation.

But Samarkand, for all its glories, was just a one-generation capital, for Tamerlane's son and successor Shah Rukh moved the capital to Herat. With the move of the Timurid capital to Herat, Samarkand was left in the hands of Shah Rukh's equally talented son, Ulugh Beg. In addition to being an enlightened and tolerant governor, Ulugh Beg was a great scholar and astronomer, whose star charts became the standard work of reference on the subject in Europe until the sixteenth century as well as in the lands of Islam. After Ulugh Beg's murder in 1449, Samarkand declined, eventually being taken over by the Uzbeks under Shaybani Khan after 1500. But it was not the last of the house of Timur: indeed its greatest days were yet to come. The Timurid court continued to flourish in Herat under the successors of Shah Rukh. In particular, under Husain-i Baiqara in the latter half of the fifteenth century Herat witnessed a golden age, the age of the great poets Nawa'i and Jami and the painter Behzad and his school (Pl. 47).

The revival of the house of Timur came from the Ferghana Valley in the heartland of Central Asia with the rise of a new great conqueror in the early sixteenth century, Babur, a descendant of Tamerlane. Babur is one of the most extraordinary rulers in history—if only because of the memoirs he left behind, surely ranking with Caesar's *War Commentaries* or Lawrence's *Seven Pillars of Wisdom* as among the more remarkable war memoirs ever written. His conquest of India and establishment of the Mughal dynasty (mis-named because of the Mongol, or Mughal, element in the army) was probably the greatest legacy of the Timurid dynasty. The Mughal Empire of India is only marginal to our story. But the great Mughal Emperors—Babur, Humayun, Akbar, Jahangir, Shah Jahan and Aurangzeb—were variously mighty conquerors, brilliant generals, wise rulers, talented writers, poets, painters and builders, true successors to Tamerlane's extraordinary house (Pls 48-9). The house finally came to an end with the exile of Emperor Bahadur Shah II by the British to Burma after the Mutiny of 1857. Altogether the era of Tamerlane and his successors was a gigantic era: gigantic personalities, gigantic achievements, gigantic buildings. From Agra, Delhi and Lahore to Herat, Kabul, Bukhara and Samarkand, the Timurid legacy is one of the world's most extraordinary.

A TURCO-PERSIAN SYMBIOSIS: THE SAFAVIDS OF IRAN

The Timurid empire declined after the mid-fifteenth century, and by the beginning of the sixteenth century we see the rise of one of the last royal houses of Iran: the Safavids. In origin, the Safavid family were ethnic Turks from south-west of the Caspian. The founder, Shaikh Safi, whose burial place at Ardabil has become a major shrine (Pl. 50), was a Sufi. During the course of the fifteenth century the sect and the family increasingly commanded a large following that was eventually able to fill the power vacuum left behind after the decline of the Timurids. In 1499 the leader of this sect, Isma'il, seized power in the then capital, Tabriz, and proclaimed himself Shah. Over the next few years he extended his rule over the rest of the country, thus initiating the rule of the Safavid dynasty, one of the most brilliant dynasties ever to rule Iran. Although as a religious sect the Safavids were originally Sunni Muslim, at the accession of Shah Isma'il, Shi'a Islam was proclaimed the official religion to underline Iran's essential difference from its Sunni Arab, Mughal and Ottoman neighbours. This act was one of the most important in Iran's history: not only was it the culmination of centuries of gradual divergence from the Arabs and the Arab brand of Islam, it laid the foundation of the Islamic Revolution of our own time. Furthermore, although the Safavid family were Turkish speakers, they were the most nationalistic—the most *Persian*—dynasty to rule Iran since the Sasanians—graphic evidence of just how completely the Turkish newcomers had assimilated and become assimilated into Persian culture. Indeed, the traditional enemies of Safavid Persia were the Ottoman Turks to the west and the Mughal Turks to the east.

Shah Isma'il was succeeded in 1524 by Shah Tahmasp, who moved the capital from Tabriz to Qazvin. In 1587 he was succeeded by the greatest of all Safavid monarchs: Shah Abbas. He was as skilled in the arts of war as he was in peace. He established secure borders of Iran—which have remained virtually unchanged to this day—and thoroughly reorganised administration and government. Then in 1598, in order to be closer to the heartland of Persia, he moved the capital of Iran to the ancient Seljuk capital of Isfahan, creating in the process one of the most spectacular cities in Asia (Pls 51-2). The ensuing age of Shah Abbas and his brilliant new court at Isfahan was a new golden age for Islam, a renaissance hearkening back to the great empires of antiquity.

The great age of the Safavids lasted through the seventeenth century and the first half of the eighteenth, but the successors of Shah Abbas became increasingly dissolute. Its decline culminated in a series of devastating raids deep into the heart of Iran from the east, first by the Uzbeks, then by Afghans. In the middle of the eighteenth century it was an ordinary soldier, Nadir Afshar (the Afshar tribe were ethnic Turks from the north of Iran) who for a while looked as though he would reinstate the glories of old. Often referred to as 'the Napoleon of Persia', Nadir Shah Afshar established Mashhad as his capital and led Persian arms further east than they had ever been throughout history, conquering the old Mughal capital of Delhi in 1739. But Nadir Shah was assassinated before he could consolidate his new Persian empire, and the country collapsed into chaos once more. Order was eventually restored at the end of the eighteenth century by a new Turkish-speaking family from the Alburz region, the Qajars, who eventually emerged as unquestioned rulers. The founder of the dynasty, the very able but very cruel Muhammad Aqa, proclaimed himself shah and established a new dynasty, moving the capital from Shiraz to Tehran. The Qajars were overthrown in 1925 by Reza Khan, who established the short-lived Pahlavi dynasty (also Turkish-speaking) until its collapse under his son, Mohammed Reza, at the Islamic Revolution of 1979.

*   *   *

Of course, it would be a gross historical distortion to describe the Safavids of Persia as somehow 'Turkish' in identity—or for that matter the Mughals of India or Mamluks of Egypt (indeed, many of the latter were ethnic Circassian or Albanian). At the same time there is a common Turkish thread that runs through all. In one way or another, the Turks who had initially arrived in the Islamic world as slaves had transformed it.

Chapter 7

BEYOND THE BOSPHORUS

RISE OF THE OTTOMANS
AND THE CAPTURE OF CONSTANTINOPLE

> The incursion from the Steppe of yet another pillaging mounted horde—the Ottoman Turks, quickly converted to Islam and engaged in holy war against Christendom.
>
> *(J H Parry[1])*

We return now to the Turks' final destination and their greatest destiny as they cross the Bosphorus and enter Europe—and immediately encounter commonly held misconceptions. First, the Bosphorus, conventionally regarded as the definitive divider between Europe and Asia, has at no time in its history been that. On the contrary, throughout history it has usually been at the centre of cultures or political units—mainly both—that straddled its waters, whether it be the Turkey of today or the Ottoman and Byzantine empires of the past. The idea that the Bosphorus is somehow a perpetual marker of that vast cultural gap that is usually implied in the terms 'Europe' and 'Asia' must be renounced once and for all.

Second, it has become conventional—or at least convenient—to think of the Turkish capture of Constantinople as an Asiatic conquest: the last of the barbarian invasions. The image of the Ottoman capture of Constantinople as simply a ravening barbaric horde from Central Asia no longer holds true but is not quite dead, as the lines at the beginning of this chapter show. Just about every part that statement no longer holds: the Ottomans did not arrive from the steppe, they were no mere pillaging horde, they had been Muslim for generations, and the idea of simple Muslim-Christian confrontation was a myth before and would be again as we shall see. But it does nonetheless reflect prevalent attitudes. Although published nearly half a century ago, Parry's book is still in print and widely read in popular editions. As recently as 2000, even an historian as broad in his approach as Felipe Fernández-Armesto would perpetuate this myth by writing that 'the Ottoman Turks had arrived on horseback from the steppes of Asia.'[2]

The Turks originated in Asia as we have seen (and almost as far east from Central Asia as Constantinople is west), but Constantinople was conquered by the Turks from the *west*, not from the east: the Ottomans became a European power before they became a Middle Eastern one and remained a primarily European power throughout, ruling up to twenty percent of mainland Europe from a European power-base. Indeed, not only did the Ottomans conquer Constantinople from *Europe*, but the Middle East and even most of Anatolia itself was conquered from Europe. The Ottoman Empire is often regarded as the last of the great native empires of the Near and Middle East, the successor of the Seljuk Empire, the Arab empires of the Abbasids and Umayyads and ultimately of the Persian Empire of antiquity. Again, this is only partially true. In a sense, the Ottoman conquest of the Near East—even of the Muslim holy places of Mecca and Medina—and its subsequent eastern empire was as much a *European* conquest as the Roman empire in the east had been. True, the Turks were originally an eastern people. But the Romans too claimed eastern descent (from the Trojans). True, the Ottomans at least practised a Near Eastern religion. But so too, in the end, did the Romans.

And third, the conquest of Constantinople has become iconic as the beginning of the contact between Greek and Turk, a contact usually viewed in Manichean terms. The fallacy of the perceived Manichean nature of this relationship will be examined later, but for the moment it is worth emphasising that by the time Mehmet's armies camped before the walls of Constantinople there has been almost a thousand years of contact between Greeks and Turks—and a contact that was, as often as not, more cordial than troubled. We have already reviewed (in Chapter 5) the nature of the relationship during the Seljuk period, with intermarriage between both Seljuk and Byzantine aristocratic families and Byzantine factions employing Turkish mercenaries, a relationship

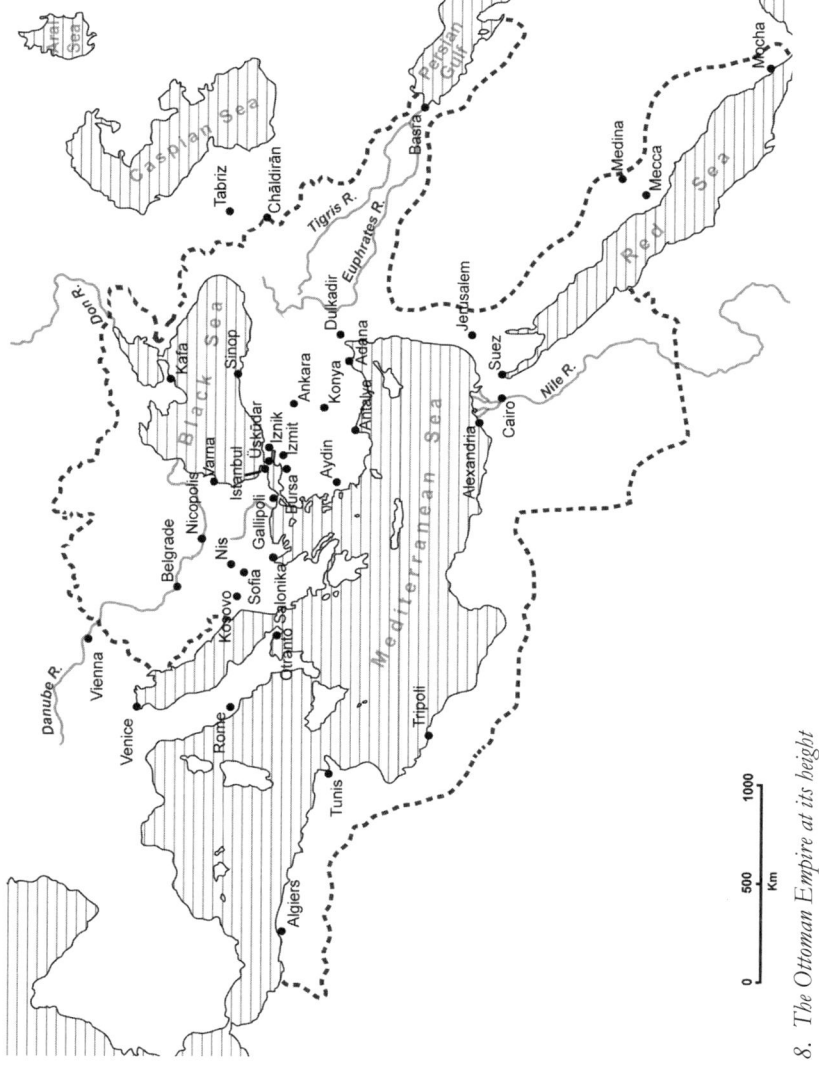

8. *The Ottoman Empire at its height*

that would be elevated in the early Ottoman period to intermarriages between both royal houses as well as continued use of mercenaries. The siege of Constantinople would even see Ottoman soldiers *within* the walls helping to defend the Byzantines against Mehmet's army outside. Long before that we saw diplomatic exchanges between Constantinople and the far-off court of the Turk Kagan in Central Asia in the sixth century, and in the early seventh century we see the first royal intermarriage between Byzantine and Turk with the marriage of the Emperor Heraclius' daughter, Eudocia, to the son of the Khazar Kagan. In the middle of the eighth century Emperor Leo III himself married a Khazar princess, and their son Constantine acquired the nickname 'the Khazar' as a result. Many other instances can be cited: the point is, these were no alien horsemen suddenly bursting unannounced from some far-off steppe who confronted the Greeks—they were well known.

A FRONTIER IN FLUX

Following the collapse of the Seljuk Empire, Anatolia dissolved mainly into tribal principalities and individual warlords—always an inherent weakness of Turk confederations in the past. Many of these became important states in their own right. The Ottomans may not have been one of these tribal groupings and was certainly not the main one, at least at first. But Osman, the eponymous founder of the house, was able to weld together the various tribes and individual leaders into an important local power in Bithynia with its capital at Bursa (Pls 53-4). To some extent this location, in the far west of Anatolia facing the Sea of Marmara, was a major factor in initial Ottoman success: it was an Islamic 'front line' facing the Christian power of Byzantium. This enabled Osman's successor, Orhan (1324-59), to attract almost inexhaustible reserves of manpower (especially from Turkish tribes in Central Asia swept westwards by the Mongols), not only with the promise of loot but the promise of pushing forward the frontiers of civilisation. With both financial and moral rewards, soldiers flocked to Orhan's banner.

But Orhan was too wise a leader to play the Islam versus Christianity card too much: it was alliances *with* Christendom as much as wars against it that contributed to many Ottoman successes, particularly after Orhan took the momentous step in 1352 of crossing into Europe, establishing the Turks as a European power for the first time. Ironically, the initiative came not from Orhan but from John Cantacuzenus, the future Emperor John VI, who established (by invitation) a group of Turkish mercenaries in a permanent camp across the Dardanelles near Gallipoli—and it was Christian Genoa that provided the ships to ferry Orhan and his troops across (Pl. 55). These Turks then offered allegiance to the Ottomans, thus acquiring the first European foothold at Byzantine invitation. Many of the freebooters who flocked to Orhan's banner were Christian Greeks themselves, either with grudges to repay or simply with a desire to share in the loot. In the words of historian Heath Lowry, 'This was a frontier society in flux. As such, it found a place for everyone, free or slave, Muslim or Christian, who had anything to contribute to its growth.'[3]

There was also *Realpolitik*. Orhan himself married into the Byzantine royal family with his marriage to a princess of the Cantacuzeni. After her marriage she was known to the Turks as Nilifer Hatun and was able to wield considerable power in the rapidly growing Ottoman Empire—and at the same time was allowed to continue being a practising Christian throughout her married life (but also endow Muslim religious establishments in the time honoured Turkish tradition of female endowments: Pl. 56). This made her particularly popular among Orhan's Christian subjects, still a majority at this time, and so Orhan's rule was particularly effective—a marriage between Muslim and Christian in more ways than one (and more than just *Realpolitik*: the evidence suggests that it was a love match). Patrick Kinross appropriately sums up the situation:

> Thus were the Ottoman Turks well entrenched with more than a foothold in Europe, not as enemies but as allies and indeed relatives of Byzantium, with a Sultan who was son-in-law of one Emperor, brother-in-law of the other—and also son-in-law of the neighbouring tsar of Bulgaria.[4]

Many Ottomans remained loyal to the Byzantines to the last: an Ottoman prince (another Orhan) with a small contingent of Turkish soldiers would later be within Constantinople helping to defend it *against* Mehmet the Conqueror in 1453. The ease by which both the Ottomans and the Christians powers formed alliances with each other prompted Kinross to describe the Turkish entry into Europe as an invitation rather than an invasion, while Norman Stone remarked that 'the year 1453 marked a synthesis, not a conquest'.[5]

Towards Constantinople

If the Mongol invasions, which swelled the Ottoman ranks with soldiers from Central Asia, were one indirect cause of Ottoman success, the Crusades were another. For the cynical Fourth Crusade had not only reduced Constantinople—Christendom's great bulwark in the east—to military insignificance, it had driven many Greeks to favour the Turks over their Latin co-religionists. The sack of Constantinople did have a logic to it, perverse though it undoubtedly was. For the real issue behind the entire Crusading movement was not so much the fight against Islam, but the supremacy of Rome and the papacy, one of the biggest issues of the European Middle Ages. The fight against Islam was simply a means towards that end: in promoting such a war the popes would be seen as the leaders of Christendom over any other claimants. And the only viable rival for the leadership of Christendom was Constantinople and the Patriarchs. Without condoning the brutality and cynicism of the Fourth Crusade, it was at least correct within its own terms.

It has also been suggested that without the Fourth Crusade Constantinople would not have fallen to the Turks: Constantinople was Christendom's eastern bastion against Islam, and its sack by the Crusaders destroyed this bastion, creating an empty shell that simply made it easier for the Turks to enter Europe when they did arrive. But perhaps it is possible to overstate the importance of the Fourth Crusade (important though it undoubtedly was to the unfortunate people of Constantinople). To begin with, Constantinople had declined to an empty shell before the Crusaders had arrived—that was one of the reasons why it was possible for them to take such an impregnable fortress in the first place. Even without the capture of Constantinople by the Crusaders in 1204, its capture by the Ottomans in 1453, one suspects, would still have taken place.

The Fourth Crusade did, however, contribute to Ottoman success in another indirect way. Religious tolerance was a central pillar of Ottoman policy, and proselytisation was expressly discouraged (if only because an important income for the Ottoman state was the poll-tax on non-Muslim populations). The occupation of Constantinople and adjacent parts of Greece by the Catholic Latins drove the Orthodox population into the arms of the Ottomans: Ottoman regard for and protection of Orthodox Christianity was contrasted with the Latin narrow-mindedness, brutality and open persecution. For the Christians of south-eastern Europe, the Muslim Turks arrived as liberators. 'Better the Sultan's turban than the Pope's mitre' as the Patriarch Gennadius remarked, and rightly so. Ottoman religious toleration (which, it must be remembered, Islam demands of its followers; modern Islamist fundamentalists betray Islam rather than represent it) stood in stark contrast to the rigid exclusivity that characterised western Christendom, a toleration that extended not only to the sultan's own subjects and minorities, but to resident foreign communities as well.

Ottoman tolerance of Christianity was to both aid its victories and characterise its rule throughout, as much in its conquests that led up to Constantinople in 1453 as in its conquest of Venetian Crete over two centuries later: in 1715, for example, the Ottoman capture of the Morea from the Venetians was viewed by the Greeks as liberation from the hated Latins. This Greek hatred of the Latins had a long history, even before the Latin sack of Constantinople in 1204. The Latins (a fairly loose term in Greek applying to any Catholic western European) were described as barbarians by many medieval Byzantine authors, such as Anna Comnena (who loathed them). In the 1170s Michael of Anchialos advised Emperor Manuel I that even subjection to the Muslims was far preferable to the Latins, described later by the historian Niketas Choniates as 'The most accursed Latins … remain forever workers of evil deeds.' Chionates further contrasts the honour, gallantry and humanity of the Muslims (in this case the Turks) with the barbarity of the 'infidel Latins'.[6] Although this special relationship between Greek and Turk eventually went disastrously sour in the nineteenth century, for most of Ottoman history the relationship was a good one (and it would be a grave mistake to transpose the modern reading of Greek-Turkish relations back into the past in any quasi-retrospective history).

Of course, one must not over-idealise the Turks—or any other aggressive imperial power for that matter. 'Imperialism is imperialism, be it Turkish or Austrian', cautions Ian Almond, and '[Ottoman] soldiers, stationed in most parts of Hungary, would probably been about as loved as a garrison of British paras in a Belfast suburb or

French police in an Algerian village' when writing of later Ottoman advances into Christendom.[7] The point is, Turkish expansion was aggressive, at times brutal (just as any other imperial power is, Muslim or Christian, ancient or—for that matter—modern), but it was never ethnic nor racist—and in the long view, nor even religious. Most of all, early Ottoman 'Holy War' is hugely overstated. In all Ottoman wars Christians fought alongside Muslim Ottomans in the rapid expansion of the empire, there was broad co-operation between the Byzantine and Ottoman Empires, intermarriage was frequent, particularly between royal houses, and religious tolerance was an active Ottoman policy. This was as true in the earliest years of Ottoman expansion as in the last years of its decline, when British and French fought alongside the Ottomans in the Crimean War, and Germans and Austrians fought alongside them in the First World War. 'The pervasive notion of permanent and irreconcilable division between the Muslim and Christian worlds at this time [fourteenth century] is a fiction' in the words of the historian Caroline Finkel.[8] As indeed it is now.

A NEW EUROPEAN POWER

The reign of Orhan's son and successor, Murat I (1359-89), thus marks a coming of age for the Ottomans when the transition from Asiatic raider to European empire was complete. Patrick Kinross writes, 'Osman's historical role was that of chieftain who gathered around him a people. His son Orhan was to weld the people into a state; his grandson Murad I to expand the state into an empire'.[9] Not only a major power, but a European one. Any doubts of this were removed when Murat discarded the old Ottoman capital of Bursa in Bithynia in favour of Adrianople (Edirne) in Thrace (Pls 57-9). This was both better to encircle Constantinople and to establish a European base for European conquest. With this move to Adrianople the Ottomans turned their back on their Seljuk legacy and directly challenged the European powers for the Roman.

The ease of the subsequent Ottoman conquests in the Balkans was unwittingly aided by the Christian West. A crusade, led by Hungary and blessed by the pope, was launched in the 1360s against *Christian* Bulgaria—Christian but of the Orthodox rite. This crusade resulted in the frequently brutal and invariably forcible conversion of the Orthodox Bulgarians to the Latin rite. Faced with this, the Bulgarians could hardly fail to welcome the Ottomans, who allowed freedom of worship and extended their protection to the Bulgarian church. Ottoman expansion into the Balkans culminated in the Battle of Kosovo in 1389, which established the Ottomans as a permanent and major power in the heart of Europe. Both Sultan Murad I and the Serb king Lazar were killed in the battle, but the Ottomans won the battle. Murad's son Bayazit I 'Thunderbolt' immediately became sultan on his father's death and was able to save the day and turn it into a great victory. Kosovo became Muslim as a result (Pl. 60).

Kosovo has recently been resurrected by the Serb nationalists as one of the great symbols of Muslim-Christian conflict in the Balkans in general and of Serb national identity in particular. With this in mind it is salutary to note the character of its victor, Sultan Bayazit 'Thunderbolt'. Bayazit had large numbers of Christian soldiers fighting on the Ottoman side and his wife was a Serb. His eldest son was called Isa—'Jesus'— admittedly a Muslim name, albeit rarely, but significant nonetheless in view of his Christian mother. Bayazit's youngest son, Yusuf (Joseph), later converted to Christianity under the name of Demetrios and entered the service of the Byzantine Emperor Manuel. Bayazit also had Serb allies fighting alongside him at Kosovo, including Prince Stefan Lazarević whose personal friendship with the Ottoman royal family stood them in good stead when he was later to save Bayazit's son, Prince Süleyman, at the Battle of Ankara. Bayazit was even powerful—and well informed— enough to interfere directly into Christian affairs when Pope Alexander VI elevated the papal envoy Nicholas Cibo to the college of cardinals on the direct intervention of Bayazit in about 1493. Prominent among the early Ottomans in their expansion into the Balkans were the warrior families of Evrenosoğulları, Mihaloğulları and Malkoçoğulları, Christian converts to Islam. The first two were Byzantine noble families from northwest Anatolia, and the last was the prominent Serb Malković family. In 1497 Milan, Ferrara, Mantua and Florence conspired to actually finance an Ottoman attack on Venice. Following that other great 'Christian-Muslim conflict', the Battle of Mohác in 1526 which resulted in the Ottoman annexation of Hungary, Ian Almond emphasises the huge Christian component—Greeks, Bulgarians, Bosnians—in the Ottoman conquering and occupying forces. Over a third of the 'Turkish' occupation of Budapest, for example, comprised Ottoman Greeks, and the number of actual ethnic Turks in the Ottoman occupation forces overall in Hungary are estimated as low as five percent.[10] Muslim-Christian confrontation—the perceived 'Holy War' symbolised by Kosovo—was simply not an issue to the early Ottomans.

In fact Bayazit's Christian allies were particularly important in his wars against rival Turkish principalities in Anatolia. Being Muslim, Bayazit could not easily use fellow-Muslims against them. Thus, the extension of Ottoman power into Anatolia—present day Asiatic Turkey—represents not only a conquest from Europe, but ironically a conquest by Christians as well.[11]

But Bayazit's victories did re-establish Islam as a European religion—and an advancing one at that, felt all the more keenly with Islam increasingly losing ground at the other end of Europe in Spain. Of course, to characterise Islam as 'European' is regarded as anathema in many quarters, with Islam's origins beyond Europe. But so too is Christianity's. Unlike Christianity, however, which took centuries to establish itself in Europe as a political power, Islam entered Europe in the first years of its outward expansion and has remained in Europe ever since. The continued existence of permanent Muslim nationalities in Europe as a result of Turkey's expansion (such as Albania, Bosnia and Kosovo), modern immigration (such as Germany), and other unrelated Muslim nationalities (such as the Tatars) leave us no doubt that Islam is also a European religion, the efforts of ethnic cleansers and the denials of modern politicians notwithstanding.* The prevailing idea that Islam is characterised as a non-European religion alien to Europe must be renounced once and for all.

The Christian powers of Europe were finally provoked into a response in 1396 when King Sigismund of Hungary led a crusade against the Turks. With an army of over 300,000 it was the largest pan-Christian army ever to put to the field, probably the largest army Europe had seen since the great days of the Roman Empire. It was far larger than any of the earlier crusades to the Holy Land, incorporating forces from England, Scotland, Flanders, Lombardy, Savoy, Poland, Bohemia, Italy and Spain. But it was their alacrity at butchering fellow Christians in the Balkans as much as Muslims that drove the Orthodox into the arms of

---

* Famously, for example, Valery Giscard d'Estaing's denial, in an interview to *Le Monde* 8 November 2002, of Turkey's and Islam's part in Europe.

the Ottomans. Sigismund's crusade culminated in the Battle of Nicopolis in 1396 where the Ottomans, with an inferior force, wiped it out.

Nothing, it seemed, could halt the Ottomans, so that by the end of the fourteenth century it looked only a matter of time—and a short time at that—before they took the greatest prize of both Christendom and the Roman legacy: Constantinople. By this time Constantinople was a sorry shadow of its former self. Once the greatest city of the greatest empire in the world, the Latin sack and occupation between 1204 and 1261 had reduced it to both insignificance and ruination. Although the emperors had regained it in 1261 and the city even enjoyed a final, late cultural flowering at the end of the fourteenth century, Constantinople possessed practically no territory beyond its walls, and large parts of the city itself were overgrown and in ruins. For a great new empire like the Ottomans, its capture surely would be as easy as it was pointless. But Constantinople was more than a pointless and powerless ruin. It was a symbol. Shadow though it was, Constantinople was still the last vestige of the greatest empire of antiquity, the Roman Empire. Its emperors, although having little more power than the magistrate of a minor city, were still the continuation in unbroken tradition of a line of emperors going all the way back to Augustus, a line that numbered some of the greatest rulers of history. And Constantinople—not Jerusalem, not Rome—was still the world's very first Christian city. The first Rome had been pagan, the second Rome Christian, the third was to be Muslim. Without Constantinople, no Ottoman victory could be deemed complete.

Historian Carole Hillenbrand comments on the irony that it was the Turks rather than the Arabs who conquered Constantinople. 'After all, medieval Arabs and Persians often looked down on the Turks, either overtly or slyly'. The urbane Arabs in particular initially viewed the Turkish newcomers with contempt: contempt for a slave people, contempt for city-less barbaric nomads of the uncivilised steppe, and contempt for new converts to Islam. For the early Arab Muslims the capture of Constantinople was seen as a religious goal, almost in messianic terms, and is even mentioned as such in the Qur'an. Hence, its capture by the Turks was a forceful reminder to the Arabs of their own religious failure, and later Arab writing subtly hijacks the Turks and recasts them as their own religious heroes. Arab recasting the Turks in heroic mould has its counterpart in earlier

Greek writing, which hijacked the Macedonian legacy and recast Alexander and his brutal suppression of the Greeks as a Greek hero.[12]

In fact Constantinople would endure three sieges by the Turks and it would take more than another half century after the Battle of Nicopolis before it would finally fall. To some extent this was due to its massive fourth century walls, the greatest urban defences in the world at the time (Pl. 61). But Constantinople was given an eleventh hour reprieve by the Battle of Ankara in 1402, where the hitherto invincible Ottoman army was defeated by a rival force of Turks under the great conqueror Tamerlane. A case of using fire to fight fire indeed! The army of Bayezit Thunderbolt, which only shortly before looked set to claim Constantinople for the Ottomans, was wiped out and Bayezit himself died in captivity. But perhaps in the long term it was the Ottomans who won at Ankara: for the Ottoman Empire lay on stronger foundations than the Timurid. Although Tamerlane was to build a great capital at Samarkand, Ottoman Constantinople was to ultimately far outshine Tamerlane's single generation Samarkand.

A NEW ROMAN EMPEROR, A NEW ALEXANDER THE GREAT

Tamerlane did not stop the Ottomans from taking Constantinople, he merely delayed the inevitable. The events leading up to this and its consequent siege, capture and immediate aftermath do not require telling here: they are well enough known and have been recounted well enough before (Pls 62-4). But the personality of the conqueror, one of the most remarkable in history who eventually did capture the second Rome, is essential in its resulting transformation into a third 'Rome', the Mediterranean's newest universal city. For Mehmet the Conqueror was only too aware of symbols, and of the symbol that Constantinople represented in particular (Pl. 65).

Mehmet announced himself as Hector's avenger. Consider the huge cultural baggage that lies behind that apparently simple remark: a hero wreaking revenge against the Hellenes for Asiatic defeat at Troy.* Like

---

* It was not only Mehmet who cast himself in that mould. The early fifteenth-century neo-Platonist philosopher George Gemistos Pleithon—who has been described as the last of the Greek philosophers—viewed the Turks as seeking revenge against the Hellenes for earlier defeats of Asiatic people at the hands of Alexander. See

many before him and many since, Mehmet had paid a visit to Troy. Like any tourist he was shown around, and the supposed tombs of Achilles and Hector pointed out to him. A ruler whom many wrote off as a barbarian invader and whom many more consider solely a part of the Islamic world, Mehmet knew only too well what Troy symbolised. In riding into the great city of Constantinople Mehmet was fully aware of the huge legacy of Greek and Roman civilisation that he had fallen heir to, as well as the Turkish and Islamic. Indeed, Mehmet regarded himself not so much as the destroyer of the Roman Empire but as its restorer and continuer, and reinstated some of the offices and institutions of the Emperor.* 'Mehmet seemed not only to want to invoke the Roman Empire, but to recreate it' as Felipe Fernández-Armesto appropriately states.[13] On entering the city he made a point of seeking out the long ruined Great Palace of the Caesars and wandered through its decaying great halls and courtyards haunted by the personalities and events of over a thousand years of Roman history. He was overheard to murmur an appropriate verse in Persian: 'The spider weaves the curtains in the palace of the Caesars; the owl calls the watches in Afrasiab's towers'.

The verse is usually attributed to the thirteenth century Persian poet Sa'di, but Sa'di's works contain no trace of these words: they are almost certainly Mehmet's own.† For in addition to Turkish, Arabic and Persian, Mehmet knew Greek, Latin and Hebrew and had a thorough grounding in both Islamic and Classical learning as well as the liberal arts. Hector's avenger? Few either before or after had so thoroughly belonged to both eastern and western worlds, was both a great conqueror and general in the field as well as a sound administrator who laid the foundations for the next four centuries of Ottoman rule. A contemporary Venetian observer described Mehmet as:

Woodhouse 1986: 92-3. But the Alexander metaphor could be used both ways as we shall see.

* In fact some in sixteenth century western Europe traced a false descent of the Turks from the Trojans, and their conquest of Greece and the Balkans as Priam's revenge. Others saw the Turks as descended from the Scythians. See Rodinson 1987: 36.

† The words are not in Sa'di's *Gulistan* or *Bustan*. A fragment that is close in sentiment in Sa'di is contained in: 'No kingdom or wealth is left for Alexander,/ Nor crown or throne remains for Faridun.' From *Kulliyat-i Sa'di*, ed. Furughi, Tehran 1351 *shamsi*: p. 876.

noble in arms, of an aspect inspiring fear rather than reverence, sparing of laughter, a pursuer of knowledge, gifted with princely liberality, stubborn of purpose, bold in all things, as avid for fame as Alexander of Macedon. Every day he has Roman and other histories read to him ... chronicles of the popes, the emperors, the kings of France, the Lombards; he speaks three languages, Turkish, Greek and Slavonic. Diligently he seeks information ... on the Pope, of the Emperor, and how many kings there are in Europe, of which he has a map showing the states and provinces. Nothing gives him greater pleasure than to study the state of the world and the science of war. A shrewd explorer of affairs, he burns with the desire to rule. It is with such a man that we Christians have to deal.[14]

As well as being compared to Alexander the Great by a Venetian, it was a Greek, George of Trebizond, who wrote to Mehmet the Conqueror proclaiming him the new Roman emperor: 'No one doubts that you are the Emperor of the Romans'. This was reflected by no less a personage than the pope, Pius II, who could not but help admire Mehmet as the logical successor to the Roman emperors, announcing publicly that if he were only to embrace Christianity Pope Pius would personally recognise this by proclaiming him 'king of the world'. The Byzantine George Critoboulos of Imbros wrote that Mehmet's accomplishments '[are] in no way inferior to those of Alexander the Macedonian' and Mehmet himself (who read Greek) included Homer and Arrian's *Life of Alexander* in his own personal library. In fact Ottoman sultans at different times styled themselves *Kaysar* ('Caesar'), *Basileos* ('Augustus') and *Padishah-i Rum* ('Roman Emperor'). Mehmet the Conqueror was far more a 'Sultan of Rome' than the Seljuks were, who actually incorporated the term into their title.[15]

The Ottomans were thus the restorer of the second Rome. For it was the Latin conquest in 1204 that destroyed Constantinople, not the Ottoman conquest in 1453. Mehmet the Conqueror's entry marked the revival of this great city, the fulfilment of its destiny marked out by its founder, Constantine. And not only for the conquerors, but for the conquered too: Byzantine and Balkan aristocrats came over to Mehmet's banner as well as Turks. A nephew of the last Roman emperor, Constantine XI, became (under his Turkish name Mesih Pasha) Admiral of the Ottoman Fleet from 1470 to 1481, then grand vizier between 1481 to 1483 and again from 1499 to 1501 when he died in office. Another of Constantine's nephews, Murad Pasha, was made governor-general of the Balkans from 1472 to 1473 when he was killed on campaign. Since Constantine XI was childless, either of these two nephews would otherwise have succeeded him as Roman emperor.* In fact the Byzantine scholar Anthony Bryer makes the wry observation that by the time of the siege there had already been so much intermarriage between the Byzantine and Ottoman royal houses that Mehmet II had at least as much dynastic claim to the Byzantine throne as many an emperor.[16] Of the grand viziers in the sixty years after the conquest, most were former Christians drawn from the Byzantine, Serbian, Bosnian and Albanian aristocracy. Mehmet the Conqueror's greatest vizier—the first Ottoman Vizier of Constantinople—was Mahmud Pasha who served as vizier from 1453 to 1468 and again from 1472 to 1474. Mahmud Pasha was a scion of the Byzantine Serbian aristocratic family of the Angelović, whose father had served as Caesar of Greece under Constantine, and was the longest serving grand vizier in Ottoman history. Ahmad Pasha Hersekzade, who became governor-general of Anatolia and served as grand vizier five times between 1497 and 1516, was similarly the son of a Bosnian duke.[17]

Just as the Christian Byzantine Empire marked a continuation of the pagan Roman, the Muslim Ottoman Empire marked a continuation of the Byzantine Roman. Accordingly, under the sultans Constantinople became the capital of a great empire once again, embellished with the most gorgeous buildings that empire could provide. It drew together the best in both eastern and western cultures at the time—both Leonardo and Michelangelo were wooed by the sultans, although in the end only Bellini came, to bequeath his sensitive portrait of Mehmet the Conqueror (Pl. 65). Indeed, Bayazıt II negotiated with both Michelangelo and Leonardo da Vinci in 1504 to build a bridge over the Bosphorus, and Leonardo proposed a huge arch spanning 350 metres, but nothing came of it (although Leonardo

---

* A niece of Constantine XI, Sofia Palaeologus, married Ivan III of Russia, who thereby proclaimed himself as heir to Byzantium.

made a sketch and Michelangelo did construct a model).[18] It was another sultan, the tenth of the House of Osman, who eventually realised both Constantine's and Mehmet's vision: Sultan Süleyman.

Chapter 8

THE MEDITERRANEAN AND THE MEDITERRANEAN WORLD IN THE AGE OF SÜLEYMAN THE MAGNIFICENT

We must not think the Turk is so unskilful
To leave that latest which concerns him first,
Neglecting an attempt of ease and gain,
To wake and wage a danger profitless.

(Shakespeare, Othello, *Act I, Scene III)*

The conquest of Constantinople in 1453 is understandably one of the greatest in Ottoman history. But Constantinople had long been reduced to insignificance—indeed, it was already an Ottoman vassal—and the Ottoman Empire already formidable without Constantinople. Militarily, therefore, Constantinople was almost a side-show to the greater conquests in Middle Europe, the Middle Sea and the Middle East. These continued unabated. Between 1454 and 1475 Moldavia was made a vassal and the Genoese colonies around the Black Sea—as well as the last Byzantine state, the 'Empire' of Trebizond—were annexed, and Caffa in the Crimea was made the capital of an Ottoman province. The Crimean Tatar Khanate under Khan Mangli Giray became an Ottoman vassal in 1475 and the Ottomans thus became a part of the legacy of Genghis Khan.* Through Crimea they were to exert influence deeper into eastern Europe: Crimea extended control over the Tatar Khanates of Astrakhan and Kazan between 1512 and 1551. Good relations were even established with far-off Muscovy because of rivalry with Poland over Moldavia, until Khan Sahib Giray of Crimea (1532-51) persuaded Constantinople of the greater threat.†

---

* The Khans of Crimea were the last descendants of the Golden Horde—to be discussed in more detail in Volume 4 in this series, *The Gates of Europe.*

† It is notable that the Ottomans refused to recognise Muscovy's title of 'Tsar'—

But the most spectacular expansions were under Sultan Selim I (1512-20) and his son Sultan Süleyman I (1520-66). Sultan Selim—known as 'the Grim'—defeated Persia and added all of the Arab Near East to the empire. In entering Cairo in 1517 Selim also added the Arabs' and Islam's own greatest title to his own: that of Caliph. Once again Europe became the seat of a caliph for the first time since the great days of the Umayyads of Cordoba, and the Caliphate was to remain European for the next 400 years under the Caesar-Caliphs of Constantinople.

UNDER THE SHADOWS OF SOLOMON AND JUSTINIAN

Under Selim's son, Süleyman the Magnificent (reigned 1520-66; Pl. 71), the Ottoman Empire reached its zenith. To the Turks he was known as 'the Lawgiver', a true successor to Justinian.* To the west Europeans he was known as 'the Magnificent'. The Venetian envoy to Constantinople in 1553 wrote of Suleyman: 'he has the reputation of being very just and when he has been accurately informed of the facts of the case he never wrongs any man. Of his faith and its laws he is more observant than any of his predecessors'.[1] In Süleyman thus several traditions come together: his name evoking the most splendid of Old Testament kings, his title evoking the lawgiving of both Solomon and Justinian (who was himself also compared to the same Old Testament king).

The age of Süleyman the Magnificent was dominated by some outstanding figures: his wife Roxelana, his architect Sinan, his admiral Barbarossa, and his grand viziers Rüstem Pasha and Sokullu Mehmet Pasha. With the exception of Barbarossa, all were intimately linked. Rüstem Pasha, grand vizier from 1544 to 1561, was married to Süleyman and Roxelana's only daughter Mihrimah; Sokullu Mehmet Pasha, grand vizier from 1565 to 1579, was married to the daughter of Selim, the son of Süleyman and Roxelana (and future sultan); Sinan built some of

---

Caesar—as it was one that the Sultans themselves claimed (*Qaysar*).

* The parallel with Justinian goes further. As well as being renowned as a lawgiver, Süleyman's marriage in 1534 to Roxelana, an ex-slave (and the first time incidentally that an Ottoman ruler married) is likened to Justinian's marriage to the low-born Theodora. Both empresses were immensely forceful personalities and Roxelana, like Theodora, was widely disapproved of and suspected of witchcraft because of the hold she held over the Sultan. See Finkel 2005: 132-3.

the finest mosques in Turkey for both viziers as well as for Süleyman, Selim, Mihrimah and Roxelana.

It was certainly a magnificent age not only for the Ottoman Empire but for Renaissance Europe as well—and in gazing further east it was also the great age of Safavid Persia and Mughal India (both ruled by Turkish speaking dynasties as we have observed). It was almost as if history paused for breath—or perhaps the world was just becoming international at last, the culmination of an internationalism that began with the ancient Persians two thousand years previously.

One must be careful of course in viewing either the age of Süleyman or the Mediterranean world as a whole in the sixteenth century with rose-tinted spectacles. Fernand Braudel sounds a cautionary note in emphasising the stark contrast between the immense wealth and prosperity of the sixteenth century and the recurrent themes of frequent famine, starvation and pestilence throughout the Mediterranean and Europe. The trade produced great wealth it is true, but it was mainly in luxury goods to enrich just the merchant houses of Antwerp, Genoa, Florence, Ragusa, Constantinople, Smyrna and Aleppo. For the rest, life was at best grindingly hard and frugal, at worst starvation. Indeed, for Christian Europe in the sixteenth and seventeenth centuries—that 'high point' between the Renaissance and the Enlightenment—historian Margaret Hunt shatters illusions when she emphasises that:

> The sixteenth and seventeenth centuries stand out as a time of extraordinary religiously inspired violence. The witch trials were very much about the belief that 'good' religion was under threat from the religion of the devil. There were the Spanish and the Portuguese Inquisitions' cruel persecutions of alleged crypto-Jews and crypto-Muslims; Ottoman massacres of Iraqi Shi'ites; the St Bartholemew's Day massacre of 1572 (it actually lasted for months) in which thousands, perhaps tens of thousands, of French Protestants were slaughtered; the long and dreadfully destructive Thirty Years' War, began over religion; the Chmielnicki massacre of the Jews; Oliver Cromwell's 1649 massacres of Irish Catholics at Drogheda and Wexford; the Savoy massacres of Waldensian Protestants in 1655; the 'Montenegran Vespers' of Christmas, 1702, when

much of the Muslim population of Montenegro was put
to the sword, and many more. Often this was violence of
the most barbarous kind. ... No group escaped unscathed
from the ravages of the sixteenth and seventeenth
centuries and rare was the faith that did not have blood
on its hands.[2]

We will also observe in the next chapter how much of the rest of
the world came to be caught up in an age of warfare. Giancarlo Casale
too sounds a cautionary note on Süleyman's reign in particular, pointing
out that while it was undoubtedly the high point of Ottoman civilisation,
his reign also marks the beginning of the undermining of the authority
of the sultan (for example—and most notoriously—the execution of
his chosen successor, his son Mustafa, at the instigation of Roxelana
his wife).[3] Like the 'Golden Age' of the Roman Empire in the second
century (Hadrian to Marcus Aurelius), the age of Süleyman marks at
once both the height and the beginning of the decline and fall.

While it is certainly important to bear these and other cautionary
notes in mind, it is equally essential to emphasise the positive aspects
of Ottoman civilisation here so as to gain a balanced view of the
Turks as a part of the complex and varied civilisation of Europe as
a whole, and to banish forever the negative idea of the Turks as the
'other', beyond the pale of anything bearing the label of 'Europe'.
Even though history may not have paused for breath (it never does),
at this point it seems appropriate that we at least do, and assess some
of the Ottoman achievements.

THE CREATION OF A MERITOCRACY

Much of the Ottoman success was due to their ability to adopt and adapt
new methods and technologies, particularly with the early adoption of
'this mischievous discovery', gunpowder and heavy artillery under Murat
II, the first to use it on a large scale in the history of European warfare.[*]
The key to European world expansion—the 'European age'—according

---

[*] 'If we contrast the rapid progress of this mischievous discovery with the slow and
laborious advances of reason, science, and the arts of peace, a philosopher, according
to his temper, will laugh or weep at the folly of mankind'. Gibbon Vol. VII: 82.

to many was gunpowder,[4] but it was the Ottomans who ushered in the 'gunpowder age' (not to mention the Chinese who invented it). They also perfected the technique of the combined naval and land pincer campaign, a forerunner of the blitzkrieg. The capture of Lepanto from Venice by Bayazit II in 1499, for example, was a combined naval and land campaign superbly executed by Bayazit's great captain Küçük Davut Pasha.

Perhaps their most important innovation in the military field was the creation of the Janissary corps through the *devşirme* system. This was both the continuation of an older Turkish tradition and the creation of a new one. We have already noted how the first Turks to arrive in the Middle East were slave units of the Arab armies. However, the conventional idea of slavery does not apply here: such 'slaves' were never an under-class, but on the contrary formed a military and social elite. It was the Turks themselves who refined and continued this tradition of training slaves to become soldiers, leaders and even rulers—both India and Egypt at different times were ruled by Turkish 'slave' dynasties as we have observed. The Ottoman *devşirme* system was an adaptation of this, whereby officials would periodically tour through the non-Muslim subject communities to levy a draft on promising young boys (usually Christians) to be converted to Islam and raised and trained exclusively for the service of the state. Even though Islamic law theoretically forbade the enslavement of Christians or Jews, the purpose behind this was to create an elite that completely avoided the minefield of class, family or tribal loyalties: the state was the sole allegiance.

The *devşirme* has been pilloried by propagandists as an example of Ottoman enslavement of Christian subjects: 'oriental' brutality with Turkish troops storming unannounced into Greek villages to tear youths away from their families never to be seen again. Such brutality did undoubtedly occur and we should not underestimate a poor family's loss of a son, but the reality was usually different. Strict rules were observed governing the *devşirme*: advance notice of the levy had to be given; only boys that showed particular talent and promise would be chosen, sons of widows must not be taken, nor boys from single son families; most of all no distinctions were made between rich or poor families, peasant or landowner, merchant, artisan, sailor, beggar or robber, Christian, Jew, Greek, Slav, Armenian, Arab, Berber, black or white: talent and talent alone was the only consideration.

And far from hiding their sons and avoiding the levy, many families saw it as a means of advancement for their sons: potential advancement, furthermore, to the highest offices of the state. Historian Philip Mansel wryly remarks of the *devşirme*: 'A hundred years ago, might not selected Irish Catholic youths have felt a similar pride, if they had been converted to Protestantism, sent to Eton and then told to govern the British Empire as servants of the Queen Empress?'[5] We shall see in the next chapter how ordinary people in Christian Europe from as far away as Scotland might voluntarily convert to Islam so as to enter Ottoman service and rise in the state.

For the boys, once taken, were given an education and training of the highest level to form an elite owing allegiance directly to the sultan. Their individual talents and potential would be strictly observed and channelled into particular areas, with the brightest being reserved for the highest posts. On 'graduation', they would be streamed into two main areas: the army and the administration. For the administration this created the first professional civil service in European history, a civil service moreover that, having no vested interests of landed or tribal or mercantile families behind it, was wholly a supreme meritocracy trained since childhood. Few societies have achieved as much. The Ottoman emphasis on meritocracy rather than noble descent was noted by non-Turks, such as Prince Dmitri Cantemir of Moldavia in the early eighteenth century or the Habsburg ambassador at the court of Süleyman in 1555, Ogier de Busbecq, who thus observed:

> In all that great assembly no single man owed his dignity to anything but his personal merits and bravery; no one is distinguished from the rest by his birth, and honour is paid to each man according to the nature of the duty and offices which he discharges. Thus there is no struggle for precedence, every man having his place assigned to him in virtue of the function which he performs. The Sultan himself assigns to all their duties and offices, and in doing so pays no attention to wealth or the empty claims of rank, and takes no account of any influence or popularity which a candidate may possess; he only considers merit and scrutinizes the character, natural ability, and disposition of each. Thus each man is rewarded according to his

deserts, and offices are filled by men capable of performing them. In Turkey every man has it in his power to make what he will of the position into which he is born and of his fortune in life. Those who hold the highest posts under the Sultan are very often the sons of shepherds and herdsmen, and, so far from being ashamed of their birth, they make it a subject of boasting, and the less they owe to their forefathers and to the accident of birth; the greater is the pride which they feel. They do not consider that good qualities can be conferred by birth or handed down by inheritance, but regard them partly as the gift of heaven and partly as the product of good training and constant toil and zeal. Just as they consider that an aptitude for the arts, such as music or mathematics or geometry, is not transmitted to a son and heir, so they hold that character is not hereditary, and that a son does not necessarily resemble his father, but his qualities are divinely infused into his bodily frame. Thus, among the Turks, dignities, offices, and administrative posts are the rewards of ability and merit; those who are dishonest, lazy, and slothful never attain to distinction, but remain in obscurity and contempt. This is why the Turks succeed in all that they attempt and are a dominating race and daily extend the bounds of their rule. Our method is very different; there is no room for merit, but everything depends on birth; considerations of which alone open the way to high official position.[6]

For the army, the *devşirme* created the corps of Janissaries, Europe's first standing professional army since the Romans—and as formidable. Ogier de Busbecq, when visiting an Ottoman military camp, was astonished at the discipline: the general silence, the rigorous cleanliness that was enforced and the overall order. He goes on to compare:

I tremble when I think of what the future must bring when I compare the Turkish system with our own; one army must prevail and the other be destroyed, for certainly both cannot remain unscathed. On their side are the resources of a mighty empire, strength unimpaired, experience and practice in fighting, a veteran soldiery, habituation to victory, endurance of toil, unity, order, discipline, frugality, and watchfulness. On our side is public poverty, private luxury, impaired strength, broken spirit, lack of endurance and training; the soldiers are insubordinate, the officers avaricious; there is contempt for discipline; licence, recklessness, drunkenness, and debauchery are rife; and, worst of all, the enemy is accustomed to victory, and we to defeat. Can we doubt what the result will be?[7]

The *devşirme* was thus one of Ottoman civilisation's greatest institutions, at once a meritocracy that ruled all subjects fairly and a leveller through which all subjects shared in their own rule. Of the forty-five grand viziers at the height of the Ottoman Empire between 1453 and 1625, five were Turks, ten were of unknown origin and the remainder were of Christian origin, including six Greeks, eleven Albanians, one Italian, one Armenian and one Georgian. By the seventeenth and eighteenth centuries the Ottoman preference for newly converted Europeans over the older Muslims of the East— especially the Arabs, but even for Anatolian Turks as well—had become a matter of open criticism. (Indeed when the Arab Receb Pasha was appointed commander-in-chief of the army in 1689 'it was rare if not unprecedented for an Arab to rise so high').[8] With the virtual complete absence of a controlling aristocracy in the early Ottoman centuries, it was a meritocracy created by the institution of the *devşirme*.

Süleyman's great vizier, Rüstem Pasha, is a typical example of the *devşirme* system at its best. Rüstem was the longest grand vizier of his reign and eventual son-in-law (married to Mihrimah Sultan, Süleyman's only daughter by Roxelana), was originally a Catholic Croat swineherd from near Sarajevo.* Another grand vizier, Mahmud Pasha, negotiated

---

* The story is told of an ordinary Greek sailor who, on shore leave in Constantinople, would regularly head for the taverns of the Golden Horn and become drunk, in the manner of sailors all the world over. He would then stagger up the hill to the palace of the grand vizier and demand loudly to be let in. There the palace servants had standing orders to allow him in, put him into a room to sleep it off. The following morning the Vizier himself would personally invite him to share breakfast and then send him on the way with a purse of money and the parting words: 'And give my love

33   *The Karatay Madrasa at Konya.*

34   *The tomb and associated mosque complex of Rumi at Konya.*

35   The Gök Medrese at Sivas in eastern Turkey, one of the finest of Seljuk architecture.

36   The mosque at Divriği in eastern Turkey, the most richly decorated of all Seljuk monuments.

37   *The plain simple lines of the Hunat Hanım Medrese in Kayseri are in contrast to the more elaborate decoration of the previous monuments.*

38   *The gavit (annex) of the eleventh century Church of the Holy Apostles in the Armenian capital of Ani added in the thirteenth century under the Seljuks and built in the Seljuk style.*

39   The Qutb Minar at Delhi, the highest minaret in the world, built in 1204 by Qutb ud-Din Aibak.

40   The massive walls of Tughluqabad outside Delhi.

XX

41   *The Mosque of Ibn Tulun in Cairo.*

42   *The Mamluk Mosque of Sultan Hasan in Cairo.*

43   *The ancient site of Afrasiab in Samarkand, with the massive bulk of the Bibi Khanum Mosque in background.*

44   *Tamerlane's tomb, the Gur-i Amir in Samarkand.*

45   The Timurid necropolis of Shah-i Zindeh in Samarkand.

46   The massive Shrine of Ahmad Yassavi at Turkestan in Kazakhstan.

47   The Tomb of Queen Gawhar Shad, Tamerlane's daughter-in-law, in Herat.

48   The Taj Mahal from the Great Fort at Agra.

49   *The extraordinary syncretic tomb of Akbar at Sikandra outside Agra.*

50   *The Shrine of Shaikh Safi, founder of the Safavid dynasty, at Ardabil.*

51   The centrepiece of Shah Abbas' new city of Isfahan, the Royal Square.

52   Shah Abbas' Royal Mosque at Isfahan.

53 The Ottoman dynastic necropolis at Bursa.

54 Interior of the Great Mosque at Bursa.

55   *The Dardanelles, scene of the first Ottoman crossing into Europe, with the Ottoman fortress of Kilit Bahır, 'Keys to the Sea,' in the foreground.*

56   *The Nilifer Hatun religious complex at Iznik.*

57   The city of Edirne, dominated by the massive Selimiye, masterpiece of the architect Sinan.

58   The Bayazit I complex at Edirne.

59   The Old Mosque at Edirne.

60   An Ottoman mosque at Gjakove in Kosovo.

XXX

61 *The Theodosian Land Walls of Constantinople, where the army of Mehmet the Conqueror finally broke through.*

62 *Rumeli Hisar, the fort on the European shore of the Bosphorus built by Mehmet the Conqueror.*

63   Anadolu Hisar, the corresponding fort on the Asian shore.

64   Part of the Byzantine chains that were used to block off the Golden Horn during the siege (now in the Istanbul Archaeological Museum).

a favourable settlement with the Serbs in 1457 on behalf of the sultan. That he was able to negotiate such a favourable settlement was due to the fact that he spoke fluent Serbo-Croat—and that his opposite number in the Serbian court with whom he conducted the negotiations, the Grand Voyvod ('Prime Minister') Michael Angelović, was his own brother. Probably the most talented grand vizier of Süleyman's and his successors reigns was another former *devşirme* boy, Sokullu Mehmet Pasha (whose small but exquisite mosque in Istanbul is one of the greatest gems of Ottoman architecture: Pl. 76), was also a Serb, whose brother was the first Archbishop of Peć, an archbishopric which Sokullu himself had revived.[9] Sokullu was also the architect of a new world order that we will discuss in the next chapter.

BUILDINGS FOR ALL

There was another Ottoman institution that formed a similar levelling function—and gave Ottoman civilisation its most visible expression. This was the *külliye* or mosque complex, endowed by successive sultans as well as by senior Ottoman officials. Like much else in Ottoman civilisation, it was both rooted in traditional Muslim practice and transformed by the Turks into a distinct institution. The mosque is, of course, universal to Islam: specifically each urban centre having a single Friday Mosque for the weekly prayer gatherings—very approximately the equivalent to the Christian cathedral—as well as numerous subsidiary mosques. The Ottomans transformed this in two ways. First, instead of one single great mosque for a city—*ulu cami* in Turkish—each sultan's reign would be marked by the construction of a grand mosque bearing his name, so that a city—usually the imperial capital—would end up with many. This tradition extended to the sultan's prime ministers, his mother, his daughters and ultimately to many senior officials, in Istanbul as well as in the provinces (Pls 72-8). To some extent this was the result of Islam's commandment—one of the five binding commandments of Islam—to give to charity. By endowing a religious establishment one is thereby not only fulfilling a religious duty, but in setting aside land for its up-keep one also ensures that the land—not to mention one's descendants who

---

to the rest of the family'. Like all good stories, this is almost certainly apocryphal, but does illustrate the nature of the *devşirme*.

remain as guardians of both land and endowment—are exempt from confiscation or taxation.

The second departure from the traditional Islamic mosque was that each of these great endowments would be much more than just a mosque. A *külliye* (deriving from the Arabic root word *kull* meaning 'all') incorporates many different functions: places of learning, both religious and secular; libraries; the tomb of the founder; and many charitable foundations, such as hospitals, asylums and kitchens for feeding the poor.* By the eighteenth century the *külliyes* of Istanbul were feeding thirty thousand people a day. To some extent these Ottoman *külliyes* have their counterparts elsewhere in the Islamic world with Islam's emphasis on charitable works, and the model for these religious endowments was set in the Seljuk period as we have seen. Equally, it drew upon the Byzantine tradition, particularly in Constantinople itself, where many of its great monasteries incorporated places of learning and charitable institutions. The sultans combined both traditions and elevated the idea to new levels. The larger *külliyes*, such as the Süleymaniye in Istanbul, would occupy—and give their name to—entire city quarters, combining the functions of places of learning and community centres that incorporated every level of society from religious establishment and intelligentsia to the poor, the homeless, the sick and the insane. Like the *devşirme*, the *külliye* served both to extend Ottoman civilisation throughout the provinces and to enable all walks of society to partake in that civilisation.

A SPLENDID BUILDING OF MANY STRANDS

The Süleymaniye in Istanbul is certainly an appropriate place to pause underneath this magnificent monument and reflect upon the many different strands that we have reviewed so far that this building draws together. It is, first, probably the greatest architectural masterpiece of Süleyman's reign, an achievement of his great architect Sinan (Pl. 74). Just over a half of the 3,523 craftsmen who worked on it—fifty-one percent—were Christian, so as well as a symbol of

---

* It is interesting to observe how some of these *külliye* kitchens in Istanbul today—that in the Süleymaniy for example—still continue their original function: but as up-market restaurants to feed the rich!

Islam it also stood for official Ottoman religious tolerance.[10] Evliya Çelebi describes that:

> [in addition to] four great medreses ... there is also a Hadith school, a Koran recitation school, a medical college, a primary school, a hospital, a soup kitchen and dining hall, a guesthouse, a caravanserai for travellers, and a palace for the Janissary Agha; markets for goldsmiths, button makers and boot makers; a resplendent public bath; quarters for theological students; and 1,000 houses for servants. 1,001 domes can be counted in the vicinity of this mosque. ... There is a total of 3,000 servants attached to it'.[11]

Architecturally, its great domed interior pays direct homage to the Emperor Justinian's cathedral of Haghia Sophia (whose plan Sinan adapted), thus representing a culmination of Byzantine and Islamic traditions as well as evoking another link with Süleyman's illustriuous predecessor. The name of the Cathedral of Haghia Sophia—or Holy Wisdom—was itself a direct reference to the Goddess of Holy Wisdom, Athena, thus making Byzantine Constantinople a new Athens, as well as a new Rome and a new Jerusalem. Now, with a great mosque echoing Haghia Sophia, Constantinople would also be a new Baghdad and a new Mecca. The name and epithet of its builder—Süleyman the Lawgiver—evoked, as we have seen, both Justinian and Solomon. Süleyman's actual title (along with all Ottoman rulers since Selim I) was both sultan and caliph, thus combining the positions of secular ruler and Islamic authority. This latter position—a secular ruler who at the same time embodied religious authority—recalls an earlier dynasty of Turk kings, the Northern Wei of China (reviewed in Chapter 2). The Tabgach Turk kings of the Northern Wei were the first to adopt an element in Mahayana Buddhism which invests the authority of the Buddha in the secular ruler as we have seen. This was manifested at the Yungang caves near Tatung in the late fourth century by each king erecting a gigantic statue of Buddha that represented both himself and the authority of the Buddha at the same time, the first time that giganticism had been introduced into Buddhist art. Such Buddha images were repeated most famously a short time later by another Turk dynasty at Bamiyan in Afghanistan (pls 8, 9 and 12). Iconographically, the image of the standing Buddha has been traced back to the image of standing statues of the Emperor Augustus: the authority of the emperor being translated into the authority of the Buddha in Buddhist art. In Constantinople, therefore, we come back full circle: a city created by Roman emperors and continued by sultans evoking Roman emperors. And the Ottomans, one recalls, were unique among Muslim dynasties as being the only one where each successive ruler built a mosque complex representing both his own reign and the religious authority invested in him as caliph: Turkish sultans continuing in Europe a tradition began by Turkish Buddhist rulers in China.* No other city in world history has bridged so many civilisations, nor has brought so many cultural strands together.

THE DREAM OF BYZANTIUM

The period also saw a minor 'Byzantine renaissance' under the sultans. After the Conquest the population of Constantinople remained primarily Greek. Many official Ottoman documents were bilingual in Greek and Turkish until the early sixteenth century. This Greek revival, mainly after 1714, was focussed on the Phanar quarter of Constantinople overlooking the Golden Horn, which flourished under the Ottomans, becoming probably the wealthiest community in the empire (Pl. 83). The Phanariots of Ottoman Constantinople consciously maintained their essentially Greek character and Byzantine traditions, making a conscious effort to recall the great days of the Byzantine Empire—a 'dream of Byzantium'—in their lifestyles, their sentiments and even the family names of many of the great houses. Indeed, when some of the Phanariot families were made princes of Wallachia and Moldavia under the Ottomans, they saw themselves as heirs to the Caesars, as the only Christian rulers left in former Byzantine lands. The life of Prince Dmitri Cantemir of Moldavia, for example, embodied this 'dream of Byzantium', and he can almost by styled 'the last of the Byzantines'.†

---

* Traditionally an Islamic city has just one single major Friday Mosque—roughly the equivalent of the position of the cathedral. Occasionally they would proliferate, but Constantinople is unique in having many 'Friday Mosques' as nearly every successive Sultan endowed one in their own name. Exceptions were Selim II, Murad III and Mehmed III, although Selim II did build the most splendid of all mosques in Edirne; Ahmet I was the last to build an imperial mosque.

† Prince Dmitri Cantemir defected to Peter the Great in 1711 during Russia's war with

Prince Alexander Mavrocordato, the Ottoman Prince of Moldavia from 1782 to 1785 and a scion of one of the grandest Greek families of Constantinople, in his refusal to Catherine II of Russia's offer to enter Russian service, could still write: 'It is better that Her Majesty regard me as a friendly Turk, which does not detract from my quality as a Christian, but on the contrary my Christian faith orders even me to be faithful to my Emperor'.[12]

Even the Byzantine Christian obsession with holy relics continued under the Ottomans: the collection of Muslim relics in Constantinople by the Ottomans (now preserved in the Topkapi Palace)—the Mantle of the Prophet, his sword, etc.—was very much in the tradition of the Byzantine policy of protecting Constantinople with Christian relics. Outside Constantinople, such a practice is rare in the Islamic world. In this context it is worth noting that the Ottomans did not change the name of Haghia Sophia (Ayasofya) cathedral even after its conversion to a mosque; indeed, contrary to popular misconception, the name of Constantinople was not changed to 'Turkish' Istanbul, but remained 'Constantinopolis' or 'Qustantiniyya' right down until the twentieth century (and 'Istanbul' is in any case a Greek name, not Turkish: a corruption of *Eistanpolis* meaning 'to the city'). Ottoman civilisation was as much a continuation of Byzantine as its replacement.

Süleyman reintroduced Roman-style spectacle into Constantinople once again with spectacular displays on state occasions and triumphal processions in the hippodrome. In 1534, for example, on the occasion of his marriage to Roxelana (the first time an Ottoman sultan was married), tournaments (the later equivalent of gladiatorial combats) featuring both Muslim and Christian knights, wild beast displays, juggling and acrobatic performances were held in the hippodrome, resurrected as its original purpose (and the hippodrome to this day remains the scene of demonstrations and discontented gatherings, recalling its other Byzantine function).

Turkey, but Prince Constantin Brancoveanu of Wallachia remained staunchly loyal to the Ottomans, despite overtures from Russia. See Runciman 1968: Chapter 10; Finkel 2005: 405-6.

A DREAM OF JERUSALEM

In addition to the protection that the sultan extended to the Orthodox Church, the position of Jews in the Ottoman Empire was in stark contrast to their status elsewhere in Europe. Following the Spanish *reconquista* culminating in the fall of Granada in 1492, Spanish Muslims and Jews were faced with the choice of forcible conversion or expulsion. Most decided to leave, with North Africa providing an obvious homeland to the Spanish Muslims. But the Jews had no obvious homeland to return to. The sultan encouraged the Spanish Jews to settle in the Ottoman Empire, even providing grants. Hence, a Spanish rabbi wrote to his brethren:

> Here in the land of the Turks we have nothing to complain of. We possess great fortunes; much gold and silver are in our hands. We are not oppressed with heavy taxes and our commerce is free and unhindered. Rich are the fruits of the earth. Everything is cheap and every one of us lives in peace and freedom. Here the Jew is not compelled to wear a yellow star as a badge of shame as is the cast in Germany where even wealth and great fortune are a curse for a Jew because he therewith arouses jealousy among the Christians and they devise all kind of slander against him to rob him of his gold. Arise my brethren, gird up your loins, collect all your forces and come to us.[13]

Even before the Spanish *reconquista* the English expelled their Jews in 1291, the French in 1343, many German states in the early fifteenth century. A tide of intolerance that swept across Renaissance Europe in the sixteenth century resulted in floods of persecuted Jews seeking refuge and protection in Ottoman lands, not only from the Spain and Portugal of the Inquisition, but from Italy, the Netherlands and elsewhere as well. Although the Turks were not exactly alien to prejudice themselves, anti-Semitism utterly baffled the Ottomans. In 1556 the sultan intervened personally with the pope to save twenty-four Jews of Ancona, whom the pope had ordered to be publicly burnt to death, but to no avail.[14] Ottoman Salonika in particular became a major Jewish centre, and remained so until the Second World War: where the

Inquisitors of fifteenth-century Spain failed, the SS of twentieth-century Germany succeeded.

There were occasional outbreaks of religious intolerance towards the Jews in Constantinople—but invariably from the Christian population, not the Muslim. Riots by Christian groups against Jews as late as 1874 were usually caused by the 'psychotic frequency' of Christian accusations against the Jews of ritual kidnapping, murder and eating of Christian children, accusations which, after 1554, all had to be referred directly to the sultan (who invariably quashed them as the nonsense they were). Jews still enjoyed the direct protection of the sultan against Ottoman Christian persecution until the end of the nineteenth century. 'In Constantinople the words pogrom, ghetto, inquisition had no meaning' in the words of Philip Mansel. Jews remain the largest minority in Istanbul today. [15]

Protection of other persecuted religions became an active policy of the Ottomans. The Ottoman Empire at its height contained seventy-two and a half nationalities (Gypsies were counted as a half a nationality—which is at least a half more than many modern European states consider them). Hungarian and Transylvanian Calvinists, Silesian Protestants and Russian Old Believers were all at different times given sanctuary in Ottoman Turkey.[*] Turkey received Polish refugees following the partition of Poland in 1795, and again—together with Hungarian refugees—following the failed 1848 revolution. Following the Russian occupation of the Caucasus in the 1860s some 600,000 Circassians, Chechens and other Russian Muslims fled into the Ottoman Empire to escape Russian persecution in the Caucasus. They were resettled throughout the Ottoman Near East and remain as distinct communities in the Middle East to this day. The Republic of Turkey to a large extent continued this policy with its absorption of Balkan Muslims in the early twentieth century; even as late as the 1980s Turkey provided a new home for a tribe of Kirghiz refugees from Soviet-occupied Afghanistan. Ottoman Constantinople also included many major Genoese families such as the Doria, the Testa, the Draperi and the Fornetti, and the Ottoman Empire accommodated asylum seekers from large parts of Europe, such as Old Believers and Circassians from Russia, Protestants from Poland and Jews from everywhere. Evliya Çelebi even records a Hindu quarter in sixteenth

---

[*] The only religious minority that was persecuted in the Ottoman Empire were fellow Muslims: the Shi'a.

century Constantinople, complete with temple and *ghat*.[16] The empire was never an 'anti-Europe' or counter-Christendom.

THE LIVES OF OTHERS: WOMEN IN OTTOMAN LANDS[17]

Probably the one reason above all others—apart from religion—why Turkish culture and society is regarded as separate from the European mainstream is the position of women in Ottoman society. Few other questions form such a source of deep-seated prejudice as attitudes to Ottoman women, marriage, and sexual mores generally, and the subject of women still colours attitudes to Muslim societies today: seclusion, veiling, polygamy, the harem, female suppression—all perceived as alien to 'European values'.

Such attitudes were determined above all by a fascination with the Ottoman imperial harem. This fascination, amounting to an obsession, was backed up by a huge eighteenth and nineteenth century West European vogue for lascivious 'orientalist' art depicting vaguely titillating harem scenes and other mild erotica, let alone an only slightly more serious (but equally misleading) fashion for operas ranging from Mozart's *Il Seraglio* to Rossini's *Italian Girl in Algiers* (and a huge number of others).

Of course, sex is an endless source of fascination—and prejudice—for all societies, and not just Christian attitudes towards Muslims,[*] and polygamy the main institution that appeared to set Ottoman marriage and women apart from Christian Europe. But the imperial harem was a unique institution completely unrepresentative of Ottoman society—or even of Ottoman aristocracy. It has been calculated that only about five percent of the Muslim population in the empire, or about two percent of all marriages, were polygamous in the eighteenth century. In such instances where marriages were polygamous, two wives were the norm, rarely the four allowed by the Qur'an and not the vast stable of scantily clad houris of popular fantasy. Even Muslim law, which condones polygamy (which in fact has now virtually disappeared in most Muslim

---

[*] In this context it is worth noting that perhaps the biggest source of prejudice of extreme Islamicists today towards 'Western' societies is the perceived sexual mores of its women

countries or even outlawed*) hedges it with strict rules stipulating full agreement of and equality among all parties, and strict property, legal and housing arrangements: a man could not take a second wife, for example, without the written permission of the first. The lack of such permission would be legal grounds for the wife suing for divorce, and such cases were frequent occurrences in Ottoman law courts. Polygamy in any case, where it was practised, was often a way in traditional Muslim societies of taking care of unwanted females, such as widows or orphans, who would otherwise fall through society's loops. The alternative in most Christian European societies was usually the convent or the asylum for the elite—or the street for the rest.

Polygamy was more tolerated in the aristocracy, but to begin with, the Ottomans did not have an 'aristocracy' as it is understood in most other European countries: the elite were generally the product of the *devşirme* which, as we have seen, were drawn from all walks of society, usually the lower. In addition, leading members of the elite were often rewarded by marriage to an imperial princess (of which there was always a plentiful stock to draw upon, being daughters of the sultan's vast stable of concubines). Being 'high born' (even though a princess would, like the sultan himself, invariably be the child of a non-Muslim slave), imperial princesses usually insisted upon strict monogamy, stipulating divorce of the first wife if her husband-to-be was already married, even if the first wife was a love match. And *no* senior Ottoman civil servant or officer would dare turn down the 'reward' or requests of such a marriage alliance to the sultan, whatever the attributes of the lady herself, be she houri or hag.

Similar misconceptions surround the largely mythical ideas of female seclusion in Ottoman society, again based largely on the fascination for the imperial harem. The imperial harem was, of course, hugely secluded—and as often as not for Ottoman princes as well as for the

---

* Informal polygamy is now effectively legal in Britain as well as many other societies, in that it is now perfectly acceptable—indeed, commonplace—for unmarried couples to live together, with the children of such unions enjoying as much full social and legal rights as those from marriages. There is, therefore, effectively no legal barrier to prevent anyone from entering into long-term liaisons with multiple partners, male or female. The fact that it does not commonly happen, despite the huge—indeed, increasing—number of monogamous unmarried partnerships, clearly suggests that polygamy is a rare occurrence in this, Muslim or any society, even when possible in practice.

womenfolk. But the harem can in no way be taken as typical Ottoman family life as we have emphasised. In practice, women in Ottoman Europe were hardly more secluded than women in most Christian European societies before the nineteenth (or, in some instances, the twentieth) century: female seclusion—or at least severe restriction—to a greater or lesser extent was the norm throughout Europe. And, of course, women throughout pre-modern Europe—Catholic, Protestant, Orthodox, Jewish, Muslim—wore the head-scarf or some other form of head-covering in public. Ottoman women took their leisure in public parks, socialised among themselves, shopped in the streets, attended public baths and visited their relatives, just as elsewhere in Europe. Segregation was stricter, but only in elite classes and hardly stricter than elites in Christian societies at the time.

Divorce and adultery are other common misconceptions. Ottoman women enjoyed considerable divorce rights: they could initiate divorce proceeding (for example domestic violence, abuse of property rights, or a husband taking a second wife without permission were all valid grounds for divorce) long before this was allowed in most other European countries, and Islamic law enforced provision by her ex-husband for a divorced woman's financial support commensurate with the standard she had enjoyed while married. Few women elsewhere in Europe enjoyed such rights until the nineteenth century. It also awarded divorced women custody of the children: boys until the age of seven, girls until puberty. Information on adultery is notoriously difficult to obtain in this or any society, but contrary to popular misconception, judicial execution of adulterous women was practically unknown in the Ottoman Empire (or, indeed, most places in the Islamic world) in the modern period until the advent of Wahabbism in the late eighteenth century (which did not spread much beyond Arabia until the late twentieth century)—and certainly less than in Christian Europe. Informal vigilante 'honour' killings—as opposed to judicial—did of course exist, in both Christian and Muslim societies.[*]

Property laws for women in the Ottoman Empire were in advance of any in most European countries before the nineteenth century, so much so that even Christian women in the Ottoman Empire generally

---

[*] And technically was only outlawed in France in 1975 and Italy in 1981; that part of the law that still condones it in Jordan is borrowed from the Code Napoléon. See Hunt 2010: 118-9.

preferred the Muslim courts over their own Orthodox ones (usually run by the clergy) because of the fairer deal they would receive. For example, following the conquest of Cyprus in 1571 the number of women flocking to the Muslim courts was a matter of considerable concern to the Orthodox clergy. The Seljuks too accorded particular prominence to women in their courts.[18] Successful recourse to the law courts became standard practice for women of all classes—and religions—in Ottoman lands from the fifteenth century onwards, a practice entrenched in traditional Islamic law. Historian Margaret Hunt cites, for example, that of the approximately 10,600 court cases between 1603 and 1627 in Kayseri in Anatolia, seventeen percent of the litigants were women, usually in cases involving property but also divorce and domestic violence.[19]

Indeed, women generally enjoyed superior property rights in Turkish lands, both in terms of inheritance and independent control of assets. Many could become major investors, patrons and philanthropists in their own right in a way that few women in Christian Europe (with the possible exception of Portugal) could ever dream. In the same statistics for Kayseri cited above, forty percent of all property cases were brought by women. Up to a third of all buyers of commercial property and investors in Aleppo in the mid-eighteenth century were women, and many women in general in the Ottoman Empire grew immensely wealthy in their own (as opposed to their husband's) right and became major property owners.

This frequently achieved physical form in the surprisingly large number of mosques, madrasas and charitable institutions that were endowed by women. This practice began as far back as the Seljuk period when many major architectural religious complexes in Anatolia were endowed by or dedicated to leading Seljuk women (e.g., Pl. 37). The Seljuk tradition of female endowments was continued by the Ottomans: of the six mosque complexes built in Istanbul by Süleyman the Magnificent's family, three—a half—were endowed by women of the royal house. Hafsa Sultan—Süleyman's mother—built a complex in Manisa comprising a mosque, madrasa, hospice, primary school, kitchen, hospital and bath-house, altogether employing a staff of a hundred, while Mihrimah—his daughter—built similar complexes both at Uskudar (opposite Istanbul) and at the Edirne Gate of Istanbul (Pl. 77, both complexes designed by Sinan). Haseki Hürrem (Roxelana)—

his wife—endowed mosque complexes in Istanbul, Edirne, Jerusalem, Mecca and Medina, the Jerusalem complex alone comprising a mosque, a fifty-five room hospice, a bakery, kitchen, cellar, granary, woodshed, refectory, lavatories, inn and a stable. The Yeni Valide Mosque on the Golden Horn—the last of the great imperial mosque complexes in Istanbul and now one of the city's more visible landmarks—was begun by Safiye Sultan, the mother of Sultan Murad IV and completed by Turhan Sultan, and included a mosque, a bazaar (the Egyptian Bazaar), madrasa, fountain, library, mausoleum and caravanserai (Pl. 78).

The rights of women in Ottoman society to a large extent are grounded in traditional Islam, as already observed. But it is also derived from a separate Turkish tradition reaching further back into their Central Asian nomadic roots, a tradition that continued under the Ottomans. By its very nature a nomadic tradition demands a far greater social status for women than amongst sedentary populations: a nomadic lifestyle requires active participation by the womenfolk at virtually every level, with women even on occasion fighting alongside men (hence the Central Asian origins of the legends of the Amazons). In Turkish Central Asia many great buildings were accordingly dedicated to or endowed by women. Samarkand's greatest mosque, the Bibi Khanum, comes to mind, as does the great funerary complex of the Shah-i Zindeh, which commemorates mainly women of the Timurid household, or the huge complex built by Queen Gawharshad at Herat (Pls 43, 45, 47). The Turks brought the tradition with them into Anatolia, and the conquest of India by a separate group of Turks, the Mughals, resulted in what is probably the most famous building in the world dedicated to a woman: the Taj Mahal (Pl. 48). Turkish civilisation, in other words, was both Islamic and supra-Islamic, reaching out to all sectors of society—and confounds much of the traditional Western image of Islam, Turks and women.

Such views were by no means universal. Voltaire, for example, in contrasting Ottoman women's freedom with their lack in France in 1765 wrote that in Islam, women 'are by no means slaves; they have property; they can make wills, they are able to request a divorce on occasion; they have their time to go to the mosque—and to their rendezvous'.[20] This is not to say that a woman's lot was not a happy one in Christian Europe but a bed of roses in Muslim Europe—far from it. But it does show that the differences—not only in women's rights but at all levels of society—were far more complex than the stereotypical images. And that to talk about 'Europe' one has to include *all* of Europe, not just selective parts to favour this or that view.

*   *   *

We have, of course, ranged far beyond the Ottoman Empire and far beyond the reign of Süleyman the Magnificent in this chapter. But to describe the Ottoman Empire and the Mediterranean world in the sixteenth century with reference to Süleyman is nonetheless appropriate. Of the civilisation which Süleyman's reign represented, Andrew Mango writes: 'Ottoman civilization was the common product of distinct religious communities speaking many different languages, coexisting within the same society while keeping their separate corporate identities'.[21] Patrick Kinross thus sums up the age and the man:

> It was a fitting end, in the fullness of age and the moment of victory, for a campaigning sultan who reigned over a great military empire. Suleiman the Conqueror, the man of action, had expanded and secured it; Suleiman the Legislator, the man of order and justice and wisdom, had perfected it, through the strengths of his institutions and the humanity of his policies, into an enlightened structure of government; Suleiman the Statesman had won for it the commanding status of a world power. The tenth and perhaps the greatest of the Ottoman sultans, he had raised their empire to a peak of unsurpassed power and prestige. ... Suleiman, the Grand Turk, was a prince of the Renaissance, outdoing in the magnificence of his court and the style of his living many of those in this Golden Age of Western Christian civilization.[22]

Chapter 9

WHEN TURKEY RULED THE WAVES

FROM STEPPE HORSEMEN TO SEA ROVERS

> Stated simply, it asks: 'Did the Ottomans participate in the
> Age of Exploration?' The answer, also stated simply, is yes.
>
> *(Giancarlo Casale[1])*

It is remarkable just how quickly the Turks—traditionally a land people—became a naval power. A naval power, moreover, that successfully challenged and defeated the far older maritime powers of the Mediterranean. Indeed, under the great admiral Hayrettin Paşa—'Barbarossa'—in the mid-sixteenth century (Pl. 84), the Turks defeated the combined Catholic forces of the entire Mediterranean (with the notable exception of France). Long before that, Turkish mastery of the waves had proved one of the most decisive elements in the extension of their power, and soon after the capture of Constantinople it had become the greatest maritime power in the Mediterranean.

It is not necessary here—nor possible—to catalogue the various stages in the Turks' rise to naval supremacy. But several aspects of Turkish maritime history and its effect are worth highlighting in the context of its interaction with the rest of Europe as well as to challenge the traditional view that overseas maritime expansion—the 'European Age of Expansion'—was a solely Western European phenomenon. We have already reviewed in the first volume of this series how the Arabs were active participants in and challengers to this view. Here, it can be shown that the Turks were as well, as Casale's remarks quoted above suggest.

THE MEDITERRANEAN AND THE AGE OF BARBAROSSA

In 1535 Francis I of France entered into a military alliance with Sultan Süleyman against the Hapsburgs. Accordingly, in 1543-4 Toulon in France was made an Ottoman naval base under Barbarossa by agreement with the French, becoming effectively—albeit temporarily—an extension of the empire. The citizens welcomed this move by entertaining Barbarossa to a grand civic banquet in their city. For the first time since the collapse of Granada the call to prayer rang over a West European city—and for the second time Toulon became a Muslim city.* From Toulon the Ottoman fleet went on to capture Nice from the Hapsburgs, mutual enemy of both the French and the Turks.

Elsewhere, much of Turkish naval activity was exercised indirectly through their allies in North Africa. The great age of the Algiers privateers—the 'Barbary Corsairs'—was between about 1560 and 1630. They raided throughout the western Mediterranean (Pl. 85), often with formidable fleets of galleys numbering several hundred vessels. In other words they were organised campaigns which had to be properly fitted out and planned some time in advance, not mere random pirate raids—officially an arm of the Ottoman state, albeit distantly so. Crews comprised mainly Berbers and Andalusians, but they also included Turks and even Greeks as well as the occasional North European. Algiers was the main centre of operations and became wealthy and polyglot as a result, with a cosmopolitan population that included Portuguese, Flemish, Scots, English, Hungarians, Danes, Irish, Slavs, French, Spanish and Italians, as well as Greeks, Turks, Berbers, Arabs, Egyptians, Ethiopians—even some Japanese and Chinese are recorded. No mere robbers' nest, this was as open and as cosmopolitan a city as any in the Mediterranean (Pl. 86.) In 1610 a 'Barbary' pirate ship operating out of Tunis was reported to be fifty percent Moor and fifty percent English.[2] As late as 1803 at the time of the fledgling US Navy's attack on Tripoli (the first overseas naval campaign by the newly independent United States, still remembered in the US Marines' song 'From the Halls of Montezuma to the Shores of Tripoli'), the 'corsair' commander of Tripoli's fleet was a Scot. In fact a Scottish captain of a Moorish fleet opposing the US navy (or raiding the Firth of Forth) was no more a phenomenon than a Moorish captain of a

---

* The first time being its capture in 940 by Arabs—see Volume 1 in this series.

Venetian fleet (such as Shakespeare immortalised) besieging Ottoman Cyprus might have been.

If Tripoli, La Goulette, Algiers, and the other bases of the Barbary Corsairs were 'pirate' centres (Pls 86-7), so too were Malta, Leghorn, Naples and Palermo—not to mention Bristol and London. Christian sea captains committed just as many random raids on foreign shipping and coasts with little or no reference to London or Madrid as Barbarossa did in relation to Constantinople. Indeed, Mediterranean shipping in particular was prey to English pirates: 'in the same way that many Britons knew Muslims only as Barbary Corsairs, so did many Muslims know Britons only as infidel pirates'. [3] When that indomitable old Turk, Khair ud-Din Barbarossa, both pirate chief and lord high admiral of the Ottoman navy, died in Constantinople in July 1546 at ninety years of age, he and the power he represented were unchallenged masters of the Mediterranean (Pl. 84.)

The Great Siege of Malta in 1565 and the repulse of Turkey's great armada from its shores by the heroic defence of the Knights has been seen as a turning point in Ottoman fortunes, and perhaps rightly so. But from the West European point of view, the real importance of Malta was not so much that it held, but that it came to within an ace of falling (and may well have done so if not for the premature death of its commander, the formidable admiral Dragut Pasha). It was certainly a very close thing. If it had fallen, the Turks once established on Malta—with the security of its incomparable Grand Harbour (Pls 88-9)—would have had the western Mediterranean at its feet. Vienna, which the Turks battered themselves against three times (1529, 1532 and—most famously—1683), would have been rendered irrelevant to the masters of the Mediterranean. Of course, questions of 'what if' are always the most pointless of all for an historian. But it was certainly not a pointless question for the defenders of Malta. For after the victory there was no rest, no complacency, and the Great Siege continued to haunt the Knights—and much of the rest of Christian Europe—despite their victory. In one of the great cases of locking the stable door after the horse had bolted, the Knights of Malta embarked upon a frenzy of fortification building immediately after the Turks departed that continued unabated for the next two hundred years. Out of it, Valetta and the Grand Harbour emerged as probably the most heavily fortified city in the world—testimony indeed to the near paranoia held by Western Europe for the power of the 'Terrible Turk' (Pls 88-9).

THE ATLANTIC AND BEYOND

Not since the Roman Empire had so much of the Mediterranean fallen under just one power. But unlike the Romans, Turkish naval power extended well beyond the Mediterranean. In answer to the question of the Ottoman Empires 'oft lamented failure' to explore the Atlantic and stake a claim in the New World, historian Giancarlo Casale points out that they were in fact no different in this to the European seaboard powers: like the Ottomans, it was the East that was their primary concern (at least at first), not the New World.[4] Columbus' voyage was, after all, an experiment to find a shortcut to *Asia*, not in search of any New World (and to his dying day he consistently maintained that it was China he had sailed to, not a New World); the Portuguese discovery of Brazil was entirely an accident while on a voyage around Africa to India; many of the Dutch, English and French early expeditions to North America (and even later ones, such as Captain Cook's in the late eighteenth century) were not so much explorations of the New World but searches of the north-west passage to the Far East. For the Ottomans, all of this was simply unnecessary: they already had access to Asia—but at the same time they by no means turned their backs upon the Atlantic as we shall see (and even helped themselves to a few New World plums as well). Indeed, it must be emphasised that the Ottoman Empire was the *sole* Mediterranean power that entered the Atlantic, for it must also be remembered that *none* of the other Mediterranean powers—Hapsburg Austria, the Papacy, Venice, Genoa (Columbus' Genoese citizenship proves the point: he had to go to Spain), Malta—took to the Atlantic or the New World. The only exceptions were France and Spain, which also had Atlantic coasts—and Turkey.

True, the New World was to become the source of fabulous wealth for the Atlantic powers far beyond the dreams of the Ottomans. But in the beginning nobody realised this, least of all the colonising powers themselves—and even as late as the end of the seventeenth century New World colonisation could be unmitigated financial disasters as the Scottish attempt at Darien showed, not to mention earlier Dutch and English failures in North America. Ottoman intelligence (which, as we shall see below, was second to none) would have been aware of such pitfalls in American colonisation and so be in no hurry to join any bandwagon. And, as Casale points out, there is not one of these

European seaboard powers who (at least at the beginning) would not have instantly swapped all of their New World possessions for the greatest plum of all: Egypt, which the Ottomans captured in 1517.

THE SULTANS' CARTOGRAPHERS[5]

Ottoman interest in the world beyond the Mediterranean was graphically demonstrated as early as the beginning of the fifteenth century with the revolution in cartography that was brought about by the development slightly earlier of the portolan charts in southern Europe, maps that for the first time were designed to be practical guides rather than merely illustrations. Some of the finest early fifteenth century portolan charts in existence are found in Ottoman archives, based upon both new Western European and older Arab geography. In the late fifteenth-century a world map was made by George Amirutzes for Mehmet the Conqueror. This was based upon Ptolemy, but incorporated the latest Arab, Greek and Latin geographical knowledge as well.

A far more up-to-date map of the world was made in 1513 by the great Turkish navigator and cartographer Piri Reis. While only a portion of this map survives, it does chart most of the eastern coasts of north and south America with astonishing accuracy just two decades after Columbus. This is only the third such world map ever made to have survived. Whilst it does not, of course, suggest that Piri Reis or other Turkish navigators sailed to America (at least then), it does demonstrate a profound knowledge of the seas, its strategic value and first-hand intelligence—as well as access to the latest sources. This makes it all the more regrettable that the Asian portion of the Piri Reis map is lost, for as well as European sources, Piri Reis used oriental sources for his map, sources that the Western European powers would not have had access to. In 1526 Piri Reis also published his *Kitab-i Bahriye* or *Book of the Seas*, a compendium of all the latest up-to-date geographical and navigational knowledge of the known world, both New and Old. He also made a second and updated version of his map in 1529, again regrettably surviving only in fragmentary form. Both are in the Topkapi Library in Istanbul. In fact Piri Reis was one of the sixteenth century's greatest navigators. He came from a venerable maritime tradition: his uncle, with whom he served his apprenticeship, was the noted Ottoman mariner Kemal Reis who campaigned successfully in the eastern Mediterranean in the late fifteenth century, and following Kemal's death Piri Reis joined forces for a short time with the great Barbarossa. As well as his contributions to the navigational theory Piri Reis was an active sea captain, commanding Ottoman naval campaigns both in the Mediterranean and in the Indian Ocean against the Portuguese (see below) as late as the middle of the sixteenth century. However, despite an almost perfect record of success, he was executed in 1552 for a single failure in the Persian Gulf.

The *Book of the Seas* was by no means the only Ottoman sea manual. In 1525 Süleyman's grand vizier, Ibrahim Pasha, commissioned a navigational and military report from the navigator Selman Reis in Cairo of the entire Indian Ocean littoral ranging from East Africa to Indonesia detailing the potential vulnerabilities and difficulties of Ottoman conquest. Although Giancarlo Casale's view of this document as 'a blueprint for future Ottoman expansion in the Indian Ocean' is perhaps an overstatement,[6] it does nonetheless demonstrate that the supposedly 'land lubber' Turks rated maritime expansion—and intelligence—just as highly as landward.

The greatest navigational achievement of the early sixteenth century was, of course, the first circumnavigation of the world by Magellan and his crew, completed in 1522. But it must be noted that the only surviving copy of the map made of this voyage exists in the Ottoman archives in the Topkapi—a map that is, furthermore, the first ever polar projection of the globe. Whilst this can hardly be claimed as an achievement of Ottoman navigation, it does demonstrate how closely they followed others' achievements—and an Ottoman map of the Indian Ocean dating to about 1580 (now in Baltimore) is surprisingly accurate and shows little if any influence from other European map-makers, so it is presumably based upon first hand intelligence.

Sometime between 1580 and 1582 there was published in Constantinople an extraordinary anonymous work, the *Tarih-i Hind-i Garb* or *Tarih-i Iklim-i Cedid*, the *History of the West Indies* or *History of the New World*, lavishly illustrated with miniatures in the classic Turco-Persian style, but depicting Spanish conquistadors and the exotic 'occidental' New World and its creatures. Later in the sixteenth century there was a massive increase in Turkey in geographical and navigational literature. These ranged from new editions of earlier Turkish works (such as Piri

Reis' *Book of the Seas*) and new Turkish translations of the old Arab geographers to entirely new Turkish works. There was also an increase in the production of maps and atlases, including the aforementioned earliest known Ottoman map of the Indian Ocean.

ATLANTIC PRIVATEERS

Turkish interest in the Atlantic went beyond the mere theoretical. In the early seventeenth century Murat Reis, an Ottoman naval captain trained by Barbarossa, raided the Canary Islands and the North Atlantic as far as the coasts of Baffin Island and Newfoundland before turning back. In 1623 an Ottoman privateer fleet of fifteen ships captured Lundy Island in the Bristol Channel and occupied it until 1625 (when they threatened Ilfracombe) and then intermittently until 1635, using it as a base to raid the English Channel and ports in the Netherlands, Denmark, Sweden, Norway, Ireland and even as far as Greenland. The well-preserved thirteenth-century castle on Lundy is still known as Marisco Castle (i.e., Morisco or Moorish) from this time, or perhaps after the de Marisco family (which means the same thing) who built the castle in the thirteenth century (who were, in any case, known to be pirates; Pl. 90.) Other corsairs were known to raid in the opposite direction as far as the Cape of Good Hope and the Indian Ocean (see below.) Both booty and slaves were captured in these raids. In 1627 the entire population of West Manöe Island off Iceland, together with their priest Olaf Eigilssen, were captured and sold as slaves. Between 1610 and 1640 Devon and Cornwall lost a fifth of its entire shipping to the Barbary Corsairs, and in 1625 over a thousand seamen from Plymouth were captured.[7]

Scotland also was prey to Ottoman corsair raids. In 1645 (during the year of the Civil War) 'a large armed vessel of peculiar rig and aspect entered the Firth of Forth, and came to anchor in Leith Roads. By experienced seamen she was at once pronounced to be an Algerine rover, and dismay spread all over the city.' The corsairs entered the city of Edinburgh and advanced as far as the Canongate. The terrified citizens of Edinburgh agreed to a huge ransom, but then a most unexpected development occurred. The corsair leader was himself originally a Scot from Edinburgh, one Andrew Gray, who had been condemned to be executed for his part in an uprising against the city provost soon after the accession of Charles I. Gray escaped and fled the city, joining the corsairs and becoming a Muslim (neither the first nor the last Scot to become a Moorish corsair captain, as we have seen). On returning years later to avenge himself against the magistrates of the city, he discovered that one of them was his own relative. He married the daughter of the provost and settled down and remained in a property in the Canongate, which henceforth and to this day was known as 'Morocco Land'. A relief of a Moor still stands there commemorating that event (Pl. 91.)[8]

FROM ARABIA AND AFRICA TO THE FAR EAST[9]

The Ottomans were no more limited by the Atlantic than they had been by the Mediterranean, and their naval power extended across the Indian Ocean as well. The Ottomans first arrived on Indian Ocean shores in 1517 with the capture of Egypt and its all important Red Sea ports with Indian Ocean access by Sultan Selim 'the Grim'. But Ottoman eyes were set on India and beyond right from the beginning. Immediately after the conquest of Egypt, Selim announced the construction and launch of an armada of seventy ships from bases in the Red Sea so as to extend operations in the Indian Ocean. This resulted in the successful capture of Yemen by 1527 as a part of a naval operation from Egypt. From bases established at Mocha on the Red Sea coast of Yemen (Pl. 92) and Shihr on the Arabian Sea, the Ottomans were able to put into practice a much broader Indian Ocean policy.

Much of Ottoman policy in the region was determined by their ally, the Sultanate of Gujerat, and the need to protect them against the Portuguese, and Gujerat was to figure largely in the subsequent history of the Ottomans in the Indian Ocean. But a number of other alliances were also formed with Indian Ocean littoral states. As early as 1528 direct trade in spices was established by the Ottomans with Sumatra, and Atjeh in Sumatra was to figure as highly as Gujarat. The Ottoman lobby in Gujerat was formed mainly by the large expatriate Ottoman merchant community established at Diu (as well as at other Indian Ocean ports), backed up in 1531 by the presence of six hundred Ottoman soldiers and over a thousand Arab auxiliaries. The Ottoman presence in the region in other words was as large as that of their great rivals, the Portuguese (and interestingly, both the Indians and the Portuguese referred to the Turks as 'Romans': *Rumi* or *Rumes*.) This force, aided by their heavy artillery and commanded by the Ottoman sea captain Mustafa Bayram, together with the local Gujeratis was able to successfully repulse a Portuguese siege of Diu in 1531, resulting in a Portuguese rout.

In 1531 the Ottomans began digging a Red Sea-Nile canal in order to circumvent Portuguese control of the Cape route, and three thousand fighting men and eight hundred ships of war were made ready for the Indian campaign. In the end they were diverted to the war against Safavid Iran in Iraq, viewed as a higher priority by Sultan Süleyman, and the canal was never finished. In fact Casale views this war (completed in 1534) in any case as part of a broader Indian Ocean policy, aimed at preventing a Safavid-Portuguese alliance and establishing Ottoman naval bases at the western end of the Persian Gulf so as to open up a second Indian Ocean front against the Portuguese.[10] Whether or not this was so, it did result in the capture of Basra, a permanent Ottoman window on the Persian Gulf, and the brief establishment of the Ottoman province of Lahsa on the southern side of the Gulf. However, the Turks were never able to dislodge the Portuguese from the Gulf, with their massively fortified base on Hormuz controlling the straits (as well as more Portuguese forts on Qeshm, Bahrain and elsewhere on the Gulf.) The Red Sea, on the other hand, remained firmly Ottoman and the Portuguese were excluded, with the establishment of the Ottoman province of Habeş (Abyssinia) on its southern side.

The late 1530s were dominated in the Indian Ocean by the extraordinary octogenarian eunuch viceroy of Egypt, Hadim Süleyman Pasha. Sultan Süleyman's orders to Hadim were quite specifically for a naval campaign to liberate India: 'you will cross over to India and capture and hold the ports of India. You will free that country from the harm caused by the Portuguese infidels.'[11] By 1538 Hadim had established a ring of alliances between the Ottoman Empire and friendly Muslim powers around the Indian Ocean from Gujerat, Calicut and Atjeh to Ottoman possessions in the Persian Gulf and Red Sea. He presided over the construction of seventy warships in Suez (despite the lack of timber: every plank and spar had to be imported from distant Ottoman sources, a logistical triumph in itself), probably the largest fleet seen in the Indian Ocean since the Ming Emperor Yongle's 'treasure ships' a century before. Assembling a force of nearly ten thousand soldiers,

Hadim and his armada set sail for Gujerat to recapture the fortress of Diu from the Portuguese (to whom it had been lost in 1535.) In the end the war proved a stalemate: the Ottomans failed to recapture Diu, but a Portuguese campaign launched from Goa in 1541 against the Red Sea ended in disaster before Suez. However, the Ottomans gained more in the long term. The coast of Arabia was firmly secured from the Red Sea northwards along the Arabian Sea as far as Dhofar, and Hadim's 'diplomacy … had for the first time joined Muslims from East Africa to Southeast Asia in an active military alliance … and a permanent Ottoman military presence in the Arabian Sea.'[12] In 1541 the sultan rewarded Hadim Süleiman with promotion to grand vizier.

During the 1540s the status quo hardly changed. There was an indecisive proxy war fought in Ethiopia by the Ottoman ally Ahmad Grañ aided by a small force of Ottoman musketeers against the Ethiopian emperor with his small force of auxiliaries supplied by Portugal, but the ultimate failure of the Portuguese to gain a foothold in the Horn of Africa was entirely to the Ottomans' advantage. On the one hand Portuguese official records note worryingly an increase in Ottoman trading activities all over the Indian Ocean from East Africa to Southeast Asia, but on the other hand the Turks failed for the second time in 1546 to take Diu, this 'Indian Vienna', despite a sizeable Ottoman force.

The late forties and early fifties of the sixteenth century in the Indian Ocean are dominated by two great figures of Turkish maritime history. The cartographer and navigator Piri Reis we have already encountered and, following the successful defence of Basra against a Portuguese attack, Piri Reis took command of an Ottoman fleet from Suez that wrested Muscat from the Portuguese in 1552, successfully defeating a superior Portuguese force. He also attempted to capture the great stronghold of Hormuz, but his failure in this as well as several lesser engagements on the Persian Gulf resulted in the execution of the great navigator.

The second figure was the flamboyant sea captain and privateer Sefer Reis, a 'Barbarossa of the East.' Sefer probably participated in the Gujarat campaign of 1538, then from the late forties took command of a small fleet that successfully carried out raids against Portuguese shipping all over the Indian Ocean from his base in Mocha (Pl. 92)—his small, light galleys could always outrun the heavier Portuguese vessels. Following the disastrous loss of Muscat to the Portuguese in 1554 (only two years after Piri Reis' successful capture), Sefer Reis brought off one of the most daring campaigns in the history of privateering when he pursued the victorious Portuguese fleet with just four light vessels right across the Arabian Sea to India. There he not only captured four wealthily laden Portuguese merchant vessels, but even managed to capture them a second time after they had been seized back by a Portuguese warship— and added the warship to his booty on top of it, sailing back to Mocha in triumph with a total of nine vessels. Another daring raid on India in 1556 resulted in the capture of two more Portuguese ships, and in 1558 he heavily defeated a major Portuguese force that tried to capture his home base of Mocha. Such were the success of his campaigns that for a short while in the 1550s the spice trade coming through the Ottoman Empire outstripped that coming through Portugal. In 1565 Sefer Reis, by that time promoted to admiral of the entire Ottoman Indian Ocean fleet, set out once again from Mocha with just ten vessels to raid all of the Portuguese possessions down the East African coast with the avowed intention of cutting off Portuguese access to the Indian Ocean once and for all. However, he fell ill off Socotra and died shortly after in Aden. His epitaph was appropriately voiced by the Portuguese envoy Mattias Bicudo Furtado: 'There is no man such as he in all the lands of the East who we need so greatly fear.'[13]

In 1567 the Sultan of Atjeh in Sumatra voluntarily surrendered sovereignty to Sultan Selim II in the face of Portuguese threats: in theory Atjeh became an Ottoman province. At the same time many of the other Muslim rulers around the Indian Ocean recognised the Ottoman sultan's supremacy by having the Friday prayers given in his name. An Ottoman naval force was sent to Atjeh's aid and a joint allied attack on Portuguese Malacca was launched. Malacca held, but other Muslim uprisings in India and the Maldives against the Portuguese enjoyed some success, and Sumatran shipping to the Red Sea was given armed escorts by the Ottomans. At the same time, Selim's grand vizier Sokullu Mehmet Pasha revived plans for a Suez canal, part of a more general policy aimed at circumventing the Christian powers in the wake of Lepanto (see below). The plans for the canal once again proved abortive, as were two further attempts in the 1580s, but it does nonetheless show that the Ottomans never lacked a global vision, particularly under the very able leadership of Sokullu Mehmet's prime ministership (whose plans also called for the construction of a Volga-Don canal—also abortive—to enable the Ottoman navy to sail to the Caspian sea in order to check Russian expansion southwards and liberate the Khanate of Astrakhan).*

There was even a brief resurgence in the Indian Ocean when Mir Ali Beğ, with just one ship, captured all Portuguese possessions on the east African coast with the exception of Malindi in 1586, coming away with vast booty (although the Portuguese quickly regained Mombasa). The Turks had thus established a maritime network that rivalled that of the better-known European powers 'when, contrary to the popular image, the Ottomans were far from passive spectators to Western domination.' Never mind that the core of the navy comprised Greeks, Arabs and other non-Turks. Like the intuitive adoption of the newfangled cannon before the walls of Constantinople, the Turks had demonstrated their extraordinary ability to adopt new methods and adapt to new situations. [14]

As with the Mediterranean, it would be a grave mistake to view the Indian Ocean conflict in simple Muslim versus Christian terms. Throughout, we see various Muslim powers switching sides and allying themselves with the Portuguese, and for the Portuguese their efforts to exclude the Turks from Indian Ocean trade were only matched—and far more successfully—by their efforts to exclude their fellow Christian powers, particularly Spain. There were also pragmatic diplomatic negotiations aimed at forming mutually agreeable compromises between the two powers, notably in the negotiations of 1540 and 1547 (although both broke down).

Nonetheless, religion was still a powerful factor for both sides. For the Portuguese, the old Crusader ideal of recapturing Jerusalem and the Holy Land still provided a strong stimulus. Although Goa was a long way from Jerusalem, Ottoman Egypt was not, and Egypt and control of the Red Sea was a cornerstone of Portuguese policy. Even in far off Goa, the final resting place of St Francis Xavier, religion and conversion to Catholicism was a major factor. For the Ottomans, their obsession with maintaining control of the Red Sea at any cost was motivated as much as—or more than—the need to protect the vulnerable maritime Haj routes from all over Muslim Asia to Mecca and Medina, of which the Sultan-Caliph was official guardian, as by commercial considerations.

---

* Again this was never accomplished. It was eventually built under Stalin.

WORLD WAR: LEPANTO AND BEYOND

The Battle of Lepanto of 7 October, 1571 (Pl. 93), fought between the Ottoman Empire on one side and Spain, Venice, Genoa and the Knights of Malta on the other, is usually regarded as a turning point: the end of Turkish Mediterranean expansion and the beginning of the Ottoman's inevitable decline to the eventual 'sick man of Europe'. It was certainly one of Turkey's greatest defeats and one of the great naval battles of history, 'the greatest occasion that past or future ones can hope to see' in the words of Cervantes, who participated in the battle.* Just as the innovative use of artillery at Constantinople in 1453 had won the day for Mehmet, it was Don John of Austria's equally innovative use of ship-mounted artillery—the first gunboats—that won the day at Lepanto. Otherwise the two fleets were virtually equal: both were well commanded, both used classic text-book manoeuvres, both had well-trained crews and state-of-the-art vessels.

It was certainly a major event for many reasons, some of them not so obvious. For the Christian powers Lepanto broke the spell of Turkish invincibility, described by Cervantes as 'that day so fortunate to Christendom when all nations were undeceived of their error in believing that the Turks were invincible'.[15] There was euphoria immediately following, amounting to wild fancies that this was the turn of the tide: extravagant claims were made to turn back the Muslims and hopes were raised for recapturing Jerusalem or even Constantinople itself.

In fact Lepanto changed very little: the Ottomans remained a great power and even continued to expand. To begin with, the Ottoman grand fleet bounced back as large and as threatening as before only a year afterwards: the imperial shipyards of the Golden Horn had worked overtime. Ottoman borders did not shrink. On the contrary they continued to expand, westwards and northwards as well as eastwards. Having taken the second Rome, the Ottomans attempted the first Rome as early as 1580, less than a decade after Lepanto, when an Ottoman army disembarked at Otranto in Italy and began to march on Rome (it did not in the end reach there—but the threat was enough for the pope to prepare an evacuation of Rome). In 1638 Baghdad was conquered

---

* Thus paraphrasing Cassiodorius on the Battle of the Catalaunian Fields against the Huns in 451 when he wrote: 'a conflict … such as could not be paralleled either in the present or in past ages.' Quoted in Gibbon 1901, III: 464.

from Persia and as late as 1647 Crete was conquered from Venice. The Catholic powers, on the other hand, did not expand into Ottoman territory, despite Lepanto.

Lepanto *was* nonetheless a symbol, but of an entirely different kind. It was almost the last of a type of naval warfare—the Mediterranean galley—that stretched all the way back to the Battle of Salamis between the Greeks and the Persian Empire in the fifth century BC. It also marked the beginning of the end of the Mediterranean itself. After Lepanto it was the type of shipping and its control of the seas which changed, with the rise of the Atlantic seaboard powers: the Portuguese and Spanish, followed soon by the English, the Dutch and the French. It was their control of the great oceans that by-passed the ancient trans-continental land routes and the Mediterranean who were the real winners. Turkey *did* in the end decline after Lepanto, but not because of it. Lepanto equally marked the beginning of the decline of the victors, particularly Venice.[16] It was a decline of the Mediterranean as a whole rather than of its individual maritime powers, 'the death of the old queen of the world, the Mediterranean, dethroned by the new king, the Atlantic' in the words of Braudel.[17] Spain and France were the only Mediterranean powers apart from Turkey that continued to expand, but they increasingly turned their backs on the Mediterranean as they became Atlantic powers. By the end of the sixteenth century the English and the Dutch were beginning to supplant the Venetians, Genoese and Florentines in the eastern Mediterranean with their favourable commercial agreements with the Ottomans (the 'capitulations'). Even if the Turks had won Lepanto, nothing much would have changed.

To some extent the gradual eclipse of the Mediterranean maritime powers after Lepanto by the Western European seaboard powers had been in progress long before due to the rise of the north European trading centres in the Middle Ages: the Champagne trade fairs, Bruges, Antwerp, Amsterdam and Nuremburg, Lübeck and the rise of the Hanseatic ports, and places further away in Scandinavia and Russia. Indeed, this move was anticipated as far back as the beginning of the ninth century by the creation of Aix-la-Chapelle as the capital of a new 'Roman Empire' by Charlemagne that turned its back on the Mediterranean and the old Roman centres—or even before that by the import of silver from the Abbasid Empire into Russia, Scandinavia and elsewhere in northern Europe.

In fact Lepanto was just one relatively minor episode in a much larger war, viewed by Fernand Braudel as a part of a far broader conflict with the Battle of Lepanto simply the event that brought many of the strands together. Its origin was the revolt of the Moriscos of Granada, descendants of the Spanish Moors who remained covertly Muslim, between 1568 and 1570. In itself it was only a relatively minor internal conflict, but the Moriscos threatened to call Morocco, Algiers and—most ominously—the Ottoman Empire to their aid, a threat which Spain had to take seriously. Morocco had become a client with the installation of an Ottoman puppet on the throne in 1574. Constantinople did send a small force of six hundred Ottoman musketeers to aid the Moriscos, and in 1574 Sokullu Mehmet Pasha despatched Ottoman agents to the Protestants of the Netherlands to propose they attempt an alliance with the Moriscos against Spain.[18]

Since Ottoman Turkey was at this time distracted by a war against Persia being fought in Mesopotamia and Azerbaijan, Spain felt confident in pre-empting the Moriscos' call by declaring war. Hence, a local revolt escalated into the War of Granada that was fought most immediately between Ottoman Turkey on one side and Spain and other Catholic powers on the other (but my no means all: France, for example, notably stayed neutral). But this is still only the smaller picture, for more distantly other related theatres of conflict involving the two main protagonists broadened the theatre immensely. Turkey was already involved in a war against Iran as we have seen, and was also aiding its ally, the Crimean Khanate, in a war against Russia to retake Astrakhan, in addition to fighting on other Ottoman fronts in the Red Sea, Yemen and Ethiopia. The Crimean and Ottoman war against Russia in 1569 was one of the reasons that led Ivan IV to negotiate with Shah Tahmasp of Iran, leading to a Russian-Persian alliance, arguing that the capture of Astrakhan would directly threaten Iranian Azerbaijan. The other reason for Ivan's negotiations with Tahmasp was that Russia itself was also distracted by a war on another front, the Swedish war of 1562 to 1572, begun by Sweden to prevent Russia's expansion into Estonia, a war that eventually involved all of Scandinavia.

Further afield, by the 1580s the war had spread to the Indian Ocean with the Ottoman naval captain Mir Ali Beğ fighting Spain's ally Portugal from India to East Africa as we have seen. The Spanish, for their part, at the same time as the War of Granada were fighting on a second front in the Netherlands. (Indeed, there is some evidence that the outbreak of the Netherlands revolt against Spain in 1569 was at Ottoman encouragement.)[19] This was the intensely bitter Spanish-Dutch War of the 1560s and 1570s that eventually resulted in independence for the Netherlands, but in 1585 England formally entered the war on the side of the Dutch after two decades of undeclared war involving privateering between Spain and England.* This culminated in the launch of the Armada against England in 1588—aimed as much at controlling the Indies as the Netherlands, according to its commander. Hence, the war spread to the Atlantic and the Caribbean.

While these are usually viewed as separate wars, the fact of two great powers being the main protagonists—Spain and Turkey—ultimately connects all the wars. 'Failure to recognise the fact that the theatre of war stretched from Gibraltar and the Maghreb to the Red Sea, the Black Sea, the Caspian and the Indian Ocean would be to misunderstand the significance of the military conflict between Christianity and Islam at the period …. The conflict was beginning to assume global proportions' in the words of the historian Franco Cardini.[20] The Mediterranean, Spain, the Netherlands, England, the Atlantic, the Caribbean, the Middle East, southern Russia, Scandinavia, the Caucasus, Persia, Eastern Africa, the Indian Ocean—this was a war that was fought on a far broader world stage than the First World War, truly a far earlier 'first world war'. The revolt of the Moriscos of Granada between 1568 and 1570 might hardly have been the cause of this war or even a major part. But the threat, real or imagined, of Ottoman support for the revolt, not to mention the deeper dread by the Spanish (again probably largely imagined) of their greatest spectre, the re-establishment of Islam in Spain, was perhaps one of the main reasons why it broadened into the wider confrontation that culminated in Lepanto, with a ripple effect over much of the world (a confrontation that, with England fighting Spain and Russia negotiating with Iran, was never Islam versus Christendom.) This war, a 'very first world war' illustrates just how inter-connected the 'eastern' and 'western' worlds were by this time.†

---

* The 'Dutch' armies opposing the Spanish in any case consisted mainly of German, English, French and Danish soldiers—see Hale 1993: 111.

† A possible earlier 'world war' in the sixth century has been discussed in Volume 2 in this series. Casale (2010: 80) describes the Ottoman-Portuguese conflict of 1538-46 in the Indian Ocean as 'history's first world war.' Boxer (1969: 108-9) identifies the struggle between the Portuguese and the Dutch between 1660 and 1663 a 'First

The historian Giancarlo Casale argues that these interconnections were largely the product of a 'soft empire' that was essentially the creation of the great sixteenth-century grand vizier, Sokullu Mehmet Pasha, who remained in office under three sultans (Süleyman, Selim II and Murad III): a complex system of alliances, spheres of influences and connections stretching from Western Europe (England, Netherlands) to India and the Far East (Atjeh), and from Central Asia (Samarkand, Astrakhan) to East and Central Africa.[21] This may be over-interpreting the evidence, but certainly by the time of Sokullu's untimely assassination in 1579, the Ottoman Empire's influence over the affairs of the Indian Ocean at least was unequalled by any other single power in the past. Sokullu himself was an international statesman with a global vision and grasp of affairs that in many ways anticipated the great geopolitical statesmen of the eighteenth and nineteenth century European imperial powers.

The inter-connections of such wars were recognised by contemporaries: the ruler of remote Daghestan in the north Caucasus, for example, wrote to Sultan Murad III in 1589 in alarm at a possible Russian attack in response to Georgian appeals for Russian aid, warning that the cities Turkey had seized from Persia would then be wide open to attack, prompting a Russia-Persia-Georgia alliance against the Ottomans which in turn would encourage a French-Spanish alliance to attack

---

World War' if only because it was fought worldwide in four continents—in Flanders, the North Sea, the Amazon, Angola, Timor and Chile—and involved at different times the English, the Danes, the Congolese, the Persians, the Indonesians, the Cambodians and the Japanese. The period of the Napoleonic Wars from 1792 to 1815 could perhaps be described as another pre-First World War 'world war', fought as it was throughout Europe as well as in North America (1812-14), India, Egypt and the Levant. Although one must caution against defining 'wars' merely as an artificial construct. In an interesting paper, Barry S. Strauss (1997) points out that the Peloponnesian War, for example, was solely Thucydides' construct, hence ours; from other viewpoints it was a series of separate wars, not one. The Vietnam War, another example, is solely a US construct: from the Vietnamese point of view it was the 'American War' and even then only a part of a much longer anti-colonial war that ran from 1945 to 1974, while from a geo-political point of view it was only a part of the Cold War. It might be argued that the war of the sixteenth century was far too long to be cast as a 'first world war'. But we have as long or longer wars: the Hundred Years War, for example, or the Thirty Years War. 'Wars' of such length might be seen as something of the past, when time was slower, but in our own era we have the Cold War, from 1945 to 1990.

from the west: '… the Russians will unite with the Persian shah and the Georgian king, and then they will march on Istanbul from here and the French and Spanish kings [will march in] from the other side …'[22] The war in the Caucasus against Iran, which began in 1578, was to continue intermittently until 1639. The broader picture was, in other words, often recognised by even the smallest player. It was the position of Turkey as a great power—and as a maritime power—that internationalised the conflict far beyond its immediate causes. It was this that makes Lepanto one of the high-points of Turkey's rise, despite losing the actual battle. From forest dwelling iron-workers of Siberia to horse-riding nomads of innermost Asia and now sea-faring mariners with a word-wide reach whose language did not even possess a word for 'sea', the Turks had indeed come a long way. If nothing else, Lepanto symbolises just how much these forest-dwellers had become a world power.

*   *   *

Of course Barbarossa, the Barbary pirates, the Indian Ocean Corsairs, the Gujerati and Atjeh merchants, Süleyman's great architect Sinan, most of the grand viziers and many of the other leading Ottomans of the sixteenth century might not have been 'Turks' in the ethnic sense of the word (and as far as strict ethnicity is concerned, very few of the inhabitants of Turkey look remotely like the original Turks of the Altai in any case.) For that matter, neither were the sultans themselves, whose blood had been so diluted by inter-marriage with their non-Turk subjects that they were eventually probably more Greek or Slav than Turk. But that is irrelevant: they were all *Ottomans*. The Ottoman Empire was never a Turkish national state but, like all great civilisations, was truly eclectic.

Chapter 10

THE SICK MEN OF EUROPE

Myths of confrontation and decline

> The myths described here—the "Age of Heroes," the battle for Europe and the fear of the Turk—all began with real triumphs and real fears. But over time that history has dwindled to nothing while the myths and legends have survived and flourished.
>
> *(Andrew Wheatcroft*[1]*)*

The Battle of Lepanto has been taken as the beginning of Ottoman decline, a decline viewed as irreversible after the failure of the second siege of Vienna in 1683 (Pl. 94.) Indeed, even a Turkish account pulls no punches when assessing their defeat before Vienna as 'a calamitous defeat of such magnitude that there has never been its like since the first appearance of the Ottoman state'.[2] For the Christian powers it broke forever the myth of the prestige and power of the Ottoman Empire. But the ability of the Ottoman state and military to recover after the most disastrous of reverses, such as Lepanto in 1571 and Vienna in 1683—both reverses which Christian triumphalism otherwise trumpeted as the end of the Ottoman Empire—confounded the prophets of doom. The idea that after Vienna 'Christendom could begin slowly rolling back Ottoman power', that it marked the beginning of 'Ottoman decline', were myths that were largely products of Christian European wishful thinking. *

---

* Another one of the myths of the Siege of Vienna is that the stores of coffee

To begin with, 'Christendom', in the form of many of the Protestant powers and even some of the Catholic, such as France, continued to support the Ottomans. The Ottoman army itself included some hundred thousand Hungarians as well as numerous Greek, Armenian and Slav Christians. As for perceived decline, the Ottoman Empire was characterised by extraordinary tenacity and an ability to survive (when compared, for example, to formerly powerful European states such as Poland or Sweden) and 'one cannot properly speak of the decadence of the Turkish Empire before the first decades of the nineteenth century' as Braudel remarks.[3] By the eighteenth century the supposedly declining Ottoman Empire was still having almost as profound an effect upon events in Europe as in the height of its power in the sixteenth century.

THE CONCERT OF EUROPE AND THE MYTH OF DECLINE

The Ottomans became major power brokers—or at least major players—in the European scene very early on. This comes as no surprise: they were, as we have already emphasised, a major European power from the beginning when 'The Ottoman state became an important component of the new European state system' as the historian of the Ottomans, Halil İnalcik, emphasises.[4] As early as the end of the fifteenth century the Ottomans held the balance of power between rival papal, Hapsburg and French interests: in 1494, for example, when Charles VIII of France was preparing to invade Italy, the pope was hoping to receive Ottoman support against the French. But the great Ottoman victories of the sixteenth century brought it to the heart of European politics: Belgrade in 1521, Rhodes in 1522 and the Battle of Mohác in 1526 which saw an Ottoman victory over the forces of Louis II of Hungary and Bohemia. The removal of Hungary as a buffer state after the Battle of Mohác put the Ottomans in direct confrontation with the Habsburgs for the next century and a half. Emperor Charles V hurriedly placed his brother, Ferdinand of Austria, on the throne of Hungary, but Sultan Süleyman,

---

abandoned by the retreating Turks introduced this beverage into Vienna for the first time, thence throughout Europe (e.g., Ferguson 2011: 56). In fact coffee drinking was first introduced into France by the visit in 1669 of the Turkish ambassador Süleyman Ağa to the court of Louis XIV.

who held most of the territory, crowned John Zápolya, Voyvod of Transylvania, king of Hungary in 1526.

Ottoman king-making did not end in Europe with Hungary. In 1572 the Polish throne became vacant with the extinction of the Jagiellonian dynasty. Selim II (1566-74) immediately intervened, insisting that he would not tolerate any candidate from a neighbouring country (i.e., no Habsburg). Hence, the throne was offered to a French candidate but Selim would only accept this if no suitable member of the Polish nobility could be found.[5]

Throughout the seventeenth century the Ottomans were directly involved in complex diplomatic negotiations throughout Europe involving, at different times, powers as far spread as Spain, England, Netherlands, Sweden, Poland and Russia, as well as their neighbouring protagonists such as Venice and Austria. In 1760, for example, Charles XII of Sweden appealed to the Ottomans for a joint alliance against Russia. Turkey, in other words, was regarded as much a European power as any of the others; its religion was hardly at issue. By 1829 the Duke of Wellington even stated that 'the Ottoman Empire stands not for the benefit of the Turks but of Christian Europe'. The Treaty of Paris formally marking the end of the Crimean War in 1856 recognised the Ottoman Empire as an equal power in the 'Concert of Europe' and the Ottoman Empire was formally admitted to 'the Public Law and System of Europe'.[6]

The term 'sick man of Europe' was coined for Turkey,* but as well as branding it as stagnating, the term implies a tacit recognition by the other European powers of something more subtle: Turkey was viewed 'of *Europe*' rather than of Asia. But Ottoman 'decline' after 1683 and its reputation for degeneracy and decay was a carefully constructed myth, mainly by the Habsburgs in a series of elaborate publications that achieved wide popularity throughout Europe. This myth carefully misconstrued and falsified eighteenth-century history into a series of Habsburg triumphs against the infidel. The myth, however, belied the vigour left in the old empire, and even further expansion. Most of Crete

---

* Supposedly coined by Sir Stratford Canning, British Ambassador to the Porte in 1851, although other sources ascribe it to Tsar Nicholas I at about the same time. Interestingly, the term was first used in 1558 by a Spanish ambassador to describe not Turkey: but England! (following the succession of Protestant Elizabeth from Catholic Mary. See Hale 1993: 6.)

was captured from the Venetians in 1647, although Candia withstood a twenty-year siege before the island was finally subjugated in 1699. The Aegean became an Ottoman lake. Many of the Cretans converted to Islam as the Turks were seen as liberators from Catholic rule (and later sought refuge in Ottoman lands: Damascus and Tripoli—in Lebanon—still have communities of Cretan Muslims). The Turks were not necessarily less oppressive than the Venetians, but they did restore the rights to the Orthodox Church, which had been suppressed by the Catholic powers. Although the period was characterised by weak sultans it was dominated by the great vizirial family of the Köprülü, particularly Mehmet the father and Ahmet the son. It was Ahmet Köprülü who completed the capture of Candia and did so much to revive the great age of Süleyman the Magnificent while weak and ineffective sultans did so much to destroy it. Under Ahmet Köprülü Ottoman rule was extended over the Cossacks in 1672 into the Ukraine (Pls 95-6) and to the borders of Poland when Kamenisto was captured and the Cathedral of St Peter and Paul there converted to a mosque. It was to be the last great expansion of Ottoman power, for only five years later they were forced to retreat back west of the Dniestr, ceding their short-lived Ukrainian province—Podolia—to the Russians (although not without leaving their mark: the fortress of Kamenisto still had a minaret with a Qur'anic inscription in 1763 according to a Turkish traveller).

In a major study of the Ottoman Empire and the outside world, the historian Suraiya Faroghi regards the differences in the sixteenth and seventeenth centuries as minimal and largely exaggerated. She regards the Ottoman Empire as essentially part of the same world as Christian Europe bound together by a common economy and common interests. Even the wars which appeared to dominate the history—such as Lepanto—are to some extent illusory, as the era is marked as much or more by long periods when both sides worked together (mainly through trade), not to mention when Christian fought Christian and Muslim, Muslim. Both sides were more alike than is usually thought.[7]

One reason why the Ottoman Empire is usually not viewed as a part of the European mainstream is that it did not participate in the European Enlightenment of the eighteenth century. This is also frequently cited as a major reason for Ottoman decline. But how much of the rest of Europe actually participated in the Enlightenment? Certainly not the peasants, the servants, the artisans, the serfs, the labourers, the slaves transported to America, the convicts deported to colonial gulags, the 'witches' burnt at the stake, the ordinary soldiers used as gun-fodder for the endless petty wars and the numerous other swathes of society in the eighteenth century. Nor did most of their masters who actually transported the slaves, reaped the fruits of their labour, condemned convicts to transportation for petty theft, ordered the witch-burnings and began numerous wars often for the pettiest of reasons inflicting untold miseries on all that they touched. The Enlightenment—or lack of it—in no way made Ottoman Turkey outside Europe.

The Ottoman Empire, particularly in its period of perceived decline, has often been regarded as introverted and isolationist—indeed, in a classic circular argument, this has frequently been put forward as both a reason for and a manifestation of their decline. But Ottoman awareness of and participation in the outside world is a natural result of their own origins as nomads originally from the opposite end of the world, belying the myth that the Turks were inward looking. Piri Reis' world maps of the early sixteenth century are a manifestation of this, as is Katib Çelebi's world geography, the *Cihannüma* of the mid-sixteenth-century, Evliya Çelebi's travels of the seventeenth century and various ambassadorial reports (the *sefaretname*) beginning in the seventeenth century. There was a renewed Ottoman outwardness and interest in the world beyond throughout the eighteenth century. This was brought about by two matters. First, they became increasingly aware that their military defeats were to a large extent a result of new superior military technology and techniques by the other European powers. Hence, the desire to learn (and this, as we have seen, characterised Ottoman successes right at the beginning). But second and more important, their military defeats meant that there was more to be gained by negotiation and diplomacy, and this resulted in increasing numbers of diplomatic missions being sent throughout Europe and a need to understand the enemy.

Significantly, the period also marks the beginning of a new brand of Turkish awareness of themselves, of the rest of Europe and of their own part in the world at large. Eighteenth century Turkish ambassadors to the Christian powers applied Ibn Khaldun's theories of the decline and decadence of dynasties and states to what they observed in Europe. The Ottoman ambassador to Paris between 1806 and 1806, Halet Effendi, for example, wrote of the European powers that 'Napoleon is a mad dog, striving to reduce all states to the same disorder as his own accursed nation ... Talleyrand is a spoilt priest ... and the rest are mere brigands'.[8] In other words at the same time that the Western European powers were observing Ottoman decadence and forecasting its decline, Ottoman observers were making precisely the same observations and predictions of the Christian powers. History would tell who collapsed first.

CHRISTIANS, MUSLIMS AND THE MYTH OF CONFRONTATION

The idea of the 'Terrible Turk' was another carefully nurtured myth throughout Europe that was constantly being revised and exaggerated. As early as the end of the fifteenth century the image had become an anachronistic metaphor in European art for the evil 'other' transposed retrospectively into ancient history. Giovanni Mansueti's 1499 painting of *The Arrest and Trial of Saint Mark* depicts the oppressors in Turkish costume, and Albrecht Dürer's 1508 painting of *The Martyrdom of the Ten Thousand* depicts the supposed massacre of Roman Christian soldiers by their pagan officers for refusing the official sacrifice to Rome and Augustus, but the 'Roman' officers are depicted here in Turkish garb. Tintoretto's *Abduction of Helen* (of Troy) of 1580 again depicts the rapacious Trojan abductors as Turks, and by the mid-seventeenth century even paintings of Biblical themes anachronistically depicted characters in Ottoman dress.[9] Thus, art is brought into play to reinforce popular prejudice in much the same way that ancient Greek vase painting suddenly started depicting Trojans anachronistically in Persian dress after the Persian wars.[10]

The spectre of the Terrible Turk was largely a creation of the Habsburgs but was also relayed by the French, the Dutch and the English. Ottoman warfare was, to be sure, brutal and barbaric, and it would be a mistake to look upon them through rose-tinted spectacles. But so too was that of its Christian opponents, who equally practised torture, impalement, beheadings, routine massacres of civilian populations and summary executions of unsuccessful commanders. The reputation of Prince Vladimir III of Wallachia, for example (1431-76), better known as 'Vlad the Impaler' or simply Dracula, has reached mythic proportions. Much of the idea of the Terrible Turk was bound up in the myth of Holy War: the idea—still prevalent—that the main object of Islam is to kill or convert Christians.* Even today, relations with Islam are routinely described in terms of 'clashes' and 'confrontations'.† The Ottomans may have adhered rigidly to Islamic religious doctrine, but in this they were no different from any of the other powers in eighteenth and even nineteenth-century Europe: Catholic, Protestant or Orthodox— indeed, the British viewed its empire in terms of the dissemination of Christianity, Russia promoted itself as the champion of Orthodoxy, as the French did of Catholicism (and the hugely bloody French Wars of Religion of the seventeenth century were still a recent memory in the eighteenth). Such religious stances by the Christian powers led directly to the Crimean War: it is notable that the Ottomans were the only power in that war who did not have a religious issue. Ottoman religious persecution may have worsened during the eighteenth century, but so did others—indeed, Austrian Catholic persecution and enforced conversion of its Orthodox subjects prompted a stream of refugees into the protection of the Ottoman Empire following the Treaty of Passarowitz in 1718 and again after the war of 1737-9. Dmitri Cantemir may have defected to Peter the Great in 1711 during Russia's war with Turkey, but Prince Constantin Brancoveanu of Wallachia remained staunchly loyal to the Ottomans, despite overtures from Russia.[11] The Habsburgs in any case also displayed much of the trappings of Holy War, such as when they launched their disastrous campaign of 1737 (and, like Ottoman practice, beheaded their commander Doxat when it failed). At least the Ottomans never burned witches.

Indeed it would be the gravest folly to overstate the wars between the Ottomans and the European powers in terms of Muslim-Christian confrontation. Even in the age of Lepanto inter-Mediterranean relations were characterised as much by relations between Christian and Muslim powers as they were by warfare. France had good relations with the Ottomans, and the trading states of Venice, Genoa and Ragusa had more to gain than to lose, whilst after 1577 even Spain negotiated a series of treaties with Constantinople. But it was the new Protestant powers above all who saw in Islam a natural ally—fellow 'strict monotheists'—

---

* Even today, the main response on mentioning a visit to a Muslim country is 'but is it safe there?' The present author overheard recently a foreign tourist refusing to enter a provincial Turkish mosque on the grounds that 'they all just want to kill us'.
† For example, 'Since the eruption of Islam from the Arabian deserts in the seventh century, there have been repeated clashes between West and East' (Ferguson 2011: 50)—Islam is described as an 'eruption' and 'West and East' in terms of 'clashes'.

against the Catholic powers. This to some extent was reciprocated by the Ottomans, who saw in many elements of Protestantism—their renunciation of figural representation, for example—a Christianity that was much more akin to Islam than to Catholicism (which in any case characterised their main enemy, the Hapsburgs). The Ottomans certainly went out of their way to extend protection to Protestant minorities in the parts of Europe they occupied, which in turn was to be viewed with considerable favour by the newly emergent Protestant powers in Europe. The triumph of Lutheranism in Germany between 1521 and 1555, for example, has been attributed in part to Ottoman pressure on Catholic Austria. Hence, the Dutch Calvinist saying of 1574, *Liever Turck dan Paus*, 'Better the Turk than the Pope', thus echoing Patriarch Gennadius 'Better the Sultan's turban than the Popes's mitre' of over a century before.[12]

Indeed, in 1574 Elizabeth I of England formed an alliance with Sultan al-Mutawakkil of Morocco and by 1588 was making overtures to Constantinople. English aid was even extended to Morocco in its conquest of Niger in order to counter-balance Spanish power in the region, and the Emir of Morocco, al-Mansur, responded positively in 1603 with the astounding proposal to Queen Elizabeth for a joint Moroccan-English attack on the Spanish West Indies, to culminate in the expulsion of the Spanish and the opening up of the West Indies to Moroccan colonisation. Nothing, of course, came of Moroccan plans for colonising America (although it is notable that Morocco was the first country in the world to recognise the newly independent United States of America in 1786.)[13]

In other words, both sides—Christian Europe and the Ottoman Empire—paid only token lip service to the idea of 'holy war'; in practice relations between Christian and Muslim were usually better than either with their own heretics, who were persecuted with a savagery rarely seen in wars between Christian and Muslim powers. A prisoner of war of the main Christian or Muslim protagonists would expect nothing worse than a spell in the galleys. Not exactly a holiday, admittedly—but better than being burnt at the stake or impaled, the fate of their own heretics.

As well as inter-European alliances that cut across the religious divide, one must also remember that the period also sees Christians fighting fellow Christians and Muslims other Muslims—and as often and as bitterly as any Christian-Muslim conflict. The Ottomans not only fought Safavid Iran (whom, being Shi'a, they regarded as heretics) but fellow Sunni Muslims as well: petty Turkish and North African principalities, all of whom were firmly Sunni. In Christendom on the other hand, the two main Catholic powers, France and Spain, were constantly at loggerheads, often at war. All Christian powers at one time or another negotiated with the Ottomans, even on occasion the Papacy and Habsburg Spain, their traditional enemies.

Turkish rule in Europe towards the end may have been inept and incompetent, even at times brutal and cruel. But this was never an Islam versus Christianity affair, for Turkish rule of its Christian subjects was no worse—indeed it was usually far better—than Turkish rule in the Arab Muslim Near East. A Greek or Bulgarian had more to thank his Ottoman overlord for than an Arab did. This is illustrated by the remarkable career of Midhat Pasha, one of the more able officers of late Ottoman history. Midhat Pasha initiated radical new reforms when he was made governor of the newly created Danube Province in 1864. He instigated new public works and factories, with agricultural credit co-operatives that enabled peasants to borrow at low interest. Such reforms were practically unknown elsewhere in Europe. He also granted non-Muslims full equal rights with Muslims, created mixed Christian and Muslim schools, and recognised Bulgarian as the official language alongside Ottoman Turkish, with newspapers allowed in both languages. [14]

Midhat Pasha was regarded as too radical by Constantinople, and in 1867 was transferred to Baghdad. However, as late at 1893, a Bulgarian's favourable view of Ottoman rule was still remembered:

> What strikes a Bulgarian when he enters Turkey is, before everything else, the air of freedom that one breathes. Under a theoretically despotic government, one definitely enjoys more freedom than in a constitutional state … One almost does not feel that there is a government … The absence of an irksome police, of crushing taxation, of very heavy civic duties here is what the non-Muslim subjects of the sultan would appreciate …[15]

Of course, it would be a grave mistake to belittle Balkan nationalism, Ottoman misrule and the genuine struggle to be free of imperial rule. But at the same time, the historian of the Ottomans, Caroline Finkel, stresses that 'Accounts of the Ottoman nineteenth century have too often treated the emergence of nationalism in the Balkans as though it were the inevitable result of Ottoman "misrule" in the region—as though the Balkan Christians had heroically resisted their Ottoman masters for centuries while awaiting the right moment to break free'.[16] When witches and heretics were still being burnt alive in public in Christian Europe down until the eighteenth century, 'The Turks do not compel anyone to renounce his faith' wrote George of Hungary in the fifteenth century, and 'There is no country on earth where the exercise of all sorts of Religions is more free and less subject to being troubled, than in Turkey' wrote the French traveller de La Motraye in the seventeenth century.[17]

THE SPECTRE OF NATIONALISM

The Turks had been so successful in the Balkans by acting as champions—or at least liberators—of Christian Orthodoxy against the oppression of the Latins. After the eighteenth century, however, Orthodox Christianity found a new champion in Russia, particularly after the rise of Peter the Great and the Russian goal of restoring Constantinople to the Greeks (or at least to Greek Orthodoxy, which was not quite the same thing.) The *Philiki Etairia*, the Greek secret nationalist society that launched the Greek war of independence, was founded in 1814 in Odessa, mainly by Black Sea and Russian Greeks rather than by Greeks within the Ottoman Empire. It had the direct support of Russia. The Russian Foreign Minister, Count Capodistrias, one of its mainstays, was a Greek originally from Corfu.* Parallel to this was the rise of the Western European Romantic movement which romanticised ancient Greek history as the roots of European civilisation, with the modern Greeks cast in the role as the torchbearers of the legacy of Pericles, Alexander and Plato. Lord Byron and other Western romantics, such as Lord Lytton (who was even offered the crown of Greece by a group of Greek exiles in 1863), cast the Greeks in heroic mould, and

---

* It is interesting to note that in 1817 Russia had two Foreign Ministers, Count Nesselrode and Count Capodistrias. The later, whilst 'Russian', was an ethnic Greek and a passionate Hellenophile dedicated to Greek liberation from Ottoman Turkey, and later became the first President of Greece.

their struggle for independence against the 'Asiatic' Turk was equated in their minds with the struggle of the ancient Greeks against the Persians (a perception that was revived again during the Second World War with the Greek liberation against the Nazis—it is notable that it attracted the participation of British Classicists). The forces unleashed by the French Revolution also had an effect on Balkan nationalism. Hence, the Turks were demonised from all sides. The result was tragedy, as much for the Turks as for the Greeks themselves, and a wedge was driven between Greek and Turk that has dominated Balkan politics to our own era. It culminated in the Greek revolt of 1821 and the hanging of the Patriarch Gregory at the gates of the Patriarchate. Sir Steven Runciman, the great Byzantinist, wrote that 'The contract made between the Conquering Sultan and Gennadius [the first Patriarch under Ottoman rule] had been broken by the Patriarchate. The Turks were no longer willing to trust the Orthodox'.[18] The result was a poisoning of relations between the two peoples with such a long shared history that still plagues politics in the region today.

When looking back at this tragic culmination of the eight centuries or so of the Greek-Turkish symbiosis it is important first, not to reinterpret all of past history in terms of nineteenth and twentieth century events and impose an invented retrospective history to the relationship.* And second, to emphasise the difference between the Ottoman Empire and present day Turkey. Today, many view Turkey essentially as a Middle Eastern state, and perhaps rightly so (albeit very distinct); the Ottoman Empire, on the other hand, was essentially a *European* power right from its beginning. True, it had an eastern empire, but so too did other European powers, such as France or Great Britain. As such, the Greeks were not so much opponents of as participants in the Ottoman Empire—far more so than the Ottomans' fellow-believers, the Arabs, were. Even before the Ottomans, Seljuk power was very much a partnership with the Greeks as we have noted, and the subsequent Ottoman Empire was never a Turkish nationalist state. Indeed, many have regarded Ottoman civilisation as 'Byzantine-Turkish'. But this is only partially true: it was dominated by the Turks of course, but it was far more, involving

---

* For example, I have heard myself how tourists visiting Greece today have been shown some mythic 'cave' where the Greek language was 'secretly kept alive' during the centuries of 'Turkish repression', as all use of the Greek language had supposedly been banned by the Turks.

Albanians, Slavs, Armenians, Egyptians, Arabs, Berbers and others as well as Greeks and Turks: it was supra-national. The rise of European nationalism after the eighteenth century drove a wedge between the Turks and the other nationalities (as much between Greek and Turk as between Arab and Turk—and both Greek and Arab nationalism are still major political issues in the region today). Hence, it all started to go wrong. As Sultan Abdulhamid exclaimed bewilderingly when confronted with the nationalist movements: 'but we are all Ottomans'.

The two-edged sword that nineteenth-century European thought inflicted upon the world was nationalism. On the one hand it was cited as a universal human right at the Versailles Peace Treaty, on the other hand it debased into the worst form of extremism under Nazism, not to mention many other problems formed out of extreme nationalism that still plague world politics today. But just as nineteenth-century nationalism was the bastard child of eighteenth-century romanticism, late twentieth-century nationalism has in turn given birth to another bastard child: extreme 'ethnicism', manifest in its worst forms in the Balkans, the Middle East and elsewhere.

The expulsion of all the Greek communities from Anatolia in the 1920s, mainly from Smyrna and Trebizond and their respective hinterlands, is usually—and rightly—condemned as an act of intolerance. But that is to miss the point. To begin with, they were not unilateral, but were exchanges—exchanges, furthermore, provoked by the Greek invasion of Turkey and then initiated by Greek expulsion of Turks. It is also important to remember that in the early years of the twentieth century there were violent revolts by Muslim populations throughout Anatolia as well as by Arabs in Syria and Arabia (the Arab Revolt), and not just Greek and Armenian. In 1909, Muslim leaders in Adana denounced the Armenian massacres and openly expressed their solidarity with the Armenian church.[19] More importantly, the very fact that Greeks and Armenians *had* survived for so long in Anatolia was precisely because of Turkish toleration: their explicit recognition of their distinct religion, culture and identity, and their consequent respect for and protection of their communities. Steven Runciman writes that 'Right up to the end of the Balkan War in 1913 they [the Greeks within the Ottoman Empire] were far more numerous than their fellow-Greeks living within the boundaries of the Kingdom of Greece, and on average more wealthy'. Many Ottoman Greeks left the Empire for the Greek 'homeland' in the middle and later years of the nineteenth century. But Greece did not have the sophistication or wealth of the Ottoman Empire—or economic opportunities—so many returned.[20]

The massacres of Armenian populations in Ottoman lands as the empire was collapsing at the end of the nineteenth and beginning of the twentieth centuries is rightly regarded by the Armenians themselves as a tragedy of unequalled scale (and a fact still not properly faced by most Turks). But almost as tragic was the loss of faith in each other by both peoples, so that now their entire history is viewed as some eternal hate-filled Manichean struggle against each other. Until the massacres, this was far from the case. For example in Armenia today the destruction of the medieval Armenian capital of Ani is attributed solely to the Seljuk conquest in 1064: in fact it was destroyed before that by the Byzantine conquest in 1045 under Emperor Constantine IX Monomachus of the Macedonian dynasty and the consequent savage persecution of Armenian Monophysitism by the Orthodox Byzantines. A further irony is that the mis-named 'Macedonian' dynasty of Byzantine emperors were in fact Armenian. The Seljuk conquest of 1064 resulted in the *restoration* of Ani and the freedom of religious worship (many Armenians welcomed the Turks as liberators from Orthodox suppression, as the prominent historian of Armenia and 'Armeniophile', David Marshal Lang, is careful to point out),[21] with particular emphasis placed on commercial buildings, as surviving remains there attest (e.g., Pl. 97). Furthermore, throughout the Ottoman period the Armenians enjoyed probably a higher lobby at the court in Constantinople than any other group with the possible exception of the Greeks, and certainly far out of proportion to their numbers (Pl. 36). The sad fact is that the twentieth century is littered with the death tolls from the collapse of imperial powers: up to a million and a half Armenians (and at least the same number of Turks) with the collapse of the Ottoman Empire, perhaps two million with the collapse of Britain's Indian Empire, a million (give or take) with the collapse of France's empire in Algeria, and estimates of between five and fifteen million from Belgium's Congo. Of course, history is more than body counts or league tables of deaths and it is wrong to make comparisons, but neither does that make it right to single out any one atrocity in order to gloss over others.

In the Russo-Turkish War of 1877-78 the Ottoman Empire lost over a third of its European territory and much of its Christian population.

It was only then that for the first time in its history Muslims and not Christians formed a majority in the Ottoman Empire. Ironically, it was the European Christian powers who forced the Ottomans to become more 'Islamic' under Sultan Abdülhamid II (1876-1909) with their insistence of 'protection' over the Christian communities in the Empire: the Russians of the Orthodox and the French of the Catholics. This was reinforced by the rise of European nationalism, Russian pan-Slavism and pan-Orthodoxy, the Romantic invention of pan-Hellenism, and the Western powers' insistence upon ethnic and religious national distinctions generally. Hence, the Western powers encouraged and facilitated the breaking away of the non-Muslim parts of the empire. All of this combined to make Abdülhamid emphasise the Islamic aspect of the Ottoman state through his title of Caliph and thus a leader of all Muslims, both within and outside the empire—a role not until then emphasised by previous sultans. In 1903, for example, Sultan Abdülhamid proposed to celebrate the four-hundredth anniversary of the transfer of the Caliphate to the Ottomans, an anniversary never previously celebrated simply because it had never before been deemed important. The construction of the Hejaz Railway after 1900 was a part of this Ottoman 'Islamisation'.[22]

In the end it would be 'the triumphal entry of industrialized, active and insatiable Europe, blundering as it were in this troubled world, [that] would sound the death-knell of Ottoman greatness' as Fernand Braudel observed.[23] But the Ottoman Empire clung on almost despite itself, partly because it became within the interests of big-power rivalries to keep it propped up, partly due to a few capable sultans such as Mahmut II and a few capable grand viziers such as Ahmet Köprülü. Almost to its own surprise, the Ottoman Empire in the end outlasted them all: it outlasted all of its traditional enemies: the Republic of Venice, the Spanish Empire, the Knights of Malta, the Papal States, the Austrian Empire, the Russian Empire, the Persian Empire; it even outlasted its traditional friends: the Kingdom of France and the German Empire. Even in its final dying moments the Ottoman Empire still managed to inflict two defeats upon the greatest power in the world at the time, the British Empire, when it defeated British forces at both Gallipoli and Kut al-Amara during the First World War. In the end the final death blow was delivered by none of these powers but by a blue-eyed Turk from Macedonia. At once both a European and a Turk, both a Westeriser and a Turkish nationalist, Mustafa Kemal Ataturk's transformation was entirely in keeping with the previous thousand years of Turkish and European symbiosis.*

*   *   *

To end, therefore, we may return to the first words of this book: the title. Reference to the Roman Empire is not only implicit in its title, but throughout: with reference to the Seljuk state, Mehmet the Conqueror, the character of Ottoman Constantinople, the professional Ottoman army, and Turkish naval power. The comparison is no chance one. 'In its own essence the composite realm of the Ottoman Empire was indeed to become, through its eclectic policies, a true successor to the Empire of Rome' in the words of Patrick Kinross.[24] Perhaps nothing else demonstrates more just how much a people originally from the Far East could become so thoroughly champions of Europe's own greatest legacy.

---

* Appropriately, a Turkish historian citing a British historian writes: 'Arnold Toynbee wrote that, indeed, Mustafa Kamal was defending the most exalted principles of the West against the West itself.' (İnalcik 2006: 83.)

65   Bellini's portrait of Mehmet the Conqueror. (© National Gallery, London)

66   Çinili Kiosk, the only part of the Topkapi Palace from the time of Mehmet the Conqueror.

67   The Baghdad Kiosk in Topkapi Palace, built to mark the conquest of Baghdad by Selim I.

68   Sultan Süleyman I in the Mohacs battlefield. (Hünernâme, Topkapi Museum)

69   Tuğra of (seal) Süleyman the Magnificent (in the Museum of Islamic Art, Istanbul).

70   Bronze medallion of the Emperor Charles V 'haunted' by Sultan Süleyman (© British Museum).

71   Turks at St Mark's: a mosaic over the entrance of St Mark's Basilica, Venice, depicting Ottoman traders.

72   *The Selimiye Mosque commemorating the reign of Selim the Grim.*

73   *The Şehzade Mosque complex commemorating Süleyman's eldest son, the first great mosque complex built by the great sixteenth-century architect Sinan.*

74   *The Süleymaniye Mosque complex dominating Istanbul's skyline in the background, with the Rüstem Pasha Mosque in the foreground, both built by Sinan.*

75   *The Mosque complex of Ahmet I, the last of the great mosque complexes of Istanbul.*

76   The Mosque of Sokullu Mehmet Pasha in Istanbul, one of the gems of the great Ottoman architect Sinan.

77   The Mihrimah Mosque built by Sinan for Süleyman's daughter.

78   *The Yeni Valide Mosque on the Golden Horn.*

79   *The Tomb of Süleyman with the great bulk of the Süleymaniye rearing up behind.*

80   The Tomb of Roxelana.

81   The mosque built by Sinan in Gezlev, modern Evpatoria, in the Crimea.

*82   The mosque built by
Sinan in Vlora on the Adriatic
coast in Albania. Both this and
the above illustrate the spread
of both the Empire and its
architect.*

*83   The nineteenth-century Greek school in the
Phanar quarter of Istanbul.*

*84   Modern statue of Barbarossa
in Istanbul.*

85 *A watchtower at La Rocella on the north coast of Sicily, one of many such fortifications built in the seventeenth century around the western Mediterranean as defence against the Corsairs.*

86 *The old harbour fortifications of Algiers, parts of which date from the time of Barbarossa.*

87   *The former Ottoman fort of Tripoli in Libya.*

88   *The Grand Harbour of Valetta in Malta.*

89   The Fort of St Elmo in Valetta, scene of the heaviest fighting in the Great Siege of Malta.

90   Marisco Castle on Lundy Island in the Bristol Channel. (© the Landmark Trust)

91 *'Morocco Land' in the Canongate in Edinburgh.*

92 *The port of Mocha in Yemen which throughout the sixteenth century was a major Ottoman naval base that launched attacks upon Portuguese interests throughout the Indian Ocean.*

93   The Battle of Lepanto, a late sixteenth-century painting by H Letter hanging in the
Queen's House, Greenwich.

94   The siege of Vienna.
(Hünernâme, Topkapi Museum)

95   *The Ottoman Black Sea 'triangle': the fortress of Yeni Kale in Crimea guarding the 'Cimmerian Bosphorus,' the modern Straits of Kerch between the Black Sea and the Sea of Azov.*

96   *The huge Ottoman fortress of Ak-kerman at the western end of the Black Sea on the mouth of the Dniestr, modern Belgorod-Dniestrovsky in Ukraine.*

97   *Ottoman decadence: the huge and costly nineteenth-century Dolmabahçe Palace on the Bosphorus, built by Armenian architects.*

98   *End of Empire: sunset over Istanbul.*

NOTES

PREFACE

1 Hale 1993: 3.
2 Lemaire 2000: 38-9.
3 Hobson 2004; Headley 2008; Lewis 2008; Pagden 2008; Goody 1996, 2003, 2006, 2009a, 2009b; Morris 2011; Fernández-Armesto 2000, 2006, 2009.
4 Ferguson 2011: xxv-xxvi.
5 Cunliffe 2009: vii; Ferguson 2011: 12.
6 Ferguson 2011: 14.
7 Hunt 2010: 376.
8 Darwin: 162, 164, 360.
9 Roberts 1996: 212.
10 For example, page 44.
11 Braudel 1981-4, 3: 19.

1 INTRODUCTION: TURKS AND TURKISHNESS

1 Doğan Kuban in Çağatay and Kuban (eds) 2006: 14.
2 Gibbon Vol VII: 79.
3 Roxburgh 2005; Çağatay and Kuban 2006.
4 Cited in Heather 2009: 15.
5 See Kessler 1993: 70. This is discussed further in Chapter 2 below.
6 Many of these inscriptions are quoted at length in Barfield 1992: 146-50.
7 For example, Nizam al-Mulk 1960: 104, 139, 158-9, 160-1.
8 Peacock 2010: 65; Çelebi 2010: 108.
9 Quoted in Peacock 2010: 60.
10 *Le Monde*, 8 November 2002.
11 Rietbergen 2006: 482.

12 Wheatcroft 2008: 266-7; Almond 2009: 140.
13 Almond 2009: 140.

2 DESCENDANTS OF THE SHE-WOLF

1   Sinor 1990 is the best summary of Turk origins.
2   See Kessler 1993: 70.
3   Grousset 1970: 60-6.

3 THE TURKS MOVE WESTWARDS

1   Sinor 1996: 327.
2   Khodarkovsky 2002.
3   Kohl in Peterson, Popova & Smith 2006: 5; Kohl 2007: 18.
4   Mainz in Amitai & Biran 2005; Parry 1962: 6.
5   Notably by Klimburg-Salter 1989: 134-6.
6   Sinor 1990: 315-6.

4 THE LURE OF ISLAM

1   Quoted by Golden 2011: 72.
2   Tetley 2009: 3, 27-8.

5 THE SULTANS OF ROME

1   Cahen 2001: 9 and 123. Italics added.
2   Tetley 2009: 4-5.
3   Hillenbrand 2007: 5.
4   Hillenbrand 2007: 7, 15.
5   Ibn al-Jawzi (d. 1200), quoted by Hillenbrand 2007: 40.
6   Hillenbrand 2007: Chapter 5.
7   Cahen 2001: 9.
8   Unofficially so at first: the first to use the title 'Sultan of the land of Rome' officially was Kılıç Arslan I, Süleyman's son. See Cahen 2001: 136-7.
9   Hillenbrand 1994: Ch IV.
10 Peacock 2010: 119-27.

11 Tetley 2009: 41-2.
12 Cahen 2001: 123.

6 A Turkish World

1   Kuban in Çağatay & Kuban: 14.
2   Finkel 2005: 188.
3   Runciman 1951-4, 3: 315.

7 Beyond the Bosphorus

1   Parry 1963: 6.
2   Fernández-Armesto: 352.
3   Lowry 2003: 93.
4   Kinross 1977: 40.
5   Kinross 1977: 38, who writes of it as an invitation. The quotation is from Norman Stone's review of Lowry in *Cornucopia* 29, 5: 26-8.
6   Browning in Harrison (ed.) 2002.
7   Almond 2009: 142, 145.
8   Finkel 2005: 15.
9   Kinross 1977: 30.
10 Almond 2009: 151-3.
11 Rodinson 1987: 34; Lowry 2003: 136-7; Finkel 2005: 18-19.
12 Hillenbrand 2007: 172-7. On the hijacking of the Alexander legacy, see Chapter 4 of *Towards One World* in this series.
13 Fernández-Armesto 2009: 108.
14 The Venetian Giacomo de' Languschi, cited in Wheatcroft 1993: 25-6.
15 See Kinross 1977: 112; Cardini 2001: 133-4; Lowry 2003: 119; Finkel 2005: 80.
16 Bryer 1981.
17 Lowry 2003: 116-126.
18 Leonardo's proposals are preserved in the Topkapi Archives. See Brotton 2002: 204; Inalcik 2006: 58; Necipoğlu 2005: 88.

8 THE MEDITERRANEAN AND THE MEDITERRANEAN WORLD IN THE AGE OF SÜLEYMAN THE MAGNIFICENT

1   Quoted in Finkel 2005: 116.
2   Hunt 2010: 245.
3   Braudel 1972, 1: 328-9; Casale 2010: 34.
4   Cf. Diamond 1997.
5   Mansel 1995: 18.
6   De Busbecq 2001: 39-40.
7   De Busbecq 2001: 72, 101-2.
8   Lewis 1982: 191; Finkel 2005: 305.
9   Mansel 1995: 19.
10 The statistic is cited by Mansel 1995: 122.
11 Çelebi: 15.
12 Quoted by Mansel 1995: 161. See also Rodinson 1987: 35.
13 Quoted in Mansel 1995: 15.
14 Mansel 1995: 124-7.
15 Mansel 1995: 16, 122-4, 265.
16 Evliya Çelebi 2010: 24.
17 For much of this section I am indebted to Hunt 2010.
18 A point emphasised by Tetley 2009: 14-15.
19 Hunt 2010: 4, 38-9, 196-7.
20 Quoted in Hunt 2010: 69.
21 Mango 1999: 7.
22 Kinross 1977: 255, 259.

9 WHEN TURKEY RULED THE WAVES

1   Casale 2010: 4.
2   Matar 1999: 60, 63.
3   See Matar 1999: 55-63.
4   Casale 2010: 11.
5   For much of the ensuing information is I am indebted to Özen 2006 and Casale 2010.
6   Casale 2010: 39-40.
7   The Icelandic raid and an account of their slavery was described by Eigilssen himself in his *Eigilson Litil Saga un Herlilasup Tyrkjan*. For this and Lundy see *Museum News* (Naval Museum Istanbul) Year 2, Issue 8, March 1999. See also the official Lundy website http://www.lundyisland. co.uk/history.htm; Matar 1999: Ch. 2; Goody 2004: 44.

8   Grant, 1881-3(?), *Vol III:* 6-7. I am indebted to Wendy Ball for bringing
    this extraordinary story to my attention.
9   Much of the following account of Indian Ocean exploration is based
    upon Casale's (2010) ground breaking study.
10 Casale 2010: 50-1.
11 Quoted in Casale: 2010: 82.
12 Casale 2010: 65-6.
13 Casale 20101: 126.
14 Boxer 1969: 57-8; Braudel 1972: 543-70; Peacock 2010: 10; Finkel 2005:
    136-8.
15 Quoted in Kinross 1977: 270-1.
16 The Venetians were acutely aware that the Portuguese were by-passing
    the Mediterranean and themselves as early as 1501. See Chaudhuri 1985:
    64-5.
17 Braudel 1972: 567-8.
18 Braudel 1973: 1055-87; Finkel 2005: 168-9; Casale 2010: 138.
19 Mansel 1995: 126.
20 Cardini 2001: 60-1.
21 Casale 2010: 149-51.
22 See Khodarkovsky 2002: 36; Finkel 2005 172-3.

10   THE SICK MEN OF EUROPE

1   Wheatcroft 2008: 252-3.
2   Quoted in Lewis 1982: 41-2.
3   Braudel 1981-4, 3: 482.
4   İnalcik 2006: 44.
5   Faroghi 2004: 142.
6   Mansel 1995: 248, 272.
7   Faroghi 2004.
8   Quoted by Lewis 1982: 214.
9   See, for example, Mack 2002: 160; Lemaire 2005: 27-9, 36-7.
10 See *Towards One World* in this series, 10.
11 Finkel 2005: 405-6.
12 Boxer 1965: 42; Cardini 2001: 144-51; Inalcik 2006: 220-1; Almond 2009:
    158-61.
13 Rodinson 1987: 34-5; Matar 1999: 9-10, 19-23; Goody 2004: 42-44.
14 Finkel 2005: 464.
15 Quoted by Andrew Mango, *Atatürk* (1999): 17.
16 Finkel 2005: 428.

17 Both quoted in Mansel 1995: 47.
18 Runciman 1968: 406.
19 Finkel 2005: 507-8, 518.
20 Runciman 1968: 407; Finkel 2005: 487.
21 Burney & Lang 1971: 210.
22 Finkel 2005: 491-9.
23 Braudel 1981-4, 3: 483.
24 Kinross 1977: 59.

BIBLIOGRAPHY

Abu Lughod, Janet, *Before European Hegemony*. Oxford 1989.

Allen, *Russian Embassies*.

Almond, Ian, *Two Faiths, One Banner: When Muslims Marched with Christians Across Europe's Battlegrounds*. London 2009.

Amitai, Reuven and Biran, Michal (eds), *Mongols, Turks, and Others. Eurasian Nomads and the Sedentary World*. Leiden 2005.

Asimov, A.S. and Bosworth, C.E. (eds), *History of civilizations in Central Asia. Volume IV. The age of achievement: A.D. 750 to the end of the fifteenth century*. Paris1998.

Baldick, Julian, *Animal and Shaman. Ancient Religions of Central Asia*. London 2000.

Barfield, Thomas J, *The Perilous Frontier. Nomad Empires and China 221 BC to AD 1757*. Cambridge (Mass) 1989.

Barthold, W, *Turkestan Down to the Mongol Invasions*. London 1977.

Beckwith, Christopher, *Empires of the Silk Road. A History of Central Asia from the Bronze Age to the Present*. Princeton 2011.

Biran, Michael, *The Empire of the Qara Khitai in Eurasian History. Between China and the Islamic World*. Cambridge 2005.

Bosworth, C E, *The Ghaznavids. Their Empire in Afghanistan and Eastern India, 994-1040*. Oxford 1963.

Bosworth, C E, *The Later Ghaznavids. Splendour and Decay. The Dynasty in Afghanistan and Eastern India, 1040-1186*. Oxford 1977.

Boxer, C R, *The Portuguese Seaborne Empire 1415-1825*. London 1969.

Bradford, Ernle, *The Sultan's Admiral. Barbarossa—Pirate and Empire-Builder*. London 1969.

Braudel, Fernand, *Civilization and the Rise of Capitalism*. 3 vols. London 1981-4.

Braudel, Fernand, *The Mediterranean and the Mediterranean World in the Age of Philip II*. 2 vols. London 1972.

Brotton, Jerry, *The Renaissance Bazaar. From the Silk Road to Michelangelo*. Oxford 2002.

Bryer, A, 'The Case of the First Byzantine-Ottoman marriage', in Davis, H and Wallace-Hadrill, J (eds), *The Writing of History in the Middle Ages*. Oxford 1981.

Burney and Lang, *Peoples of the Hills*. 1971.

Çağatay, Ergun and Kuban, Doğan, *The Turkic Speaking Peoples. 2,000 Years of Art and Culture from Inner Asia to the Balkans*. Munich, Berlin, London, New York 2006.

Cahen, Claude, *The Formation of Turkey. The Seljukid Sultanate of Rūm: Eleventh to Fourteenth Century*. London 2001.

Campbell, Caroline and Chong, Alan, *Bellini and The East*. London 2005.

Cardini, Franco, *Europe and Islam*. Cambridge 2001.

Casale, Giancarlo, *The Ottoman Age of Exploration*. New York and Oxford 2010.

Chaudhury, K N, *Trade and Civilisation in the Indian Ocean. From the Rise of Islam to 1750*. Cambridge 1985.

Christian, David, *A History of Russia, Central Asia and Mongolia. Volume I. Inner Eurasia from Prehistory to the Mongol Empire*. Oxford 2008.

Christian, David, *A History of Russia, Central Asia and Mongolia. Volume I. Inner Eurasia from Prehistory to the Mongol Empire*. Oxford 2008.

Cunliffe, Barry, *Europe Between the Oceans 9000 BC–AD 1000*. New Haven 2009.

Darwin, John, *After Tamerlane. The Rise and Fall of Global Empires, 1400–2000*. London 2007.

de Busbecq, Ghislain Ogier, *Turkish Letters*. London 2001.

Di Cosmo, Nicola, *Ancient China and its Enemies. The Rise of Nomadic Power in East Asian History*. Cambridge 2002.

Diamond, Jared, *Guns, Germs and Steel. A Short History of Everybody for the Last 13,000 Years*. London 1997.

Elliott, J H, *Imperial Spain 1469-1716*. London 1963.

Evliya Çelebi, *An Ottoman Traveller. Selections from the* Book of Travels *of Evliya Çelebi*. Translation and Commentary by Dankoff and Kim. London 2010.

Faroghi, Suraiya, *The Ottoman Empire and the World Around It*. London 2004.

Ferguson, Niall, *Civilization. The West and the Rest*. London 2011.

Fernández-Armesto, Felipe, *1492. The Year Our World Began*. London 2009.

Fernández-Armesto, Felipe, *Civilizations*. London 2000.

Fernández-Armesto, Felipe, *Pathfinders. A Global History of Exploration*. Oxford 2006.

Findley, Carter Vaughn, *The Turks in World History*. Oxford 2005.

Finkel, Caroline, *Osman's Dream. The story of the Ottoman Empire, 1300 – 1923*. London 2005.

Freely, John, *Istanbul the Imperial City*. London 1996.

Geary, Patrick J, *The Myth of Nations. The Medieval Origins of Europe*. Princeton 2002.

Gibbon, Edward, *The History of the Decline and Fall of the Roman Empire*. 7 vols. Ed. J. B. Bury. London 1900.

Goffman, Daniel, *The Ottoman Empire and Early Modern Europe*. Cambridge 2002.

Golden, Peter B, *Central Asia in World History*. New York and Oxford 2011.

Goodwin, Godfrey, *A History of Ottoman Architecture*. London 1971.

Goody, Jack , *Renaissances. The One or the Many?* Cambridge 2009.

Goody, Jack , *The East in the West*. Cambridge 1996.

Goody, Jack , *The Eurasian Miracle*. Cambridge 2009.

Goody, Jack , *The Theft of History*. Cambridge 2006.

Goody, Jack, *Islam in Europe*. Cambridge 2004.

Grant, James, *Old and New Edinburgh. Its History, its People and its Places. Vol III*. Edinburgh 1881-3(?).

Grousset, René, *The Empire of the Steppes: a History of Central Asia*. New Brunswick 1970.

Hale, John, *The Civilization of the Renaissance in Europe*. London 1993.

Halliday, Fred, *Islam and the Myth of Confrontation*. London 1996.

Harmatta, J and Litvinsky, B A, 'Tokharistan and Gandhara under Western Türk rule (650-750)', in Litvinsky 1996: 367-402.

Headley, John M, *The Europeanization of the World. On the Origins of Human Rights and Democracy*. Princeton 2008.

Heather, Peter, *Empires and Barbarians. Migration, Development and the Birth of Europe*. London 2009.

Hilenbrand, Robert, *Islamic Architecture*. Edinburgh 1994.

Hillenbrand, Carole, *Turkish Myth and Muslim Symbol. The Battle of Manzikert*. Edinburgh 2007.

Hobson, John M, *The Eastern Origins of Western Civilisation*. Cambridge 2004.

Holt, P.M., Lambton, Ann K.S., and Lewis, Bernard (eds.), *The Cambridge History of Islam*. 2 vols. Cambridge 1970.

Hunt, Margaret R, *Women in Eighteenth Century Europe*. London 2010.

İnalcık, Halil, *Turkey and Europe in History*. Istanbul 2006.

Kaeuper, Richard W, *Chivalry and Violence in Medieval Europe*. Oxford 1999.

Kessler, Adam T, *Empires Beyond the Great Wall. The Heritage of Genghis Khan*. Los Angeles 1993.

Khodarkovsky, Michael, *Russia's Steppe Frontier. The Making of a Colonial Empire, 1500-1800*. Bloomington 2002.

King, Charles, *The Ghosts of Freedom. A History of the Caucasus*. Oxford 2009.

Kinross, Patrick, *The Ottoman Centuries. The Rise and Fall of the Turkish Empire*. New York 1977.

Klimburg-Salter, Deborah, *The Kingdom of Bāmiyān. Buddhist Art and Architecture of the Hindu Kush*. Naples, Rome 1989.

Koestler, Arthur (undated), *The Thirteenth Tribe. The Khazar Empire and its Heritage*. London.

Kohl, Philip L, 'The Early Intefration of the Eurasian Steppes with the Ancient Near East: Movements and Transformations in the Caucasus and Central Asia', in Peterson, Popova and Smith, *Beyond the Steppe and the Sown. Proceedings of the 2002 University of Chicago Conference on Eurasian Archaeology*. Leiden 2006.

Kohl, Philip L, *The Making of Bronze Age Eurasia*. Cambridge 2007.

Lane-Poole, Stanley, *The Barbary Corsairs*. London 1896.

Lattimore, Owen, *Inner Asian Frontiers of China*. New York 1940.

Lemaire, Gérard-Georges, *The Orient in Western Art*. Paris 2005.

Lewis, Archibald R, *Nomads and Crusaders. A.D. 1000 – 1368*. Bloomington 1998.

Lewis, Bernard, *The Muslim Discovery of Europe*. London 1982.

Lewis, David Leavering, *Islam and the Making of Europe, 570-1215*. New York 2008.

Litvinsky, B.A. (ed.), *History of civilizations in Central Asia. Volume III. The crossroads of civilizations: A.D. 250 to 750*. Paris 1996.

Lowry, Heath, *The Nature of the Early Ottoman State*. Albany, 2003.

Mack, Rosamond E, *Bazaar to Piazza. Islamic Tradition and Italian Art, 1300-1600*. Berkeley 2002.

Maenchen-Helfen, Otto, *The World of the Huns: Studies in their History and Culture*. Berkeley 1973.

Mainz, Beatrice Forbes, 'Nomad and Settled in the Timurid Military', in Amitai and Biran 2005.

Mak, Geert, *The Bridge. A Journey Between Orient and Occident*. London 2008.

Mango, Andrew, *Atatürk. The Biography of the Founder of Modern Turkey*. New York 1999.

Mango, Andrew, *The Turks Today*. London 2004.

Mansel, Philip, *Constantinople. City of the Word's Desire, 1453-1924*. London 1995.

Matar, Nabil, *Turks, Moors, and Englishmen in the Age of Discovery*. New York 1999.

McCarthy, Justin, *The Ottoman Turks. An Introductory History to 1923*. London, 1997.

Morris, Ian, *Why The West Rules—for Now. The patterns of history and what they reveal about the future*. London 2011.

Necipoğlu, Gülru, *The Age of Sinan. Architectural Culture in the Ottoman Empire*. London 2005.

Nizam al-Mulk, *The Book of Government or Rules for Kings*. Translated by Hubert Darke. London 1960.

Norwich, John Julius, *A History of Venice*. London 2003.

Norwich, John Julius, *Byzantium*, 3 vols. London 1988-95.

O'Shea, Stephen, *Sea of Faith. Islam and Christianity in the Medieval and Renaissance World*. London 2006.

Öney, Gönül, *Early Ottoman Art. The Legacy of the Emirates*. Izmir 2002.

Özen, Mine Esiner, *Piri Reis and his Charts*. Istanbul 2006.

Pagden, Anthony, *Words at War. The 2,500-Year Struggle Between East and West*. Oxford 2008.

Parry, J H, *The Age of Reconnaissance*, London 1963.

Peacock, A C S, *Early Seljūq History. A new interpretation*. London 2010.

Peacock, Andrew, 'Islam, trade and politics across the Indian Ocean: links between Southeast Asia and the Ottoman Empire, 16th–20th centuries', *Anatolian Archaeology* 16: 9-10 2010.

Rehman, Abdur, *the last Two Dynasties of the Śāhis. Analysis of their History, Archaeology, Coinage and Palaeography*. Delhi 1979.

Rietbergen, Peter, *Europe. A Cultural History*. London 2006.

Roberts, J M, *A History of Europe*. Oxford 1996.

Roberts, J M, *The Triumph of the West*. London 1985.

Rodinson, Maxime, *Europe and the Mystique of Islam*. London 1987.

Rogers, J M, and Ward, R M, *Süleyman the Magnificent*. London 1998.

Rogerson, Barnaby, *The Last Crusaders. The Hundred-Year Battle for the Centre of the World*. London 2009.

Roxburghe, David J, *Turks. A Journey of a Thousand Years, 600-1600*. London 2005.

Runciman, Steven, *A History of the Crusades*. 3 vols. Cambridge 1951-4.

Runciman, Steven, *The Fall of Constantinople 1453*. Cambridge 1965.

Runciman, Steven, *The Great Church in Captivity*. Cambridge 1968.

Sanping Chen, 'Turkic or Proto-Mongolian? A Note on the Tuoba Language', *Central Asiatic Journal* 49, 2: 161-74. 2005.

Schafer, Edward H,. *The Golden Peaches of Samarkand.* Berkeley 1963.

Schimmel, Annemarie, *Rumi's World. The Life and Work of the Great Sufi Poet.* Lahore 2003.

Sinor, Denis (ed.), *The Cambridge History of Early Inner Asia.* Cambridge 1990.

Sinor, Denis, 'The establishment and dissolution of the Türk empire', *The Cambridge History of Early Inner Asia* (ed. D. Sinor). Cambridge 1990.

Sinor, Denis, 'The First Türk Empire', in B A Litvinsky (ed.), *History of Civilizations in Central Asia. Volume III. The crossroads of civilizations: A.D. 250 to 750.* Paris 1996.

Strauss, Barry S, 'The Problem of Periodization: the Case of the Peloponnesian War', in Mark Golden and Peter Toohey (eds) *Inventing Ancient Culture,* London 1997.

Swanton, Michael, *The Lives of Two Offas.* Crediton 2010.

Tetley, G E, *The Ghaznavid and Seljuk Turks. Poetry as a source for Iranian history.* London 2009.

Torday, Laszlo, *Mounted Archers. The Beginnings of Central Asian History.* Durham 1997.

Ustinova, Y, 'Lycanthropy in Sarmatian Warrior Societies: The Kobyakovo Torque', *Ancient East and West* Vol 1, no 1: 102-123. Leiden 2002.

Wheatcroft, Andrew, *The Enemy at the Gate. Habsburg, Ottomans and the Battle for Europe.* London 2008 .

Wheatcroft, Andrew, *The Ottomans. Dissolving Images.* London 1993.

Woodhouse, C M, *Gemistos Plethon. The Last of the Hellenes.* Oxford 1986.

INDEX